A CORNISH

A Cornish Anthology

CHOSEN BY
A. L. ROWSE

ALISON HODGE

First published by Macmillan & Co. Ltd in 1968,
and then by Alison Hodge under ISBN 0-906720-04-4
Third edition published in 1990 by Alison Hodge,
Bosulval, Newmill, Penzance, Cornwall TR20 8XA

British Library Cataloguing in Publication Data
A Cornish Anthology. – 3rd ed.
1. English literature. Special subjects: Cornwall – Anthologies
I. Rowse, A.L. (Alfred Leslie), 1903–
820.80324237
ISBN 0-906720-23-0

Cover designed by Carole Page

The painting on the cover is *Porthgwarra*, by Ernest Procter,
reproduced by kind permission of
Newlyn Orion, Cornwall.

Printed in Great Britain by BPCC Wheatons Ltd, Exeter

To
Douglas Jay
For his love of Cornwall
and
his friendship over many years

Contents

Preface

ANTHOLOGIES should and can be a delightful form of reading. They can also be educative. For myself I can say how much pleasure I derived, and how much I learned, from such anthologies as *The Golden Treasury*, Q's *Oxford Book of English Verse*, E. V. Lucas's *The Open Road*—frequent companion of my walks in youth—and Herbert Read's *The Knapsack*.

Someone has observed that anthologies are not an exacting form of reading. Oddly enough, I have found this a most exacting form of making a book. It was nearly forty years ago that the idea first occurred to me, and that I wrote to Q suggesting that he give us a Cornish Anthology. He thought the idea a good one, but returned the compliment by suggesting that I should do it. It was then quite beyond my powers.

Nevertheless, as the years have gone by, filled with other undertakings, I find that I have been putting aside passages in prose and verse that have caught my attention and appealed to me as revealing of Cornwall in many of its aspects and of Cornishmen in various moods and characters. Altogether I hope that the book presents a representative picture, if by no means a complete one.

I am chiefly indebted, for suggestions and valued help over this book, to Professor Jack Simmons and Mr Robin Davidson.

A. L. ROWSE

Trenarren, St. Austell
March 1968

Acknowledgements

THE editor and publishers wish to thank the following, who have kindly given permission for the use of copyright material: Mr Robin Atthill for 'Christopher Wood', from *If Pity Departs*; G. Bell & Sons Ltd, for extracts from *Harvest of the Moor*, by Margaret Leigh; the owner of the copyright for 'Founding the Bishopric of Truro', from *As We Were*, by E. F. Benson; Mr Nicolas Bentley and T. Werner Laurie Ltd for 'Sir Humphry Davy', from *Biography for Beginners*, by E. C. Bentley; the Bodley Head Ltd for 'Chough', from *Poems and Contradictions*, by Rex Warner; British Railways, Western Region, for the extract from *History of the Great Western Railway*, by E. T. MacDermot; Curtis Brown Ltd for extracts from *The Old Place*, by C. C. Vyvyan; Cambridge University Press for extracts from *From a Cornish Window*, by Arthur Quiller-Couch, *Memories and Opinions: An Unfinished Autobiography*, by Arthur Quiller-Couch, edited by S. C. Roberts, and *Richard Trevithick*, by H. W. Dickinson and A. Titley; Chatto & Windus Ltd for extracts from *My Life and Times: Octave Four*, by Sir Compton Mackenzie; the Clarendon Press for extracts from *Cornwall in the Great Civil War*, by Mary Coate, *Diaries of William Johnston Temple*, by Lewis Bettany, and Arthur Quiller-Couch's Preface and passages from *Essays in Cornish History*, by Charles Henderson; William Collins, Sons & Co Ltd for the extract from *Bird Life in Cornwall*, by B. H. Ryves, and 'Mylor in War-Time', from *Memories and Gardens*, by Marion Howard Spring; Country Life Ltd for extracts from *Shrubs for the Milder Counties*, by W. Arnold-Forster; the C. W. Daniel Company Ltd for the poems from *A Cornish Collection*, by Bernard Moore; Eyre & Spottiswoode Ltd for 'The Squire of Lanarth' and 'Garden-stealing', from *Look Towards the Sea*, by Frank Baines; Faber & Faber Ltd for extracts from *A Potter's Book*, by Bernard Leach, and 'The Voyages of Alfred Wallis', from *The White Threshold*, by W. S. Graham;

the Executors of the Cecil Gray Estate and Jonathan Cape Ltd for the extract from *Peter Warlock*; Rupert Hart-Davis Ltd for extracts from *Union Street* and *Johnny Halleluia*, by Charles Causley; William Heinemann Ltd for two poems from *The Poems of Arthur Symons*; David Higham Associates Ltd for extracts from *Freedom of the Parish*, by Geoffrey Grigson, and *A Charm Against the Toothache*, by John Heath-Stubbs; Hodder & Stoughton Ltd for the extract from *Chronicles of the Eighteenth Century*, by Maud Wyndham; Hutchinson Publishing Group Ltd for extracts from *The Farington Diary*; Mr A. K. Hamilton Jenkin for extracts from *News from Cornwall*; Michael Joseph Ltd for the extract from *We Fought Them in Gunboats*, by Robert Hichens; the Editor of the *Journal of the Royal Institution of Cornwall* for the extracts from 'William Borlase', by P. A. S. Pool; Longmans, Green & Co Ltd for the extract from *Sir George Otto Trevelyan, O.M.: A Memoir*, by G. M. Trevelyan; Methuen & Co Ltd for extracts from *The Map of Clay*, by Jack Clemo, and *Twenty Years at St. Hilary*, by Bernard Walke; John Murray (Publishers) Ltd for the poem from *Collected Poems* and extracts from *First and Last Loves*, by John Betjeman, and extracts from *Kenneth Grahame*, by Peter Green; Oxford University Press for 'The Harbour of Fowey' and 'By Talland Church as I did go', from *Poems*, by Arthur Quiller-Couch; A. D. Peters & Co for the extract from *Admiral Boscawen*, by C. Aspinall-Oglander; Mr William Plomer and Jonathan Cape Ltd for extracts from *Kilvert's Diary*, edited by William Plomer; Laurence Pollinger Ltd, William Heinemann Ltd and the Estate of the late Mrs Frieda Lawrence for extracts from *The Collected Letters of D. H. Lawrence*; Mr L. T. C. Rolt and Longmans, Green & Co Ltd for the extract from *Isambard Kingdom Brunel*; the Royal Society for the Protection of Birds and the Society of Authors for the extract from *The Land's End*, by W. H. Hudson; and the Executors of the Anne Treneer Estate for extracts from *Schoolhouse in the Wind* (Jonathan Cape Ltd) and *The Mercurial Chemist* (Methuen & Co Ltd).

In a few cases the publishers have been unable to trace the copyright-holders, but they will be pleased to make the necessary arrangements at the first opportunity.

I. Prologue

1. *When I Set Out For Lyonnesse*

When I set out for Lyonnesse,
  A hundred miles away,
  The rime was on the spray,
And starlight lit my lonesomeness
When I set out for Lyonnesse
  A hundred miles away.

What would bechance at Lyonnesse
  While I should sojourn there
  No prophet durst declare,
Nor did the wisest wizard guess
What would bechance at Lyonnesse
  While I should sojourn there.

When I came back from Lyonnesse
  With magic in my eyes,
 All marked with mute surmise
My radiance rare and fathomless,
When I came back from Lyonnesse
  With magic in my eyes!

Thomas Hardy

2. Setting Cornish to Music

THE Celtic language which attracted him [Peter Warlock] above all others was the Cornish, probably because it was entirely extinct, the last person to speak it being one Dolly Pentreath, who died in the eighteenth century. He actually set himself to learn this preposterous [sic] tongue, and set a Cornish text to music in one of the best works he wrote during this period—the *Cornish Christmas Carol*, for unaccompanied chorus. There was also a shorter companion piece, likewise set to Cornish words, which he never published, but it still exists in manuscript.

'The Cornish language should be revived—nay, is being revived, for am I not myself reviving it? What more effective protest against imperialism (in art as in other matters) could you or I make than by adopting, as a pure ritual, a speech, a nationality, that no longer exist—for you to make your dwelling [Bosigran] the centre of a Celtic rebirth—the rebirth of a something that never was born? . . .

'I am writing with great enthusiasm two Cornish hymns; it is probably the first time the old language has ever been musicked deliberately (assuming that the folk-songs—of which Cornwall seems to possess practically none—generated spontaneously) but it is wonderful for singing purposes, containing many sounds almost unknown in English (except in Cornish-English dialect) which have a real musical value of their own. I have lately made a great many experiments with Celtic tunes without approaching a solution of the problem of their adequate—I had almost said legitimate—treatment. As far as I can see at present, it is unsatisfactory to use more than fragmentary quotations from them in a composition; they do not seem suitable as 'themes' for treatment—they are somehow too proud as well as too perfect, complete, and rounded for that.'

CECIL GRAY, *Peter Warlock*

4

3. *The Cornish Language*

THE principal love and knowledge of this language lived in Dr. Kenall the Civilian, and with him lieth buried; for the English speech doth still encroach upon it, and hath driven the same into the uttermost skirts of the shire.

RICHARD CAREW, *Survey of Cornwall*

4. *And Shall Trelawny Die?*

A good sword and a trusty hand!
   A merry heart and true!
King James's men shall understand
   What Cornish lads can do!

And have they fixed the where and when?
   And shall Trelawny die?
Here's twenty thousand Cornish men
   Will know the reason why!

Out spake their Captain brave and bold:
   A merry wight was he:—
'If London Tower were Michael's hold,
   We'd set Trelawny free!

'We'll cross the Tamar, land to land:
   The Severn is no stay:
With "one and all", and hand in hand;
   And who shall bid us nay?

'And when we come to London Wall,
   A pleasant sight to view,
Come forth! come forth! ye cowards all:
   Here's men as good as you.

5

'Trelawny he's in keep and hold:
  Trelawny he may die:
But here's twenty thousand Cornish bold
  Will know the reason why!'

R. S. HAWKER, Cornish Ballads

5. *The Cornish Emigrant's Song*

Oh! the eastern winds are blowing;
  The breezes seem to say,
'We are going, we are going,
  To North Americay.

'There the merry bees are humming
  Around the poor man's hive;
Parson Kingdon is not coming
  To take away their tithe.

'There the yellow corn is growing
  Free as the king's highway;
So, we're going, we are going,
  To North Americay.

'Uncle Rab shall be churchwarden,
  And Dick shall be the squire,
And Jem, that lived at Norton,
  Shall be leader of the quire;

'And I will be the preacher,
  And preach three times a day
To every living creature
  In North Americay.'

R. S. HAWKER, Cornish Ballads

6. *Emigrant Miners*

AT Ogden we changed cars from the Union Pacific to the Central Pacific line of railroad.... I had by this time some opportunity of seeing the people whom I was among.... There were no emigrants direct from Europe—save one German family and a knot of Cornish miners who kept grimly by themselves, one reading the New Testament all day long through steel spectacles, the rest discussing privately the secrets of their old-world, mysterious race. Lady Hester Stanhope believed she could make something great of the Cornish; for my part, I can make nothing of them at all. A division of races, older and more original than that of Babel, keeps this close, esoteric family apart from neighbouring Englishmen. Not even a Red Indian seems more foreign in my eyes. This is one of the lessons of travel—that some of the strangest races dwell next door to you at home.

R. L. STEVENSON, *Across the Plains*

II. Places

1. D. H. Lawrence Likes Cornwall

I like Cornwall very much. It is not England. It is bare and dark and elemental, Tristan's land. I lie looking down at a cove where the waves come white under a low, black headland, which slopes up in bare green-brown, bare and sad under a level sky. It is old, Celtic, pre-Christian. Tristan and his boat, and his horn.

* * *

I still like Cornwall. The house is a big, low, grey, well-to-do farm-place, with all the windows looking over a round of grass, and between the stone gate pillars down a little tamarisky lane, at a cove of the sea, where the waves are always coming in past jutty black rocks. It is a cove like Tristan sailed into, from Lyonnesse—just the same. It belongs to 2000 years back—that pre-Arthurian Celtic flicker of being which disappeared so entirely. The landscape is bare, yellow-green and brown, dropping always down to black rocks and a torn sea. All is desolate and forsaken, not linked up. But I like it.

D. H. LAWRENCE, *Letters*

2. St. Michael's Mount

SEPTEMBER 8, 1810.—Before breakfast made a finished sketch of St. Michael's Mount from the Star Inn. I next hired a boat with two fishermen to take me round the island, which they undertook to do and to allow me time for making sketches, for a reward of four shillings. The weather was very fine, and the sea sufficiently smooth to enable them to keep the boat nearly stationary wherever I chose to remain. This rock, with its castle, is a noble subject for a painter. The west front of it which faces the ocean is the most rugged and precipitous. The form and the colour of it is beautiful, and all the parts are so much in unison; the castle is in all respects in such harmony with the rock upon which it stands, as almost to seem a natural part of it. The general colour of the rock is grey of various degrees; such also is that of the castle; but in both there is a mixture of other tints which by their opposition give greater effect to the whole. The herbage which forms a part of the surface is of a mild and subdued colour, well agreeing with the grave hue of the castle and rock.

The Bass rock at the mouth of the Firth of Forth, and the rock of Dumbarton in the Clyde, are famed features of nature in their respective situations; but cannot either of them be compared with St. Michael's Mount, which far exceeds them in elegance of form and picturesque beauty.—

I passed a considerable time in contemplating the island from various points and in sketching; and my boatmen being satisfied with the bargain they had made, and being young and cheerful, they sung, while I pursued my purpose.

JOSEPH FARINGTON, *The Farington Diary*

3. *The Vision of the Mount*

Where the great Vision of the guarded Mount
Looks toward Namancos and Bayona's hold ...

JOHN MILTON, *Lycidas*

12

4. *Peter Warlock at Zennor*

Trewey Bungalow
Newmill
Near Penzance
[No date]

... I am living now in a little wooden house on the highest part of the moor that separates the two seas, north and south—between Zennor and Penzance. All round, on all sides, nothing but open moorland and rock-strewn hills, mostly crowned with marvellous Druidic temples. Without leaving the house I can see the sun rise at five in the morning, and watch it sink at night into the sea. The sky never grows dark; the darkness seems rather to come welling out of the earth like a dye, infusing into every shape and form, every twig and every stone, a keen, intense blackness.... In the twilight, bushes, walls, roofs, and the line of the hills all seem to become rigid and sharp against the sky, like dark blades, while the upper air remains clear and bright and the sky becomes more and more luminous as the blue deepens to a marvellous purple setting for the first stars. The hollows and lower slopes of the hills are covered with a dazzling profusion of gorse and blackthorn—I have never seen such blazing masses of gorse. Tiny lizards dart about among the violets on the sunny banks and splendid gold-and-black adders often cross one's path on the moors. The other day, looking down from the cliffs into a clear, green sea-pool, I caught sight of a lovely young seal, gambolling about under the water. Up here on the moor all the birds and beasts come so near one, not suspecting any human presence. Foxes lollop leisurely along the road, bunnies hardly take the trouble to hop out of the way when one walks by. A chorus of larks makes the air ring all day long, and there are cuckoos innumerable, piping from far and near with delightful variations of pitch and interval—sometimes two sing exactly together, on different notes. One cuckoo (I've actually seen him several times—a beautiful, bluey-grey person who bobs up and down just like the one that lives in a clock) is very fond of sitting on my roof or on the fence just outside the house in the very early morning before his throat's clear: and he can't cuckoo properly, but makes queer gurk-noises and then chortles with a peculiar laugh of which I could never have thought him capable! And on the edge of the pond near by an assembly of huge gulls holds colloquy (there is no other word for this strange croaking).

I wish you would come and live hereabouts for a bit. There is an extraordinary fascination about this little remote end of Cornwall.

CECIL GRAY, *Peter Warlock*

5. *A Cottage at Poltescoe*

AT Helston the last Cornish railway ends, on a railed motor-track coming from Gwinear Road; and from Helston to Poltescoe it is a drive of ten miles, for the last part of the way along the edge of Goonhilly Downs. As we come into Poltescoe Valley the road becomes steeper, and we climb and descend through high green hedges, until, just after the bridge, we turn aside into a narrow lane, and, after passing a double cottage and a smithy, come round a slow curve to the thatched cottage standing inside a little garden. There are fields on the slope of a hill opposite, and, lower down, where the road turns around an edge of solid rock, there is a stream, going by an old mill, and, beyond it, a steep rocky hill, with clusters of trees, bracken, gorse, and rough green foliage, rising up against the sky, between the valley and the sea.

I have never lived in so peaceful a place, and the old miller who lives by himself at the mill—'like a single plover,' he tells me—says that the people like the restfulness and do not willingly leave it. The washerwoman who has part of the double cottage along the lane says that she would go mad if she went to live in a town, and that the mere thought of it, sometimes, as she goes in and out of her door all day long, makes her feel uneasy. The miller says that the people do not notice the beauty of the place much, because they

14

are used to it; but he himself told me that, so far as he can hear, it is the prettiest place in England.

The cottage has a few disadvantages. One is that I cannot stand quite upright in either of the lower rooms. When a labourer lived in it there was, of course, a stone floor, and the wooden floor which the new landlord has put in has brought the ceiling lower. Where the ceiling is plain I can stand upright; but there are cross-beams, and the doors are lower than the cross-beams, and I have to go about stooping, for fear of dashing my head against one or the other.

Then there is that very decorative and in some ways practical thing, a thatched roof. I have always wanted to sleep under a thatched roof, but the actual experience has chilled my enthusiasm. There is the delight of looking at it from the hill going up to Ruan Minor, like a corkscrew, on the other side of the valley; and there is the delight of sitting under the eaves and hearing the sudden soft rustle of wings as the birds fly in and out of their nests among the thatch. But when you find, on going to bed, a little red worm sitting on the pillow; when black spots of various shapes and sizes begin to move and crawl on the wall and ceiling; when the open window, which lets in all the scents and sounds of the country, lets in also whatever creeps and flies among the bushes—sleep under a thatched roof becomes a less desirable thing.

But for these slight drawbacks, which have their compensations as one sits at night, reading by lamplight, in rooms so pleasantly and quaintly proportioned, and the painted butterflies and sombre moths come in at the window and dash themselves ecstatically at the light: well, I can ask no more of a cottage. And then, with the cottage, have we not the indispensable Mrs. Pascoe, and is not Mrs. Pascoe the contriver of all expedients and the journal and encyclopaedia of all local knowledge?

ARTHUR SYMONS, *Cities and Sea Coasts and Islands*

6. *Ludgvan and St. Just Contrasts*

No two things can be more opposite than the situations of Ludgvan and St. Just. In the former I have all the pleasures that a southern sun, a fine valley, a bay with a gently declining shore, trading towns, prettily planted villages, and now the Spring is come, all vegetable nature awake. In the latter there is one perpetual hue of heath, no tree to blossom nor shrub to flower. The bleak northern sea is edged by steep and craggy cliffs, the hills and valleys equally bestrewed with rocks; and what seemingly adds to the natural horror of the place is, that you everywhere meet with little growing mountains of rubbish, which are thrown up here out of tin mines, and would be so many blemishes and deformities on any other surface than this.

(Dr. Borlase to Dr. Oliver)

Oliver's reply was equally apt though more metaphorical:

Ludgvan is like a buxom girl of 18, always laughing and playing, and affording plentifully all the superficial pleasures of mirth and jollity; but St. Just is an old haggard philosopher, whose ruthful appearance would deter the soft and the luxurious from having anything to do with him, but he is full of riches within, and though they lie deep, and are come at with difficulty, yet he never fails to afford them to the hardy, the patient and the industrious.

P. A. S. POOL, 'William Borlase', in *Journal of the Royal Institution of Cornwall* (1966)

7. *Erisey*

IN the valley, across fields in which rocks like the rocks on the seashore grow naturally, with ferns and bramble about them, buried deep among old trees, murmuring with rooks, there is a decayed manor-house, now a farm, called Erisey: an Erisey of Erisey is said to have danced before James I. The road leads over many Cornish stiles, and through farmyards where cows wait around the milking-stool, or hens scratch beside the barn door, or pigs hurry to a trough. The air is heavy with scents from the hedges and with the clean, homely odour of farms; there is nothing in this wooded place to remind one that the sea lies on the other side of a few fields. And yet I have always felt some obscure, inexplicable, uneasy sense or suggestion when I come near this old house set over against a little wood, in which Mélisande might have walked; the wood has a solemn entrance, through curved and pillared stone gateways; the grass is vivid green underfoot, and the tree trunks go up straight in a formal pattern. The old house at the door of the wood seems to slumber uneasily, as if secrets were hidden there, somewhere behind the thick ivy and the decayed stone. The villagers will not go that way after dark, because of a field that lies on the road there, which they call Deadman's Field.

Sunset comes delicately into the wood at Erisey, setting gold patches to dance on the dark trunks of the trees. But it is from the downs, or from the croft which lies between the cottage and the sea, that I like best to see the day end. From the downs, or from the road just above the cottage, the sky has often that amber light which Coleridge notes in his poems; with infinite gradations of green, and a strange heaping of sullen and bodiless clouds against pure bright-ness. From the fields at Carleon, between the valley and the sea, night is seen touching the valley into a gentle and glowing harmony. The valley, a deep dell sunk into the midst of a circle of rocks covered with thin green foliage, is a nest and bower of soft trees, which rise cluster above cluster almost to the edge of the sky, where the rocky line of the field ends it. Above, you see the bars of colour left over by the sunset; the moon hangs aloft between the valley and the sea; and as the valley withdraws into the rich darkness of the earth, the sea still glitters with gray light, to where white clouds come down out of the sky and rest upon it.

Tidings of the outer world come but rarely into the valley, except by way of the sky. Once a day the old postman comes down from

Ruan Minor, and takes the letters back to the post-office. At times the sound of a siren, like the lowing of a brazen ox, comes paradoxically into the midst of the hot inland scents. At times a farm-boy following the cows, or a man sitting on the shafts of his cart, passes, whistling; and the tune will be a hymn tune, 'Jesu, lover of my soul,' or an air as old as 'Rule, Britannia,' taken very slowly. If you hear the people talking to one another in the lane, you will notice that they speak and reply in phrases out of the Bible, as in a language of which they can catch every allusion. They never pass one another without stopping to talk, and every one of them greets you with the time of the day as you pass.

All day long the tree before the door of the cottage is filled with music, and at night, when the moon is up, the sky before the windows is flooded with strange shapes and motions of light. I have never seen the moon's magic so nimbly or so continuously at work as upon that space of sky where the higher ridges of the croft ended. Kingdoms and seas of cloud passed before us under that calm radiance; they passed, leaving the sky clear for the stars; the polar star stood over the cottage, and the Great Bear flung out his paws at the moon.

ARTHUR SYMONS, *Cities and Sea Coasts and Islands*

8. Phillack

MR. EDMUND HOCKIN, the squire of Phillack, was a bachelor of almost sixty who lived in a small house at the top of the village he owned. Here, with an elderly housekeeper to look after him, he devoted himself to two passions—growing vegetables better than anybody else in Cornwall, and the preservation of old Cornish apples like Sops in Wine, Cornish Gillyflowers, Irish Peaches, Tom Putts, Sweet Larks, and many other the names of which I have forgotten. He seemed doubtful at first about letting Rivière House because it would mean parting with that acre of potatoes on the left as one entered the gates of the drive up to the house. Also there was a Canadian woman to whom he had half promised to let the house the previous year when she was visiting some relations in Hayle. However, in the end he decided to let it to us on a seven-years' lease with the option of renewal.

Rivière had been built by the chief owner of a long abandoned copper-mine at the end of the eighteenth or beginning of the nineteenth century, and it had a large copper roof. Another relic of that mine was an adit, at the back of the house, which pierced the slope above for at least a hundred yards; it was a dark, gloomy and tiring business to walk up to the end of that adit with bent head and shoulders; I need hardly add that it was an expedition I inflicted on any male guest we had.

Behind the house rose the great sweep of towans, many times larger than those between Church Cove and Cury Churchtown, and stretching for most of the length of St Ives Bay, being bounded on the west by St Ives itself and on the east by Godrevy lighthouse below the cliffs of Dead Man's Cove. To my pleasure I saw that the towans at the back of Rivière were covered with cowslips.

Mostly these towans presented to the beach a low line of serrated cliffs some thirty feet high; from time to time they would break away to gullies full of fine, drifted sand, whose small cavities hoarded snail-shells wind-dried to an ethereal lightness and rabbit-bones bleached and honey-combed by weather. The beach itself was at low water a very wide and flat and completely desolate expanse, shining near the sea's edge with whatever gold or silver was in the air, shot with crimson bars at sunset, crinkled by the wind to a vast replica of one of its own shells, ribbed and ploughed by tempests.

Beyond that acre of potatoes with which Squire Hockin had been at first unwilling to part was the walled garden sloping down to what from a gardener's point of view was a pestilent row of elms beyond which at high tide the water of the Hayle estuary glittered, at low tide presented an expanse of mud. On the other side was the town of Hayle, which had grown up round the famous Hayle Foundry, where that engineering genius Richard Trevithick had done at least as much as, if not more than, Watt and Stephenson to develop the steam engine. He married a Harvey and in 1908 there were still Harveys in control of the Hayle Foundry and Engineering Works, where once upon a time were built, besides the engines used in the lead mines, what were considered the best railway locomotives in Great Britain. By 1908 the great foundry was almost still and Hayle itself had become a small industrial town living in its past.

SIR COMPTON MACKENZIE, My Life and Times

9. Redruth

THE last two decades of that century were stirring times in West Cornwall. The Industrial Revolution was at its height and nowhere were its effects more clearly seen than in Redruth, which for a few years became a focal point from which many of the industrial and engineering developments of the modern world were destined to proceed. In 1797 Richard Trevithick was living in the town. Although best known as the pioneer of railway locomotion and for his use of high-pressure steam, he was a man so versatile in genius that pages might be devoted to the mere enumeration of his inventions. Near neighbour to Trevithick was Boulton and Watt's agent, the Scotsman William Murdock, who, in addition to a wide range of mechanical experiments, made history in the town by being the first man ever to apply coal gas to the purposes of lighting. In Redruth too James Watt himself lived for a while, revolutionizing Cornish mining with his pumping engines as elsewhere he was changing the character of England by the new force of steam.

Despite all this Redruth, surprisingly, has found comparatively small mention even in Cornish history, a fact which may be attributed to its having always been predominantly a working-class town. Visitors to the county in the past, as at the present, rarely stayed there, whilst the land-owners who frequently derived considerable revenues from its tin and copper mines eschewed it as a place of residence. In this respect it differed from Truro, Penzance and even Helston where, down to the middle of the eighteenth century, many of the neighbouring squires had their 'town houses' to which they resorted in winter, and where as a consequence theatres, concerts, balls and card parties emulated in some small degree the contemporary glories of Bath.

But Redruth knew little of the graces of life. In the early numbers of the two Cornish newspapers which came into being at the beginning of the nineteenth century such items of news as relate to the town are generally of a sombre character—of accidents among the miners from falling rock or premature explosions, of children burnt or scalded to death in overcrowded homes, and of the savage punishment of petty offences inflicted by a harsh criminal law.

Happily, there was another side to this picture. The town had its merchant and small employer class, the risk-takers of our now much abused capitalism; men who adventured their own small savings in the local mines and enterprises, who provided employment when trade was good and when times were bad relieved the ensuing distress. . . . Engaged as many of them were in the common forms of applied science, whether as engineers or assayers in the surrounding mines, they were alive to the value of education, and were prepared to extend it in some measure to the labouring masses.

A. K. HAMILTON JENKIN, *News From Cornwall*

10. *Celia Fiennes Visits Tregothnan*

So I went three miles more to Mr. Boscawen's—Tregothnan—a relation of mine. His house stands on a high hill in the middle of a park with several rows of trees, with woods beyond it. The house is built all of white stone like the rough coarse marble, and covered with slate. They use much lime in their cement, which makes both walls and cover look very white. There is a court walled round with open iron gates and bars. The entrance is up a few stone steps into a large high hall and so to a passage that leads foreright up a good staircase. On the right side is a large common parlour for constant eating in, from whence goes a little room for smoking that has a back way into the kitchen, and on the left hand is a great parlour and drawing-room—wainscotted all very well, but plain. The great parlour is cedar; out of it is the drawing-room, which is hung with pictures of the family, that goes into the garden, which has gravel walks round and across, but the squares are full of gooseberry and shrub trees and looks more like a kitchen garden, as Lady Mary Boscawen told me, out of which is another garden and orchard, which is something like a grove—green walks with rows of fruit trees.

It is capable of being a fine place with some charge; the rooms above are new-modelled, three rooms wainscotted and hung as the new way is, and the beds made up well, one red damask, another green, another wrought some of the Lady's own work and well made up, which is her room with a dressing-room by it. There is a dressing-room and a room for a servant just by the best chamber. There are two other good rooms unaltered, with old hangings to the bottom on wrought work of the first Lady's, Lady Marget's work, that was my cousin german; within that room was a servant's room and back stairs, and there was just such another apartment on the other side. Between all from the stairs a broad passage leads to a balcony over the entrance, which looked very pleasantly over the park, but in the cupola on the leads I could see a vast way, at least twenty miles round; for this house stands very high to the land side eastward, and the south was the Great Ocean which runs into Falmouth, that is the best harbour for ships in that road.

CELIA FIENNES, Through England on a Side-Saddle

11. How Many Miles to Mylor?

How many miles to Mylor
 By frost and candle-light:
How long before I arrive there,
 This mild December night?

As I mounted the hill to Mylor
 Through the thick woods of Carclew,
A clock struck the three-quarters,
 And suddenly a cock crew.

At the cross-roads on the hill-top
 The snow lay on the ground,
In the quick air and the stillness,
 No movement and no sound.

'How is it?' said a voice from the bushes
 Beneath the rowan-tree;
'Who is it?' my mouth re-echoed,
 My heart went out of me.

I cannot tell what queerness
 There lay around Carclew:
Nor whatever stirred in the hedges
 When an owl replied 'Who-whoo?'

A lamp in a lone cottage,
 A face in a window-frame,
Above the snow a wicket:
 A house without a name.

How many miles to Mylor
 This dark December night:
And shall I ever arrive there
 By frost or candle-light?

     A. L. ROWSE, *Poems of a Decade*

12. Winds at Gorran

GORRAN SCHOOL, with a house for 'master' glued to it, stood strong and symmetrical, without beauty but not mean, triumphantly facing the wrong way. It might have looked south over the distant Gruda and the sea; but this advantage was forgone in favour of presenting a good face to the road. Master's room in school, the big room as we called it, caught the north wind while the closets at the back caught the sun. I have heard that Mr. Sylvanus Trevail, the architect, who designed many Cornish schools, committed suicide in the end; but whether out of remorse for his cold frontages I do not know.

Except in thick mist or in high summer I hardly remember still air at Gorran. The wind either played or howled round our house; it rarely died altogether. It was a constant companion, in one's hair and in the leaves and in the telegraph poles, whirling the smoke down the chimneys, rattling the sash windows, and bringing the middle door to with a bang if front or back were suddenly opened. When I was told the story of Jacob wrestling with God I saw him struggling to open our heavy front door in the wind.

The wind streamed round us straight from everywhere. From whatever direction it blew it met house and swept on and round it like a sea-swirl over and around rocks. Winter gales were glorious. When the winds were really high, entering our house from the lanes was almost like getting into a beleaguered fortress. In the lanes we were protected by hedges. Then, tugging open our gate, we would advance a few yards in the shelter of the wall before running the gauntlet of the wind in the open garden. Sometimes we could only just manage to round the projecting corner of the house against which the wind would try to hurl us. It was called 'rounding the Cape of Good Hope'....

The School House and High Lanes were the windiest spots in Gorran. A wag once named the School House Gorran Lighthouse. The Churchtown, at the foot of Menaguins Hill, was sheltered; but Menaguins itself, where Will Richards had his forge, Agnes her shop, and Cap'n Lelean his coal-store, was pretty exposed. Will

24

Richards was captain of the Gorran cricket team, and my brothers' hero. We had our coals from Cap'n Math; my eldest brother once said Cap'n Math watered it to make it heavy, and Will Lelean fought him for the aspersion and won. Most of the older farmhouses were sheltered, though Trelispan, Lamledra, Tregarten and Tregerrick caught the wind. Cotna was deliciously situated; so were Trewollock, Treveague, Penare, Tredinnick, Treveor and Polsue. Trevarrick was perhaps the best of all, where the earliest snowdrops grew. The vicarage was well placed among trees, its richly cultivated garden contrasting with our wild one. . . .

The high hedges which bordered the roads and divided the fields were shelters for beasts and men. In sudden scurries of driving rain we sought a 'lew'[1] hedge. Cattle, seeking the hedges in wet windy days, would stand, their hind-quarters in comparative comfort, looking with melancholy eyes over the fields. Except for the moor-like stretches round Dodman and the Grebe, all Gorran was field and hedge. At Hemmick the poppies and corn and a lovely blue flower—I think corn cockle—grew to the cliff edge, so that the summer wind could be heard in the waves on the one hand and in the wheat or oats or barley on the other. Thomas Hardy has described the winter voice of the wind in holly and oak and other woodland trees; to hear it rustle the ripe oats is the luxury of summer.

ANNE TRENEER, *School House in the Wind*

13. From a Cornish Window

MY window, then, looks out from a small library upon a small harbour frequented by ships of all nations—British, Danish, Swedish, Norwegian, Russian, French, German, Italian, with now and then an American or a Greek—and upon a shore which I love because it is my native country. Of all views I reckon that of a harbour the most fascinating and the most easeful, for it combines perpetual change with perpetual repose. It amuses like a panorama

[1] lee.

and soothes like an opiate, and when you have realised this you will understand why so many thousands of men around this island appear to spend all their time in watching tidal water. Lest you should suspect me of taking a merely dilettante interest in the view, I must add that I am a Harbour Commissioner.

As for the house, it is a plain one; indeed, very like the house a child draws on a slate, and therefore pleasing even externally to me, who prefer the classical to any Gothic style of architecture. Why so many strangers mistake it with its modest dimensions for a hotel, I cannot tell you. I found one in the pantry the other day searching for a brandy-and-soda; another rang the dining-room bell and dumb-founded the maid by asking what we had for lunch; and a third (a lady) cried when I broke to her that I had no sitting-room to let. We make it a rule to send out a chair whenever some unknown invader walks into the garden and prepares to make a water-colour sketch of the view.

There are some, too, whose behaviour cannot be reconciled with the hallucination of a hotel, and they must take the house for a public institution of some kind, though of what kind I cannot guess. There was an extremely bashful youth, for instance, who roamed the garden for a while on the day after the late Duke of Cambridge's funeral, and suddenly dashing in by the back door, wanted to know why our flag was not at half-mast. There was also a lady who called on the excuse that she had made a life-study of the Brontës, and after opining (in a guarded manner) that they came, originally, from somewhere in Yorkshire, desired to be informed how many servants we kept. I have sometimes thought of rechristen-ing our house The Hotel of the Four Seasons, and thereby releasing its true name (The Haven) to a friend who covets it for his own.

On the whole, however, these visitors disturb the house and the view from my window very little. The upper halves of them, as they pass up and down the road, appear above my garden wall much as the shadows that passed in Plato's cave. They come, enjoy their holiday, and go, leaving the window intent upon the harbour, its own folk and its own business.

Q, *From a Cornish Window*

14. *Trenarren: Autumn 1941*

The thunder-green sea
Brings nearer the Island
On which stood the chapel
Of Michael the Archangel.

Smoke from a chimney
In the V-shaped valley,
The voices of children,
A robin on the bough:

Familiar and cheerful
Domestic noises
Speak of contentment
About me now.

But what is to come?
I ask myself, waiting
In this burial-place
Of my ancient people:

The long-headed, dark-faced
Mediterranean
Men who drove prows
Into these inlets:

Confronting the danger
That they too awaited
In the urgent whisper,
The winter sea waiting.

A. L. ROWSE, *Poems Chiefly Cornish*

15. 'The Wind in the Willows'

WHILE the Grahames were at Fowey in May and June of 1907, they made the acquaintance of an American family also on holiday there—Mr. and Mrs. Austin Purves of Philadelphia, and their five sons, Dale, Austin Jr., Pierre, Edmund, and John. Kenneth actually stood godfather to Pierre, the youngest, at his Fowey christening, which 'was unusual in that old Cornish customs were carried out, a procession to the Church and the presentation of the Kimbly cake to the first person encountered.' Grahame and Austin Purves continued to correspond regularly until the latter's death in 1915; the two families met again at Fowey just before the First World War, and after it Grahame entertained the Purves boys on various occasions both in Oxford and in Rome.

All the brothers are happily alive today; and all agree in believing that the general setting of *The Wind in the Willows* is largely derived from Fowey and the Fowey River. This is suggestive and revealing. Hitherto it has generally been supposed that Fowey only contributed 'the little grey sea town' of the Sea Rat's tale, and that the rest was unadultered Thames-side Berkshire. But it is entirely in key with his Coleridgean methods of composition that Grahame should have added elements from Fowey as well.

More specifically, the Purves brothers confirm that the opening chapter, 'The River Bank', was inspired by a boating trip up the Fowey River, undertaken by Grahame, 'Atky', and their father, 'to a little village called Golant, on the right bank, for tea. They probably hired someone else to row them.' Similarly the entire open-air sequence of 'Wayfarers All' is supposed to have been directly provoked by a walk Grahame and Austin Purves (or 'Atky') took in the near-by countryside; perhaps 'towards the west on the Fowey side, past Ready Money Cove, to St. Catherine's Castle and the hills and sea coast beyond that'.

PETER GREEN, *Kenneth Grahame*

16. *The Harbour of Fowey*

O the Harbour of Fowey
   Is a beautiful spot,
And it's there I enjowey
   To sail in a yot;
Or to race in a yacht
   Round a mark or a buoy—
Such a beautiful spacht
   Is the Harbour of Fuoy!

When her anchor is weighed
   And the water she ploughs,
Upon neat lemoneighed
   O it's then I caroughs;
And I take Watts's hymns
   And I sing them aloud
When it's homeward she skymns
   O'er the waters she ploud.

But the wave mountain-high,
   And the violent storm,
Do I risk them? Not Igh!
   But prefer to sit worm
With a book on my knees
   By the library fire,
While I list to the brees
   Rising hire and hire.

And so, whether I weigh
   Up the anchor or not,
I am happy each deigh
   In my home or my yot;
Every care I resign,
   Every comfort enjoy,
In this cottage of mign
   By the Harbour of Foy.

And my leisure's addressed
   To composing of verse
Which, if hardly the bessed,
   Might be easily werse.
And, the spelling I use
   Should the critics condemn,
Why, I have my own vuse
   And I don't think of themn.

Yes, I have my own views:
   But the teachers I follow
Are the Lyrical Miews
   And the Delphic Apollow.
Unto them I am debtor
   For spelling and rhyme,
And I'm doing it bebtor
   And bebtor each thyme.

Q, Poems

17. *The Sunken Garden at Tregrehan*

WHEN grandmother and grandfather were promoted to keep the lodge-gate at Tregrehan—'The Lodge' or 'to th' Lodge' it was referred to respectfully by the family—I think the old lady felt that she had gone up in the world. No more 'ole farmplaace with nobody and nothin' to look at year in, year out, and nobody to come fore to the door, you 'ad to get everything for yourself.' There at the Lodge she was entrenched upon the main road, with a view of everything going up and down, but at the same time a little withdrawn within the defences of the park. 'Entrenched' is the right word; for grandmother thought as much of herself as the lady at the big house. She wasn't going to open and shut the gates for

30

them as they went in or out: the gates should be opened and remain open, or they should be shut and they could open them themselves! It was a good thing for her that the family was absent through all these years, or she would perhaps not have been there long. As it was she had the place to herself. The Carlyons were away in New Zealand, and then the young heir was in the War, in which he was badly wounded; the great house was shut up and in the hands of an old butler-housekeeper, Mr. Pope, with mutton-chop whiskers and silver hair, and silvery, obsequious voice and manner.

The place opened a window in my imagination as a boy. On Thursday afternoons when the shop was shut, in the summer during the school holidays, mother and I used to drive out in the donkey-and-jingle to Tregrehan. I used to wander about the park by myself, the place full of memories of the family that had lived there—for we knew all the servants' gossip about the gentry and their strange, exotic life: how many horses the Major had kept in his heyday, when the royalties were pouring in from the mines round about, Wheal Eliza, Wheal Buckler and the rest, and it seemed that their prosperity would never come to an end; how many servants there were in the house, the grand lady that was the housekeeper, with a housemaid all to herself to wait on her in the housekeeper's room; the Major coming home from abroad on his last illness, a neat dapper little man with red complexion and black beard, elegant small feet and hands; stories of Ann Bone, the cook (still alive, good soul, a tiny little woman of between eighty and ninety, whom I went to see in her cottage at Tregrehan Mills a year or two ago, out of nostalgia for these memories which were never mine); the coming to and fro between Tregrehan and the Major's town-house in Mayfair; the shooting-parties, the mass of meat-pasties that would be made in the kitchen.

Sometimes, rather timorously, I wandered on up the drive or across the park under the fine beeches that remembered other days, and round the curve with the steep banks of grass (they seemed high then) to the gate and looked, greatly daring, into that sacred preserve: the melancholy, green gloom around the house, the long pillared portico to the front door, the big lion couchant on the grass that seemed very much on guard against small boys trespassing in those dedicated precincts. Sometimes when I thought nobody was about, the great house silently eyeing me with all its shuttered windows, I have stolen by that knowing lion, made for the path between the thick shrubs that led to a more remote paradise where I felt for a moment secure in the angle of those box-hedges. There was the sunken Italian garden, with its formal flower-beds and box-borders, the raised terraces all round with the figures of Spring, Summer, Autumn, Winter (an old man, I remember, bent beneath his burden of sticks) in white marble at the corners; the long colonnade of the south front looking down upon that empty, waiting scene with one small boy moonstruck in his nook. Silence, save for the rustle of leaves, a sigh along the nearer trees outside in the park—or was it the silk skirt of some long-dead lady, wife of the Admiral or the Major, upon the terrace?—silence and waiting accentuated by the tinkle of the fountain plashing patiently among the water-lilies of the decorated basin. When later I read

> Now sleeps the crimson petal, now the white;
> Now waves the cypress in the palace walk;
> Now winks the gold fin in the porphyry font ...
>
> Now folds the lily all her sweetness up,

it was the deserted Italian garden at Tregrehan that was always present in the back of my mind.

Once or twice I wandered a little farther, keeping carefully to the farthest walk from the house, and found my way into the deep gloom of the cedar-walk, a vista which ended with a figure of a dog agonizing on his pedestal: I assumed that it must be the grave of a favourite dog. Stealing back along the path, soft and plumb with accumulated moss, I returned by way of the sunken garden, catching sight as I passed of a shadowy figure in an upper window moving forward to shut the shutters: the ancient ritual of the venerable old retainer, as slow, deliberate, formal as some devotee in the temple of a vanished religion.

A. L. ROWSE, *A Cornish Childhood*

18. A Plan-an-Gwary: Perran Round

HARD by the edge of the sand-hills, and close beside the high road on the last rise before it dips to the coast, stands a turfed embankment surrounded by a shallow fosse. This is none of our ancient camps ('castles' we call them in Cornwall), as you perceive upon stepping within the enclosure, which rises in a complete circle save for two entrances cut through the bank and facing one another. You are standing in a perfectly level area a hundred and thirty feet in diameter; the surrounding rampart rises to a height of eight or nine feet, narrowing towards the top, where it is seven feet wide; and around its inner side you may trace seven or eight rows of seats cut in the turf, but now almost obliterated by the grass.

This Round (as we call it) was once an open-air theatre or planguary (*plain-an-guaré*, place of the play). It has possibly a still older history, and may have been used by the old Cornish for their councils and rustic sports; but we know that it was used as a theatre, perhaps as early as the fourteenth century, certainly as late as the late sixteenth: and, what is more, we have preserved for us some of the plays performed in it.

They are sacred or miracle plays, of course. If you draw a line from entrance to entrance, then at right angles to it there runs from the circumference towards the centre of the area a straight shallow trench, terminating in a spoon-shaped pit. The trench is now a mere depression not more than a foot deep, the pit three feet: but doubtless time has levelled them up, and there is every reason to suppose that the pit served to represent Hell (or, in the drama of the Resurrection, the Grave), and the trench allowed the performers, after being thrust down into perdition, to regain the green-room unobserved—either actually unobserved, the trench being covered, or by a polite fiction, the audience pretending not to see. My private belief is that, the stage being erected above and along the trench, they were actually hidden while they made their exit. Where the trench meets the rampart a semi-circular hollow, about ten feet in diameter, makes a breach in the rows of seats. Here, no doubt, stood the green-room.

The first notice of the performance of these plays occurs in Carew's *Survey of Cornwall*, published in 1602:—

Pastimes to delight the mind, the Cornishmen have guary miracles and three-men's songs: and for exercise of the body hunting, hawking, shooting, wrestling, hurling, and such other games.

The guary miracle, in English a miracle play, is a kind of Interlude compiled in Cornish out of some scripture history with that grossness which accompanied the Romans' *vetus comedia*. For representing it they raise an earthen amphitheatre in some open field, having the diameter of his inclosed plain some forty or fifty foot. The country people flock from all sides, many miles off, to hear and see it; for they have therein devils and devices to delight as well the eye as the ear; the players con not their parts without book, but are prompted by one called the Ordinary, who followeth at their back with the book in his hand and telleth them softly what they must pronounce aloud.

Our Round, you observe, greatly exceeds the dimensions given by Carew. But there were several in the west: one, for instance, traceable fifty years ago, at the northern end of the town of Redruth, which still keeps the name of Planguary; and another magnificent one, of stone, near the churchtown of St. Just by the Land's End. Carew may have seen only the smaller ones.

Q, *From a Cornish Window*

19. Near Lanivet

There was a stunted handpost just on the crest,
    Only a few feet high:
She was tired, and we stopped in the twilight-time for her rest,
    At the crossways close thereby.

She leant back, being so weary, against its stem,
    And laid her arms on its own,

Each open palm stretched out to each end of them,
  Her sad face sideways thrown.

Her white-clothed form at this dim-lit cease of day
  Made her look as one crucified
In my gaze at her from the midst of the dusty way,
  And hurriedly 'Don't,' I cried.

I do not think she heard. Loosing thence she said,
  As she stepped forth ready to go,
'I am rested now.—Something strange came into my head;
  I wish I had not leant so!'

And wordless we moved onward down from the hill
  In the west cloud's murked obscure,
And looking back we could see the handpost still
  In the solitude of the moor.

'It struck her too,' I thought, for as if afraid
  She heavily breathed as we trailed;
Till she said, 'I did not think how 'twould look in the shade,
  When I leant there like one nailed.'

I, lightly: 'There's nothing in it. For *you*, anyhow!
  —'Oh I know there is not,' said she . . .
'Yet I wonder . . . If no one is bodily crucified now,
  In spirit one may be?'

And we dragged on and on, while we seemed to see
  In the running of Time's far glass
Her crucified, as she had wondered if she might be
  Some day.—Alas, alas!

THOMAS HARDY

20. Blisland Church

OF all the country churches of the West I have seen I think the Church of St. Protus and St. Hyacinth, Blisland, in Cornwall, is the most beautiful. . . .

Perched on the hill above the wood stands Blisland village. It has not one ugly building in it and, which is unusual in Cornwall, the houses are round a green. Between the lichen-crested trunks of elm and ash that grow on the green, you can see everywhere the beautiful moorland granite. It is used for windows, for chimney stacks, for walls. One old house has gable ends carved in it. They are sixteenth or seventeenth century and curl round like swiss rolls. The church is down a steep slope of graveyard, past slate headstones and it looks over the tree tops of a deep and elmy valley and away to the west where, like a silver shield, the Atlantic shines. An opening in the churchyard circle shows a fuchsia hedge and the Vicarage front door beyond. The tower is square and weathered and made of enormous blocks of this moorland granite, each block as big as a chest of drawers. When I first saw it, the tower was stuffed with moss and with plants which had rested here and there between the great stones. But lately it has been most vilely repointed in hard straight lines with cement. The church itself, which seems to lean this way and that, throws out chapels and aisles in all directions. It hangs on the hillside, spotted with lichens which have even softened the slates of its roof. Granite forms the tracery of its windows, there is a granite holy-water stoup in the porch.

The whitewashed porch, the flapping notices, the door! That first thrill of turning the handle of the door of a church never seen before, or a church dearly loved and visited again and again like Blisland—who but the confirmed church crawler knows it?

Sir Ninian Comper, that great church architect, says that a church should bring you to your knees when first you enter it. Such a church is Blisland. For there before me as I open the door is the blue-grey granite arcade, the hardest of stones to carve. One column slopes outwards as though it was going to tumble down the hill and a carved wooden beam is fixed between it and the south wall to stop

it falling. The floor is of blue slate and pale stone. Old carved
benches of dark oak and a few chairs are the seating. The walls are
white, the sun streams in through a clear west window and there—
glory of glories!—right across the whole eastern end of the church is
a richly-painted screen and rood-loft. It is of wood. The panels at its
base are red and green. Wooden columns, highly coloured and
twisted like barley sugar, burst into gilded tracery and fountain out
to hold a panelled loft. There are steps to reach this loft, in the wall.
Our Lord and His Mother and St. John who form the rood are over
the centre of the screen. I look up and there is the old Cornish roof,
shaped like the inside of an upturned ship, all its ribs richly carved,
the carving shown up by white plaster panels. Old roofs, beautifully
restored, are to be seen throughout the church. They stretch away
beyond the cross irregularly and down the aisles. I venture in a little
further, there through this rich screen I mark the blazing gold of the
altars and the medieval-style glass, some of the earliest work of
Comper. In the nave is a pulpit shaped like a wineglass, in the
Georgian style and encrusted with cherubs and fruit carved in wood.

The screen, the glory of the church, the golden altars, the stained
glass and the pulpit are comparatively *new*, designed by F. C. Eden
in 1897, who died a few years ago. He must have visualised this
Cornish church as it was in medieval times. He did not do all the
medieval things he might have done. He did not paint the walls
with pictures of angels, saints and devils, he left the western windows clear that people might see their books; he put in a *Georgian*
pulpit. He centred everything on the altar to which the screen is, as
it were, a golden, red and green veil to the holiest mystery behind it.

What do dates and styles matter in Blisland church? There is
Norman work in it and there is fifteenth- and sixteenth-century
work and there is sensitive and beautiful modern work. But chiefly
it is a living church whose beauty makes you gasp, whose silent
peace brings you to your knees, even if you kneel on the hard stone
and slate of the floor, worn smooth by generations of worshippers.

The valley below the church was hot and warm when first I saw
this granite cool interior. Valerian sprouted on the Vicarage wall. A
fig tree traced its leaves against a western window. Grasshoppers

and birds chirruped. St. Protus and St. Hyacinth, patron saints of Blisland church, pray for me! Often in a bus or train I call to mind your lovely church, the stillness of that Cornish valley and the first really beautiful work of man which my boyhood vividly remembers.

JOHN BETJEMAN, *First and Last Loves*

21. *Autumn in Cornwall*

The year lies fallen and faded
On cliffs by clouds invaded,
With tongues of storms upbraided,
    With wrath of waves bedinned;
And inland, wild with warning,
As in deaf ears or scorning,
The clarion even and morning
    Rings of the south-west wind.

The wild bents wane and wither
In blasts whose breath bows hither
Their grey-grown heads and thither,
    Unblest of rain or sun;
The pale fierce heavens are crowded
With shapes like dreams beclouded,
As though the old year enshrouded
    Lay, long ere life were done.

Full-charged with oldworld wonders,
From dusk Tintagel thunders
A note that smites and sunders
    The hard frore fields of air;

A trumpet stormier-sounded
That once from lists rebounded
When strong men sense-confounded
  Fell thick in tourney there.

From scarce a duskier dwelling
Such notes of wail rose welling
Through the outer darkness, telling
  In the awful singer's ears
What souls the darkness covers,
What love-lost souls of lovers,
Whose cry still hangs and hovers
  In each man's born that hears.

For there by Hector's brother
And yet some thousand other
He that had grief to mother
  Passed pale from Dante's sight;
With one fast linked as fearless,
Perchance, there only tearless;
Iseult and Tristram, peerless
  And perfect queen and knight.

A shrill-winged sound comes flying
North, as of wild souls crying
The cry of things undying,
  That know what life must be;
Or as the old year's heart, stricken
Too sore for hope to quicken
By thoughts like thorns that thicken,
  Broke, breaking with the sea.

A. C. SWINBURNE

22. Tintagel in Tudor Times

THIS castle hath been a marvellous strong and notable fortress, and almost *situ loci inexpugnabile*, especially for the dungeon that is on a great and high terrible crag environed with the sea, but having a drawbridge from the residue of the castle on to it. The residue of the buildings of the castle be sore weather-beaten and in ruin, but it hath been a large thing. The castle had by likelihood three wards, wherof two be worn away with gulfing in of the sea, in so much that it hath made there almost an isle, and no way is to enter into it now but by long elm trees laid for a bridge. So that now without the isle runneth only a gatehouse, a wall, and a false bray digged and walled. In the isle remain old walls, and in the east part of the same, the ground being lower, remaineth a wall embattled, and men alive saw therein postern door of iron. There is in the isle a pretty chapel of St. Ulette *alias* Uliane, with a tomb on the left side. There is also in the isle a well, and nigh by the same is a place hewn out of the stony ground to the length and breadth of a man. Also there remaineth in the isle a ground quadrant walled as it were a garden plot; and by this wall appear the ruins of a vault. The ground of this isle now nourisheth sheep . . .

Also about Camelford, are certain old mines, wrought in times past, but of what metal it is now unknown. Within a mile above that poor village south runneth the river that goeth into the Severn Sea at Padstow, and it is the greatest river on the north side of Cornwall, and is called in the common speech there, Dunmere,[1] and in the king's grant of privilege to the Canons of Bodmin and the burgesses of the same town, Alan, it may fortune for Alaune. Some histories call it Camlan. By this river Arthur fought his last field, in token whereof the people find there in ploughing bones and harness.

JOHN LELAND, *Itinerary*

[1] Now called Camel. The chief tributary is called Allen.

23. Trebetherick

We used to picnic where the thrift
    Grew deep and tufted to the edge;
We saw the yellow foam-flakes drift
    In trembling sponges on the ledge
Below us, till the wind would lift
    Them up the cliff and o'er the hedge.
Sand in the sandwiches, wasps in the tea,
Sun on our bathing-dresses heavy with the wet,
Squelch of the bladder-wrack waiting for the sea,
Fleas round the tamarisk, an early cigarette.

From where the coastguard houses stood
    One used to see, below the hill,
The lichened branches of a wood
    In summer silver-cool and still;
And there the Shade of Evil could
    Stretch out at us from Shilla Mill.
Thick with sloe and blackberry, uneven in the light,
Lonely ran the hedge, the heavy meadow was remote,
The oldest part of Cornwall was the wood as black as night,
And the pheasant and the rabbit lay torn open at the throat.

But when a storm was at its height,
    And feathery slate was black in rain,
And tamarisks were hung with light
    And golden sand was brown again,
Spring tide and blizzard would unite
    And sea come flooding up the lane.
Waves full of treasure then were roaring up the beach,
Ropes round our mackintoshes, waders warm and dry,
We waited for the wreckage to come swirling into reach,
Ralph, Vasey, Alastair, Biddy, John and I.

Then roller into roller curled
　　And thundered down the rocky bay,
And we were in a water-world
　　Of rain and blizzard, sea and spray,
And one against the other hurled
　　We struggled round to Greenaway.
Blessèd be St. Enodoc, blessèd be the wave,
Blessèd be the springy turf, we pray, pray to thee,
Ask for our children all the happy days you gave
To Ralph, Vasey, Alastair, Biddy, John and me.

JOHN BETJEMAN, *Collected Poems*

24. *Mist on Bodmin Moor*

THE spur of Cornwall juts far into the vapours of the Atlantic, and
the rapid changes of temperature that so often visit our western
coasts bring not only thunder in winter, but sudden mists at all
seasons, especially on high ground. The dangerous fogs of Dart-
moor are well known, and those of Bodmin Moor are no less
unexpected and misleading. Men who have known the moor all
their lives can get hopelessly lost within a mile of their own doors;
and I know of one young man overtaken by mist who followed the
sound of traffic to the main road, on which he lived, and then did
not know the way to turn for home! In really thick weather it is
well to keep near a hedge, for once in the open, there will be no
indication but the feel of the ground under your feet, since the
direction of the wind, so often variable, will prove but a fallible
guide. In open rolling country, with rare streams to follow and few
features to arrest the attention, mist is a real bane to travellers, since
the moor, like some petrified ocean, must be navigated by means of
distant landmarks. Luckily the thickest mist will often rise like a
theatre curtain, revealing, if only for a moment, whole tracts of

distant country; and then we can pick up our bearings before it falls again and leaves us blind. At Trenoweth we were fortunate in having the main road with its guiding hum of traffic barely a mile away, and connecting with it, two side roads that would lead the fogbound wanderer close to home. And there were the electric standards of Durfold, which could be followed to our neighbour's hedge, and so on to our own. At night the lights of distant farms, and the glare from the Hawkstor clayworks, made useful beacons. Trembath had a brilliant lamp in his uncurtained window, which was visible for miles on the downs, and as it showed to the north of Trenoweth and rather above it, we called it the Pole Star and used it for midnight navigation. We missed it when he left, and our chief grievance against his successor was that his lamp was less bright and he kept his curtains drawn.

The sudden onset of mist would often hinder us in herding cattle, especially in summer, when the cows never come home of their own accord. I would ride out into a grey and silent world of illusion, in which nothing was clear but a narrow circle of ground underfoot, on whose rim were trailed the ghostly hems of the mist. All things encountered—boulders, bushes, boundary-posts—were changed and magnified, till they looked like men riding or cows grazing; and many a time have I gone in pursuit of some spectral Devon cow only to find that I had been hunting a lichened stone or dwarf oak. And at the end of the day I might come to a thicket of furze, and see in its shadows, fronting the west and reflecting its last pale rays, a glimmering semi-circle, supine like a crescent moon, the spreading horns of the cow Lois, the rest of whose dark recumbent shape was lost in the bosky gloom.

Our mists were mostly in rapid motion, borne on breezes or even whirled on gales. They poured across the downs in a wild and eddying torrent, as if the sea had been drained of its vapours to overwhelm the land. But every now and then, in fair calm weather, surface fog would collect in the hollows of the moor. Sometimes, when riding home at night, I have seen the upper slopes of our fields, crowned by the tall trees in the yard, stand sharp and clear against a host of stars, while the shallow dell at the bridge beyond was full of mist that lay at peace like standing water, faintly bright in the gleam of distant worlds; so that the place had the look of a peat-moss in Uist, where there is more loch than land. At a little distance from the hollow, the clear-cut edge of the mist could still be seen, but as I crossed the lip and began to descend it faded from sight, because I was actually entering; and like a cold and stealthy tide the fog crept up to my horse's belly, and then to my own breast. The rocks and bushes on either hand grew dim and blurred, like shores receding from a spent swimmer, and as the chill dark vapours closed above my head the stars wavered and went out. A moment more, and Joey's hoofs were ringing on the further slope, and I saw again the long black ridge of Trehudreth, and the bare tracery of our trees, and from east to west the jewelled arch of the sky.

MARGARET LEIGH, *Harvest of the Moor*

25. *Beeny Cliff*
March 1870–*March* 1913

I

O the opal and the sapphire of that wandering western sea,
And the woman riding high above with bright hair flapping free—
The woman whom I loved so, and who loyally loved me.

II

The pale mews plained below us, and the waves seemed far away
In a nether sky, engrossed in saying their ceaseless babbling say,
As we laughed light-heartedly aloft on that clear-sunned March day.

III

A little cloud then cloaked us, and there flew an irised rain,
And the Atlantic dyed its levels with a dull misfeatured stain,
And then the sun burst out again, and purples prinked the main.

IV

—Still in all its chasmal beauty bulks old Beeny to the sky,
And shall she and I not go there once again now March is nigh,
And the sweet things said in that March say anew there by and by?

V

What if still in chasmal beauty looms that wild weird western shore,
The woman now is—elsewhere—whom the ambling pony bore,
And nor knows nor cares for Beeny, and will laugh there nevermore.

THOMAS HARDY

26. Dozmary Pool

I had been too busy to explore the moor beyond the usual haunt of
our flocks and herds, not even having followed the main road to
Bolventor, the moorland capital. But one day in the week before
Christmas, when I had a dozen jobs on hand but no inclination to
tackle any of them, I saddled Joey and rode in search of Dozmary
Pool. The moor is little known, and has few show places; and when
you have climbed Brown Willy, the highest hill in Cornwall, there
is nothing to do but visit this curious little lake, into which Sir
Bedivere is said to have thrown the sword Excalibur.

The pool is easily found, lying close to the road from Bolventor
to St. Neot, and in summer is much frequented by tourists; but I
saw it lonely as a Highland loch and almost as beautiful. The nearly
circular sheet of water lay still and burnished under a pure sky,
where floated motionless a fleet of domed and gilded clouds, faithfully mirrored in the shining levels beneath. The moor, which is
here 'blacker' and less grassy than about Trenoweth, compassed the
pool with low and gentle undulations, except to the south, where
rose a high hill crowned by ancient barrows. There were no distant
views, and the bareness of the near sky-line was broken only by the

45

stones of a pre-historic circle and one or two looming ricks of turf, big as haystacks, which lay remote from any house, and were fenced with wire from roaming cattle. Beside the pool stood a cottage with a cowshed and ricks of hay and ferns, and all the familiar crofter's jumble of mud and fallen stones and rotten wood: and in front, at the edge of the water, a granite boat-house with an iron roof so rusty that it glowed in the sun like fire. A plume of peat smoke rose from the single chimney, but the door was fastened, and there was nothing astir but a few geese, a couple of pigs, and four or five Devon cows, which stood dreaming on the brink, gazing at their still and unbroken reflections.

Out in the middle were floating a score of gulls, motionless as their mirrored counterparts. The thin cold air of the moor was muted to a rare silence, upon which an occasional squawk or flap of a wing broke with startling reverberation. The eternal lap of water on stone had ceased for a season, and the wide surface, unwrinkled by the slightest flaw, held all the world reflected—the golden clouds and tawny boathouse roof and white inverted gulls and the looming bulk of cows on the shore. I hitched Joey to a post and sat there for a while. The pool was the centre of the moor and of its very essence, and I wished that the people who had locked the cottage door and left their fire banked up might never return, and I would go in there and hang up my hat for good.

MARGARET LEIGH, *Harvest of the Moor*

27. *The Seasons in North Cornwall*

O spring has set off her green fuses
    Down by the Tamar today,
And careless, like tidemarks, the hedges
    Are bursting with almond and may.

46

Here lie I, waiting for old summer,
    A red face and straw-coloured hair has he:
I shall meet him on the road from Marazion
    And the Mediterranean Sea.

September has flung a spray of rooks
    On the sea-chart of the sky,
The tall shipmasts crack in the forest
    And the banners of autumn fly.

My room is a bright glass cabin,
    All Cornwall thunders at my door,
And the white ships of winter lie
    In the sea-roads of the moor.

CHARLES CAUSLEY, *Union Street*

28. *The Phantom Horsewoman*

I

Queer are the ways of a man I know:
        He comes and stands
        In a careworn craze
        And looks at the sands
        And the seaward haze
        With moveless hands
        And face and gaze,
        Then turns to go . . .
And what does he see when he gazes so?

II

They say he sees as an instant thing
        More clear than to-day,
        A sweet soft scene

47

That once was in play
By that briny green;
Yes, notes alway
Warm, real, and keen,
What his back years bring—
A phantom of his own figuring.

III

Of this vision of his they might say more:
Not only there
Does he see this sight,
But everywhere
In his brain—day, night,
As if on the air
It were drawn rose bright—
Yea, far from that shore
Does he carry this vision of heretofore:

IV

A ghost-girl-rider. And though, toil-tried,
He withers daily,
Time touches her not,
But she still rides gaily
In his rapt thought
On that shagged and shaly
Atlantic spot,
And as when first eyed
Draws rein and sings to the swing of the tide.

THOMAS HARDY

29. Snowfall at Kernick

Here with a burly flutter and sting
   The snow-blast scampers winnowing,
And dribble of foam-flakes seeps and bores
   Through clay-clump thickets, under doors;
While flurry of snow-mist rises where
   The waggons tug till rails are bare.
The smoke is battered round the stacks;
   Soot falls with snow on trolley-tracks.
Even the mica-channel planks
   And narrow walls of settling-tanks
Are frilled and ice-splashed there between
   The frozen pools now sickly green.
The pit-edge merges with the fields,
   A softened gash the clay-bone shields;
Beyond it in the valley's fold
   Virginia woods loom taut and cold.

JACK CLEMO, *The Map of Clay*

30. The Isles of Scilly

Here are the islands of dead hope:
And where the bodies safely crouched,
The megaliths, empty on the headlands lie,
In the red, wind-shivering fern
High on these islands of a grim good-bye.

Here, on Samson, are the ruined hearths—
Hopes flickered there like fire—scrubbed
Of their soot by gale and rain and spray,
And the wild black rabbits run
Across the longings of a yesterday.

Here on the glistening beach
The dolphin's teeth grow loose
In the large and sand-rubbed skull,
And, in the weed, what rotting human eyes
Have never seen the safety of the day, black gull,

Or cobalt sea, or the grey holly in the drift.
O rotten in the weed, O emigrants to hope,
The islanders have graved you in their scanty sand,
Girls mourned in Lübeck, in Livonia,
By wrinkled hearts, and bloodless hand,

And wind-drunk tombstones, ordered
In our foreign land. Manured by the sea's red
Bitter weed, by sorrow's grey-skied, endless hours,
Pink lilies by the granite grow—
For foreign death such unfamiliar flowers.

Yearn, too, by the tropic gardens,
Under the ratas and the peeling gums,
The pink breasts of the figurehead,
Her blue eyes dry,
Immobile, yearning for these helpless dead.

And soon beyond the reddened fern, the rounded
Granite, gold on this green-black sea,
Day darkening with the night's destroying fear,
Must rise the flattened, huge, and butter-
Yellow moon, which cannot care.

GEOFFREY GRIGSON

III. People

1. *Theodoro Paleologus in Landulph Church*

Here lyeth the Body of Theodoro Paleologus
Of Pesaro in Italye, descended from ye Imperyall
Lyne of ye last Christian Emperors of Greece
Being the sonne of Camilio, ye sone of Prosper,
The sonne of Theodoro, the sonne of John, ye
Sonne of Thomas, second brother to Constantine
Paleologus, the 8th of that name and last of yt lyne yt
Raygned in Constantinople, untill sub-
Dewed by the Turks, who married with Mary
Ye daughter of William Balls of Hadlye in
Suffolke, Gent. and had issue 5 children Theo-
Doro, John, Ferdinando, Maria and Dorothy, and de-
Parted this life at Clyfton ye 21st of January, 1636

2. *A Natural*

IT yieldeth a large view of the south coast, and was itself, in Sir
William's lifetime,[1] much visited, through his frank invitings. The
mention of this Knight calleth to my remembrance a sometimes

[1] Sir William Bevil of Killigarth.

53

uncouth servant of his, whose monstrous conditions partly resembled that Polyphemus, described by Homer and Virgil, and lively imitated by Ariosto in his Orco; or rather, that Egyptian Polyphagus, in whom (by Suetonius report) the Emperor Nero took such pleasure. This fellow was taken up by Sir William, under a hedge, in the deepest of winter, wellnear starved with cold, and hunger: he was of stature mean, of constitution lean, of face freckled, of composition well proportioned, of diet naturally spare, and cleanly enough; yet, at his master's bidding, he would devour nettles, thistles, the pith of artichokes, raw, and living birds and fishes, with their scales and feathers; burning coals and candles, and whatsoever else, howsoever unsavory, if it might be swallowed: neither this a little, but in such quantity, as it often bred a second wonder, how his belly should contain so much: yet could no man, at any time, discover him doing of that, which necessity of nature requireth. Moreover, he would take a hot iron out of the fire with his bare hand; never changed his apparel, but by constraint, and used to lie in straw, with his head down, and his heels upwards. Spare was he of speech, and, instead of half his words, used this term Size, as, I will Size him, for strike him; he is a good Size, for man, &c. Over-sleeping, or some other accident, made him to lose a day in his account of the week, so as he would not believe but that Sunday was Saturday, Saturday Friday, &c.

To Sir William he bare such faithfulness, that he would follow his horse like a spaniel; without regard of way or weariness, wait at his chamber-door, the night-time, suffering none to come near him, and perform whatsoever he commanded, were it never so unlawful or dangerous. On a time, his master, expecting strangers, sent him, with a pannier, to his cater at the sea side, to fetch some fish. In his way he passed by a river, whereinto the tide then flowed, and certain fishermen were drawing their nets; which, after John Size had a while beheld, he casts to have a share amongst them for his master. So into the water he leaps, and there, for the space of a flight shoot, wadeth and walloweth (for swim he could not) sometimes up, and sometimes down, carrying his pannier still before him, to his own extreme hazard of drowning, and the beholders great pitying; until at last, all wet and wearied, out he scrambleth, and home he hieth, with a bitter complaint to his master of his ill fortune, that he could not catch some fish as well as the rest, where so much was going. In this sort he continued for divers years, until (upon I wot not what freak, or unkindness) away he gets, and abroad he rogues; which remitter brought him in the end to his foredeferred, and not avoided destiny: for as under a hedge he was found pining, so under a hedge he found his miserable death, through penury.

RICHARD CAREW, *Survey of Cornwall*

3. Nicholas Boscawen

THE Rev. and Hon. J. T. Boscawen, of Lamorran, was perhaps the arch-gardener of Cornwall in his day, and his talent has not died with him. In the time of Queen Elizabeth, 1597, the Chancery Proceedings afford us a delightful little vignette of Nicholas Boscawen, Squire of Tregothnan, selling certain rights that he had over the Manor of Trewarthenick. The Lord of Trewarthenick offered him money or some young apple trees growing in his nursery. Mr. Boscawen refused the money, but took the trees, professing himself 'an old foole that loved an apple', and there and then drove over with his servants and wain to fetch them. It is fitting that the only Cornish squire known to history for his interest in arboriculture should be an ancestor of the late rector of Lamorran, and the present Rector of Ludgvan his direct descendant.

CHARLES HENDERSON, *Essays in Cornish History*

4. The Parson of St. Ewe

But far more commendable is Mr. Atwell, sometime parson of Calverly in Devon, and now of S. Ewe in Cornwall: for besides other parts of learning, with which he hath been seasoned, he is not unseen in the theorics of physic, and can out of them readily and probably discourse, touching the nature and accidents of all diseases. Besides, his judgment in urines cometh little behind the skilfullest in that profession. Marry, his practice is somewhat strange, and varying from all others; for though now and then he use blood-letting, and do ordinarily minister manus Christi, and such like cordials, of his own compounding (a point fitting well with my humour, as enabling nature, who best knoweth how to work), yet mostly for all diseases he prescribeth milk, and very often milk and apples, a course deeply subject to the exception of the best esteemed practitioners; and such notwithstanding, as whereby either the virtue of the medicine, or the fortune of the physician, or the credulity of the patient, hath recovered sundry out of desperate and forlorn extremities.

This his reputation is of many years standing, and maintaineth itself unimpaired. But the same soareth to a higher pitch, by the help of another wing; and that is, his liberality. On the poor he bestoweth his pains and charges gratis. Of the rich he taketh moderately, but leaves the one half behind, in gift amongst the household, if he be called abroad to visit any: the rest, together with the profits of his benefice (rather charitably accepted, than strictly exacted from his parishioners), he poureth out with both hands 'in pios usus', and will hardly suffer a penny to sleep, but never to dwell with him.

Few towns there are in Cornwall, or any other shire between that and London, which have not in some large measure tasted of his bounty. None cometh in kindness to see him, but departed gratified with somewhat, if his modesty will accept it. Briefly, his sound affection in religion is so waited on by honesty of life, and pleasantness of conversation, that in Fabricius's voluntary poverty, he is an equal partner of his honour, and possesseth a large interest in the love of his neighbours. My love to virtue, and not any particular beholdingness, hath expressed this my testimony.

RICHARD CAREW, *Survey of Cornwall*

5. *On Sir F. Carew*

No way unworthy of his fair descent,
Careless of that brave life which we lament
All the good ends of living here acquired
Much loved, much honoured, and how much desired
His virtue past all trials shining far
Bright in the brightest sphere of fame, the war;
Submitting gladly to that fate, which oft
He had so boldly, and so bravely sought,
Here Carew lies, but, Reader, may that name
Not move thy tears, but warm thee with like flame.

SIDNEY GODOLPHIN

6. *Thomas Hobbes Dedicates the 'Leviathan'*

TO
MY MOST HONOR'D FRIEND
Mr FRANCIS GODOLPHIN
of *Godolphin*.

Honor'd Sir,

Your most worthy Brother Mr *Sidney Godolphin*, when he lived, was pleas'd to think my studies something, and otherwise to oblige me, as you know, with reall testimonies of his good opinion, great in themselves, and the greater for the worthinesse of his person. For there is not any vertue that disposeth a man, either to the service of God, or to the service of his Country, to Civill Society, or private Friendship, that did not manifestly appear in his conversation, not as acquired by necessity, or affected upon occasion, but inhærent, and shining in a generous constitution of his nature. Therefore in honour and gratitude to him, and with devotion to your selfe, I humbly Dedicate unto you this my discourse of Common-wealth.

7. *Character of Sidney Godolphin*

SIDNEY GODOLPHIN was a younger brother of Godolphin, but by the provision left by his father, and by the death of a younger brother, liberally supplied for a very good education, and for a cheerful subsistence, in any course of life he proposed to himself. There was never so great a mind and spirit contained in so little room; so large an understanding and so unrestrained a fancy in so very small a body; so that the lord Falkland used to say merrily, that he thought it was a great ingredient into his friendship for Mr. Godolphin, that he was pleased to be found in his company, where he was the properer man; and it may be, the very remarkableness of his little person made the sharpness of his wit, and the composed quickness of his judgment and understanding, the more notorious and notable. He had spent some years in France, and in the Low Countries; and accompanied the earl of Leicester in his ambassage into Denmark, before he resolved to be quiet, and attend some promotion in the court; where his excellent disposition and manners, and extraordinary qualifications, made him very acceptable.

Though everybody loved his company very well, yet he loved very much to be alone, being in his constitution inclined somewhat to melancholy, and to retirement amongst his books; and was so far from being active, that he was contented to be reproached by his friends with laziness; and was of so nice and tender a composition, that a little rain or wind would disorder him, and divert him from any short journey he had most willingly proposed to himself; insomuch as, when he rid abroad with those in whose company he most delighted, if the wind chanced to be in his face, he would (after a little pleasant murmuring) suddenly turn his horse, and go home. Yet the civil war no sooner began, (the first approaches towards which he discovered as soon as any man, by the proceedings in parliament, where he was a member, and opposed with great indignation,) than he put himself into the first troops which were raised in the west for the king; and bore the uneasiness and fatigue of winter marches with an exemplar courage and alacrity; until by too brave a pursuit of the enemy, into an obscure village in Devonshire, he was shot with a musket; with which (without saying any more, than, Oh God! I am hurt) he fell dead from his horse; to the excessive grief of his friends, who were all that knew him; and the irreparable damage of the public.

CLARENDON, *Life*

8. *Lord Treasurer Godolphin*

NEVER in the way, and never out of the way.

KING CHARLES II

LORD GODOLPHIN had conducted the Queen [Anne] with the care and tenderness of a father or a guardian through a state of helpless ignorance, and had faithfully served her in all her difficulties before she was Queen, as well as greatly contributed to the glories she had to boast of after she was so. He was a man of few words, but of a remarkable thoughtfulness and sedateness of temper; of great application to business... of wonderful frugality in the public concerns, but of no great carefulness about his own. He affected being useful without [seeking] popularity; and the inconsiderable sum of money which he left at his death showed that he had been indeed the nation's treasurer and not his own.

SARAH CHURCHILL, DUCHESS OF MARLBOROUGH,
*An Account of the Conduct of the Dowager
Duchess of Marlborough*

9. Sir Bevil Grenville

The Death of the Right Valiant
Sir Bevil Grenville, Knight

Not to be wrought by malice, gain or pride,
To a compliance with the thriving side;
Not to take arms for love of change, or spite,
But only to maintain afflicted right;
Not to die vainly in pursuit of fame,
Perversely seeking after voice and name;
Is to resolve, fight, die as martyrs do:
And thus did he, soldier and martyr too.

   He might (like some reserved men of state,
Who look not to the cause, but to its fate)
Have stood aloof, engaged on neither side,
Prepared at last to strike in with the tide.
But well weighed reason told him, that when law
Either is renounced, or misapplied by the awe
Of false named Commonwealth's men; when the right
Of King, and subject, is suppressed by might;
When all religion either is refused
As mere pretence, or merely, as that used;

When thus the fury of ambition swells,
Who is not active, modestly rebels.
Whence, in a just esteem, to Church and Crown
He offered all, and nothing thought his own.
This thrust him into action, whole and free,
Knowing no interest but loyalty;
Not loving arms as arms, or strife for strife;
Not wasteful, nor yet sparing of his life;
A great exactor of himself, and then
By fair commands no less of other men;
Courage and judgment had their equal part,
Counsel was added to a generous heart;
Affairs were justly timed; nor did he catch
At an affected fame of quick despatch;
Things were prepared, debated, and then done,
Nor rashly brook, nor vainly overspun;
False periods nowhere by design were made,
As are by those who make the war their trade;
The building still was suited to the ground,
Whence every action issued full and round.
We know who blind their men with specious lies,
With revelations and with prophecies,
Who promise two things to obtain a third,
And are themselves by the like motives stirred:
By no such engines he his soldiers draws;
He knew no arts but courage and the cause;
With these he brought them on, as well-trained men,
And with these too he brought them off again.
    I should, I know, track him through all the course
Of his great actions, show their worth and force:
But, although all are handsome, yet we cast
A more intentive eye still on the last.
When now the incensed rebel proudly came
Down, like a torrent without bank or dam;
When undeserved success urged on their force,
That thunder must come down to stop their course,

Or Grenville must step in; then Grenville stood,
And with himself opposed and checked the flood.
Conquest or death, was all his thought. So fire
Either o'ercomes or doth itself expire.
His courage worked like flames, cast heat about,
Here, there, on this, on that side; none gave out;
Not any pike in that renowned stand,
But took new force from his inspired hand;
Soldier encouraged soldier, man urged man.
And he urged all: so much examples can.
Hurt upon hurt, wound upon wound did call,
He was the butt, the mark, the aim of all:
His soul this while retired from cell to cell,
At last flew up from all, and then he fell:
But the devoted stand, enraged more
From that his fate, plied hotter than before,
And proud to fall with him, sworn not to yield,
Each sought an honoured grave, and gained the field.
Thus, he being fallen, his action fought anew:
And the dead conquered, whiles the living slew.
    ... And thou (blest soul) whose clear compacted fame,
As amber bodies keeps, preserved thy name,
Whose life affords what doth content both eyes,
Glory for people, substance for the wise;
Go laden up with spoils, possess that seat
To which the valiant, when they've done, retreat:
And when thou seest an happy period sent
To these distractions, and the storm quite spent;
Look down, and say: I have my share in all;
Much good grew from my life, much from my fall.

WILLIAM CARTWRIGHT, Poems

10. *Character of Sir Harry Killigrew*

SIR HARRY was of the house of commons; and though he had no other relation to the court than the having many friends there, as wherever he was known he was exceedingly beloved, he was most zealous and passionate in opposing all the extravagant proceedings of the parliament. And when the Earl of Essex was chosen general, and the several members of the house stood up and declared what horse they would raise and maintain, and that they would live and die with the Earl their general, one saying he would raise ten horses, and another twenty, he stood up and said, 'He would provide a good horse, and a good buff coat, and a good pair of pistols, and then he doubted not but he should find a good cause;' and so went out of the house, and rode post into Cornwall, where his estate and interest lay; and there joined with those gallant gentlemen his friends, who first received the Lord Hopton, and raised those forces which did so many famous actions in the west.

He would never take any command in the army; but they who had, consulted no man more. He was in all actions, and in those places where was most danger, having great courage and a pleasantness of humour in danger that was very exemplary; and they who did not do their duty took care not to be within his view, for he was a very sharp speaker, and cared not for angering those who deserved to be reprehended. The Arundells, Trelawnies, Slannings, Trevanions, and all the signal men of that county, infinitely loved his spirit and sincerity; and his credit and interest had a great influence upon all but those that did not love the king; and to those he was very terrible, and exceedingly hated by them; and not loved by men of moderate tempers, for he thought all such prepared to rebel, when a little success should encourage them; and was many times too much offended with men who wished well, and whose constitutions and complexions would not permit them to express the same frankness which his nature and keenness of spirit could not suppress. His loss was much lamented by all good men.

CLARENDON, *History of the Rebellion*

11. *The Beautiful Lady Robartes*

LADY ROBARTES was then in the zenith of her glory: her beauty was striking; yet notwithstanding the brightness of the finest complexion, with all the bloom of youth, and with every requisite for inspiring desire, she nevertheless was not attractive. The Duke of York, however, would probably have been successful, if difficulties, almost insurmountable, had not disappointed his good intentions: Lord Robartes, her husband, was an old, snarling, troublesome, peevish fellow, in love with her to distraction, and, to complete her misery, a perpetual attendant on her person.

She perceived his royal highness's attachment to her, and seemed as if she was inclined to be grateful: this redoubled his eagerness, and every outward mark of tenderness he could possibly shew her; but the watchful husband redoubling his zeal and assiduity, as he found the approaches advance, every art was practised to render him tractable: several attacks were made upon his avarice and his ambition. Those who possessed the greatest share of his confidence, insinuated to him, that it was his own fault, if Lady Robartes, who was so worthy of being at court, was not received into some considerable post, either about the queen or the duchess: he was offered to be made lord lieutenant of the county where his estate was; or to have the management of the Duke of York's revenues in Ireland, of which he should have the entire disposal, provided he immediately set out to take possession of his charge; and having accomplished it, he might return as soon as ever he thought proper.

He perfectly well understood the meaning of these proposals, and was fully apprized of the advantages he might reap from them: in vain did ambition and avarice hold out their allurements; he was deaf to all their temptations, nor could ever the old fellow be persuaded to be made a cuckold. It is not always an aversion to, or a dread of this distinction, which preserves us from it: of this her husband was very sensible; therefore, under the pretence of a pilgrimage to Saint Winifred the virgin and martyr, who was said to cure women of barrenness, he did not rest, until the highest mountains in Wales were between his wife and the person who had designed to perform this miracle in London, after his departure.

ANTHONY HAMILTON, Memoirs of Grammont

12. Mrs. Anne Killigrew

To the Pious Memory of the accomplished young lady, Mrs. Anne Killigrew, excellent in the two sister arts of Poesy and Painting.

Thou youngest virgin-daughter of the skies,
    Made in the last promotion of the blest;
Whose palms, new plucked from Paradise,
In spreading branches more sublimely rise,
    Rich with immortal green above the rest:
Whether, adopted to some neighbour star
Thou roll'st above us, in thy wandering race,
    Or, in procession fixed and regular,
    Moved with the heaven's majestic pace;
    Or, called to more superior bliss,
Thou tread'st with seraphims the vast abyss:
Whatever happy region is thy place,
Cease thy celestial song a little space;
Thou wilt have time enough for hymns divine,
    Since Heaven's eternal year is thine.
Hear, then, a mortal Muse thy praise rehearse,
        In no ignoble verse;
But such as thy own voice did practise here,
When thy first-fruits of Poesy were given,
To make thyself a welcome inmate there;
    While yet a young probationer,
        And candidate of Heaven.

If by traduction came thy mind,
   Our wonder is the less, to find
A soul so charming from a stock so good;
Thy father was transfused into thy blood:
So wert thou born into the tuneful strain,
An early, rich, and inexhausted vein.
   But if thy pre-existing soul
      Was formed at first with myriads more,
It did through all the mighty poets roll
   Who Greek or Latin laurels wore,
And was that Sappho last, which once it was before.
   If so, then cease thy flight, O heaven-born mind!
Thou hast no dross to purge from thy rich ore:
   Nor can thy soul a fairer mansion find,
   Than was the beautous frame she left behind:
Return, to fill or mend the quire of thy celestial kind. . . .

   Art she had none, yet wanted none,
      For Nature did that want supply:
   So rich in treasures of her own,
      She might our boasted stores defy:
Such noble vigour did her verse adorn,
That it seemed borrowed, where 'twas only born.
   Her morals, too, were in her bosom bred,
      By great examples daily fed,
What in the best of books, her father's life, she read.
   And to be read herself she need not fear;
   Each test, and every light, her Muse will bear,
   Thou Epictetus with his lamp were there.
   Even love (for love sometimes her Muse expressed)
Was but a lambent flame which played about her breast,
      Light as the vapours of a morning dream;
   So cold herself, while she such warmth expressed,
      'Twas Cupid bathing in Diana's stream. . . .

66

Now all those charms, that blooming grace,
The well-proportioned shape, and beauteous face,
Shall never more be seen by mortal eyes;
In earth the much-lamented virgin lies.
Nor wit, nor piety could Fate prevent;
Nor was the cruel Destiny content
To finish all the murder at a blow,
To sweep at once her life and beauty too;
But, like a hardened felon, took a pride
    To work more mischievously slow,
    And plundered first, and then destroyed.
O double sacrilege on things divine,
    To rob the relic, and deface the shrine!
        But thus Orinda died:
    Heaven, by the same disease, did both translate;
As equal were their souls, so equal was their fate.

    Meantime, her warlike brother on the seas
    His waving streamers to the winds displays,
And vows for his return, with vain devotion, pays.
    Ah, generous youth! that wish forbear,
    The winds too soon will waft thee here!
    Slack all thy sails, and fear to come,
Alas, thou knowest not, thou art wrecked at home!
No more shalt thou behold thy sister's face,
Thou hast already had her last embrace.
But look aloft, and if thou kennest from far,
Among the Pleiads a new kindled star,
If any sparkles than the rest more bright,
'Tis she that shines in that propitious light. . . .

                JOHN DRYDEN, *Poems*

13. *The Second Lord Godolphin*

(1735)

LORD GODOLPHIN was a very singular character, for though he was a man of undoubted understanding and strict honour yet he passed his whole life with people who had neither. Natural modesty, indolence, and laziness, made him exert himself but little in the great and the busy world; and his chief if not his only pleasures being wine and running horses, he passed almost all his time in low company, who could talk sense in no character but that of jockeys, and acted, even in that character, as little like gentlemen as they talked.

Lord Pembroke's character was a very different one. Not that he wanted sense, or that he was not very justly esteemed a man of the nicest and strictest honour, but he was quite illiterate, whereas Lord Godolphin was an extremely good scholar, and had a great deal of knowledge. The one, too, was always in bad company, whilst the other was always in the best. And as Lord Pembroke, being much known, was generally esteemed and had many friends, so the other, from the obscurity of his way of life, was so far from having many friends, that, out of the very narrow compass of his own low acquaintance, he was hardly known to exist.

LORD HERVEY, *Memoirs*

14. *On Sir John St. Aubyn*

EVERY man has his price except the little Cornish baronet.

SIR ROBERT WALPOLE

15. *Admiral Boscawen*

William Pitt: When I explain my projects to other admirals, they always raise difficulties; Boscawen alone finds expedients.

Admiral Boscawen to his wife: I now have no less than nineteen sail of the line under my command, besides seventeen frigates; and yet, with all this, I am happier at home in the arms of my darling Fanny—not but what it would hurt my glory greatly to be left behind when these great affairs was in hand.

Mrs. Boscawen to the Admiral, from Portsmouth, 'spying for sails around St. Helen's Point'.... Here I have been this last fortnight, my dear love, in daily, hourly expectation of the greatest pleasure this life can give me—the joy of seeing you arrive safe. As I think of it all day and dream of it all night, so I cannot sit quiet in my chair if anyone rings at the door, without running to the window to see who it is, for I have upon this occasion learnt all my old vivacities, and am what my father would call as great a fool as I was when we first married twelve years ago. Adieu, my love. A short adieu let it be. Spread all your sails, catch every gale, and fly to the faithful arms and tender heart of your most affectionate and entirely devoted F.B.

C. ASPINALL-OGLANDER, *Admiral's Widow*

16. *William Glanville Boscawen*

SACRED to the memory of the most lovely, the most beloved youth, William Glanville Boscawen, second son of Admiral Boscawen and of Frances Glanville his wife; who having early dedicated himself to the service of his country after the example of his father, was made a Lieutenant of the British Navy in his eighteenth year, and promised to be one of its brightest ornaments. But, alas, death cut off these hopes, and he was unfortunately drowned on the 21st day of April 1769, in the island of Jamaica. His disconsolate mother thus commemorates her lost treasure, and places this Urn—though the ashes are denied.

In St. Michael Penkivel Church

17. *Mrs. Delany's First Husband*

About this time there came on a visit to Alcander [Lord Lansdowne] an old friend and countryman of his, Gromio.[1] When he arrived we were at dinner: he had travelled on horseback, the day being excessively rainy: he sent in his name, upon which Alcander rose from table overjoyed at his arrival, and insisted on his coming in to dinner. I expected to have seen somebody with the appearance of a gentleman, when the poor, old, dripping almost drowned Gromio was brought into the room, like Hob out of the well, his wig, his coat, his dirty boots, his large unwieldy person, and his crimson countenance were all subjects of great mirth and observation to me. I diverted myself at his expense several days, and was well assisted by a young gentleman,[2] brother to Laura; who had wit and malice. Gromio soon changed his first design of going away the next day, the occasion of his coming was (*it was stated*) a quarrel he had with a gentleman[3] who had married his niece; he offered to settle on him his whole estate, provided he would after his death,

[1] Alexander Pendarves, Esq., of Roscrow, Cornwall.
[2] The Hon. Henry Villiers, second and youngest son of Edward, 1st Earl of Jersey. He died in 1743.
[3] Francis Basset, of Tehidy, Esq., married as his second wife Mary, daughter and heiress of the Rev. John Pendarves, rector of Dunsteignton, Devonshire. She was also eventually the heiress of her father's elder brother, Alexander Pendarves, of Roscrow. The eldest son of Francis, her second son, was Lord de Dunstanville.

take his name. Bassanio (his nephew's name) proud of his family, refused to comply with that part, upon which Gromio determined to dispose of his estate, and settle quietly for the rest of his life in the country.

In order to execute this design, he was going to London, and passing near Alcander's heard that the family were in the country, which determined him to make his journey one day longer by calling there. He talked of going every day, but still stayed, and I (to my great sorrow) was after some time convinced I was the cause of this delay; his behaviour was too remarkable for me not to observe it, and I could easily perceive I was the only person in the family that did not approve of it. Gromio was then near sixty, and I seventeen years of age. You may readily believe I was not pleased with what I suspected. I formed an invincible aversion towards him, and everything he said or did by way of obliging me, increased that aversion. I thought him ugly and disagreeable; he was fat, much afflicted with gout, and often sat in a sullen mood, which I concluded was from the gloominess of his temper. I knew that of all men living, my uncle had the greatest opinion of and esteem for him, and I dreaded his making a proposal of marriage, as I knew it would be accepted. In order to prevent it, I did not in the least disguise my great dislike to him; I behaved myself not only with indifference but rudeness; when I dressed, I considered what would become me least; if he came into the room when I was alone, I instantly left it, and took care to let him see I quitted it because he came there. I was often chid by my two wise aunts for this behaviour; I told them plainly he was odious to me, in hopes they would have had good-nature enough to have prevented what I foresaw; but Laura called me childish, ignorant, and silly, and that if I did not know what was for my own interest, my friends must judge for me. I passed two months with dreadful apprehensions, apprehensions too well grounded. I assure you the recollection of this part of my life makes me tremble at this day. I must relieve my spirits by concluding this letter: adieu.

LADY LANOVER, *Life and Correspondence of Mrs. Delany*

18. Dr. Borlase Remembered

I remember frequently seeing him at Castle Horneck. He used to drive a couple of bays, 'tandem', and was the only gentleman in that part of the country who ever did so. I remember his figure accurately, with his large wig and rather short stature. It was his habit, on his return from his morning drive to see his brother at Castle Horneck, to pull up at the only book-shop then in town, Hemming's, just above Mrs. Treweeke's great house, and go in and see what books had been ordered by the families in the neighbourhood, and to read the paper, while his servant, who was always with him, held his horses.

GENERAL WALTER TREMENHEERE, in P. A. S. Pool, 'William Borlase', in *Journal of the Royal Institution of Cornwall* (1966)

19. Friends

Dr. Oliver of Bath, originator of the 'Bath Oliver' biscuit:

'Tis not only with our own species that we contract the most lasting friendships in the beginning of life. I remember the name and character of every dog I used to miss school to hunt with. I could go to every little thicket which was most likely to afford game. I love the memory of a tall sycamore out of which I used to cut whistles. I have the situation of the hazel from which I obtained the best cob nuts full in my eye. And I remember with gratitude a rare apple tree, which afforded the first *regale* of the summer, and the Borlase's Pippin which, like its namesake, was a high entertainment in a winter's evening in a warm room with a good fire.

ANNE TRENEER, *The Mercurial Chemist*

20. An Eighteenth-century Gentleman

I saw very little of Sir William Pendarvis, or his lady, after Miss H—
left them; they were very little in the country, and Mr. Pendarvis
had never a very cordial kindness for Sir William. Some years after
I heard that Lady Pendarvis had acted a very generous part
towards Miss H—; for though she had disturbed her domestic
happiness in a high degree, she never made any complaint of her,
but let the affair drop quietly; indeed she did not long survive it;
after which Sir William's house was the rendezvous of a very
immoral set of men. One of his strange exploits, amongst other
frolics, was having a coffin made of copper (which one of his mines
that year had produced), and placed it in the midst of his great
hall, and instead of his making use of it as a monitor that might
have made him ashamed and terrified at his past life, and induce
him to make amends in future, it was filled with punch, and he and
his comrades soon made themselves incapable of any sort of reflection; this was *often* repeated, and hurried him on to that awful
moment he had so much reason to dread.

LADY LANOVER, *Life and Correspondence of Mrs. Delany*

21. A 'Fracas' at the Opera

SEPTEMBER 10, 1810.—In the afternoon, I walked to Penrose to
dinner, and found the family party assembled. We dined soon after
4 o'clock.—

Before dinner on my looking at a picture[1] of the late Mr. Basset,
father to Lord de Dunstanville, it led to a conversation respecting
his rencontre with the late General Johnston at the Opera House,
which was much spoken of at the period when it happened. Mr.
Basset being one of many gentlemen who according to the custom

[1] By Gainsborough.

73

of that time stood upon the stage near the scenes, was grossly insulted by Johnston, who ridiculing Mr. Basset's small figure, treated him otherways with contempt. Johnston was celebrated for his skill in fencing and being a tall man had every advantage; but on this occasion nearly lost his life; for Mr. Basset drew his sword and attacked him with such spirit as nearly to have run him through the body. They were instantly separated, but His Majesty, George 2nd, happening to be at the theatre that night, the bustle occasioned by this affray caused him to inquire into the occasion of it. He was informed that it was Major Johnston who had given the offence, on which His Majesty said, 'And *Major* Johnston he shall remain.'

JOSEPH FARINGTON, *The Farington Diary*

22. *Mr. Tillie of Pentillie*

MR. TILLIE, once the owner of Pentillie house, was a celebrated atheist of the last age. He was a man of wit, and had by rote all the ribaldry and commonplace jests against religion and scripture; which are well suited to display pertness and folly, and to unsettle a giddy mind, but are offensive to men of sense, whatever their opinions may be, and are neither intended nor adapted to investigate truth. The brilliancy of Mr. Tillie's wit, however, carried him a degree farther than we often meet with in the annals of profaneness. In general the witty atheist is satisfied with entertaining his *contemporaries*; but Mr. Tillie wished to have his sprightliness known to *posterity*. With this view, in ridicule of the resurrection, he obliged his executors to place his dead body, in his usual garb, and in his elbow-chair, upon the top of a hill, and to arrange, on a table before him, bottles, glasses, pipes, and tobacco. In this situation he ordered himself to be immured in a tower of such dimensions as he prescribed; where he proposed, he said, patiently to wait the event. All this was done, and the tower, still enclosing its

74

tenant, remains as a monument of his impiety and profaneness. The country people shudder as they go near it:

—Religio pavidos terrebat agrestes
Dira loci:—silvam, saxumque tremebant.

W. S. GILPIN, *Observations on the Western Parts of England*

23. *In Linkinhorne Churchyard*

Here we lye without the wall;
Twas full within—they made a brawl,
Here we lye, no Rent to pay,
And yet we lye so warm as they.

Cut by Daniel Gumb[1]

24. *Boswell's Friend Temple*

As Vicar of St. Gluvias, possessed of an income from combined private and professional sources amounting to over £500 a year (so Boswell reckons it in one of his letters), Temple passed the last nineteen years of his life. These years seem to have been a time of comparative comfort and contentment; though it is only fair to

---

[1] Daniel Gumb, d. 1776, was an eccentric who lived in a rock-dwelling not far from the Cheese-wring, near Liskeard. He was apparently well educated and had a gift for mathematics; a diagram on one of the rocks of his abode illustrated a problem in Euclid. He was occasionally employed in surveying and mapping estates; one of the curiosities of the neighbourhood, he was much sought out, and was a valued acquaintance of Cookworthy, who discovered china-clay in Cornwall.

remember that Temple, like a later and more distinguished Cornish clergyman,[1] never received from his bishop a single real mark of distinction. That he would have welcomed the offer of a prebend or of an archdeaconry as a visible token of his success in the Church is scarcely open to doubt. Whether he can be said to have earned it is more disputable; for, so far as we know, he was no pulpit orator, and, interested though he was in the current Theist and Socinian controversies, he certainly made no contribution to polemical divinity. But, despite his lack of preferment, he must have been too busy to be very unhappy. His clerical duties and ministrations had to be performed. His correspondence, with friends, with brother parsons, and with men of business, had to be dispatched. Parcels of books sent down from London by Dilly or the Boswells had to be examined. His newspaper, his magazine,[2] and his reviews[3]—all regularly arriving under his patron's covers—had to be studied. Local visits of ceremony, too, though always deprecated, had constantly to be paid and received. All this took up time and allowed Temple scant leisure for brooding over his disappointments, the most constant of which appears to have been his failure to secure tolerable conversation. His unremitting search for this commodity proves, I think, that he was not really a gregarious man.

Walking and riding were his regular daily exercises, never on any account to be pretermitted; drinking tea at his own or at a neighbour's house was the daily concession he made to the claims of social intercourse. Some dinners he had to give and others to accept; but he found both kinds a nuisance. Sitting long after a heavy meal was physically oppressive to him; and he took pleasure neither in the circulation of the bottle nor in the talk which it provoked. Such amusements as were accessible—a rubber of whist, a saunter in his garden, an appearance at the local Assembly, a visit to a friend to hear some competent pianist or vocalist, an attendance at the Assizes to meet the Sheriff and the Judges, or an excursion to Land's End or Fowey in search of the picturesque—he seems never to have

[1] The Rev. Sabine Baring-Gould.
[2] The *Gentleman's Magazine*.
[3] The *Critical* and *Le Journal Encyclopédique*.

disdained and sometimes even to have enjoyed. When he was quite at a loose end he would ride over to Killiow to see the Gwatkins or to Trewithen to call on Kit Hawkins.

Diaries of William Johnston Temple, ed. Lewis Bettany

25. Sir Christopher Hawkins

A large park and no deer,
A large cellar and no beer,
A large house and no cheer,
Now tell me who lives here.
Sir Christopher Hawkins lives here.

On Sunday Mr. Hawkins gave us a dinner at Argyle Street. It is not possible he can be a narrow man, mama: only think of his having at his table turbot, venison, and several other very expensive things. Yet there is a strange contradiction in his character; for in some respects he is shabby to a degree. I am sure the knives that were set were hardly good enough to be in the kitchen; and as a substitute for salt spoons they had put tea spoons. These things appear very extraordinary and inconsistent; but I can't help thinking there is a little affectation in his apparent disregard of making what is called a *genteel figure*.

NANCY TEMPLE, in *Diaries of William Johnston Temple*, ed. Lewis Bettany

26. John Opie's Beginnings

MR. PENWARNE said that Opie was born at St. Agnes, a village in Cornwall, about 4 or 5 miles from Truro. That his father was not in so low a situation as has been reported. That he was a Carpenter & Joiner in a decent situation of life. Opie's education must have been very limited, as good schools were not established in that part, but he was taught to read & write. The first time that he showed an inclination to drawing has been thus related by his sister. He was acquainted with a young man of the name of Mark Oates who is now a Captn. of Artillery.—Opie happened to call upon him and saw a drawing of a Butterfly made by him, was seized with a desire to attempt to make one like it. In this (he) succeeded so well as to become quite eager to make further attempts in drawing. His father kept a horse on which Opie rode to Truro & purchased some pencils & colours.

Penwarne told me that Opie's sister had informed him that Opie was at ten years of age a very good arithmetician, & at that early age he set up a sort of school, & taught writing and accounts to many much older than himself. Before he was twelve years of age he had for some time been under the tuition of Dr. Wolcot so far as to receive advice & instruction in painting, the Doctor having much love for the art & a few pictures in his possession. He began to paint portraits at a very early period, and when not more than thirteen years of age went to *Padstow* a town at some distance where he remained three months, and at the end of that period returned to his fathers dressed in a new suit of clothes & having twenty or thirty guineas in his pocket.

JOSEPH FARINGTON, *The Farington Diary*

27. Opie's Originality

[29 May, 1811]

FUSELI and Northcote spoke much of Opie's powers in conversation. Fuseli said he had in this greater vigour than in his painting. Northcote particularly dwelt on his originality of thinking.—'He said so many things which sunk into the mind; that which you could not forget.

JOSEPH FARINGTON, *The Farington Diary*

28. Sir Humphry Davy

Sir Humphry Davy
Abominated gravy
He lived in the odium
Of having discovered sodium.

E. C. BENTLEY, *Biography for Beginners*

Coleridge on Davy: There is an energy, an elasticity in his mind, which enables him to seize on and analyse all questions, pushing them to their legitimate consequences. Every subject in Davy's mind has the principle of vitality. Living thoughts spring up like turf under his feet.

ANNE TRENEER, *The Mercurial Chemist*

29. Sir Humphry Davy and Sir Walter Scott

BUT the most picturesque figure was the illustrious inventor of the Safety Lamp. He had come for his favourite sport of angling ... and his fisherman's costume—a brown hat with flexible brims, surrounded with line upon line, and innumerable fly-hooks; jackboots worthy of a Dutch smuggler, and a fustian surtout dabbled with the blood of salmon—made a fine contrast to the smart jackets, white-cord breeches, and well-polished jockey-boots of the less distinguished cavaliers about him.... I have seen Sir Humphry in many places, and in company of many different descriptions; but never to such advantage as at Abbotsford. His host and he delighted in each other, and the modesty of their mutual admiration was a memorable spectacle. Davy was by nature a poet—and Scott, though anything but a philosopher in the modern sense of that term, might, I think it very likely, have pursued the body of physical science with zeal and success had he fallen in with such an instructor as Sir Humphry would have been to him in early life. Each strove to make the other talk—and they did so in turn more charmingly than I have ever heard either on any other occasion whatsoever. Scott in his romantic narratives touched a deeper chord of feeling than usual, when he had such a listener as Davy; and Davy, when induced to open his views on any question of scientific interest in Scott's presence, did so with a degree of clear energetic eloquence, and with a flow of imagery and illustration, of which neither his habitual tone of table-talk (least of all in London), nor any of his prose writings (except, indeed, the posthumous *Consolations of Travel*) could suggest an adequate notion. I say his prose writings— for who that has read his sublime quatrains on the doctrine of Spinoza can doubt that he might have united if he had pleased, in some great didactic poem, the vigorous ratiocination of Dryden and the moral majesty of Wordsworth? I remember William Laidlaw whispering to me, one night, when their 'wrapt talk' had kept the circle round the fire until long after the usual bedtime of Abbotsford —'Gude preserve us! This is a very superior occasion! Eh, sirs!' he added, cocking his eye like a bird, 'I wonder if Shakespeare and Bacon ever met to screw ilk other up.'

J. G. LOCKHART, *Life of Sir Walter Scott*

30. Miss Branwell Becomes Mrs. Brontë

MR BRONTË resided here for five years; and, while the incumbent of Hartshead, he wooed and married Maria Branwell. She was the third daughter of Mr. Thomas Branwell, merchant, of Penzance. Her mother's maiden name was Carne; and, both on father's and mother's side, the Branwell family were sufficiently well descended to enable them to mix in the best society that Penzance then afforded. Mr. Branwell, the father, according to his descendants' account, was a man of musical talent.

Miss Branwell was extremely small in person; not pretty, but very elegant, and always dressed with a quiet simplicity of taste, which accorded well with her general character, and of which some of the details call to mind the style of dress preferred by her daughter for her favourite heroines. Mr. Brontë was soon captivated by the little, gentle creature, and this time declared that it was for life. In her first letter to him, dated August 26, she seems almost surprised to find herself engaged, and alludes to the short time which she has known him.

MRS. GASKELL, *The Life of Charlotte Brontë*

31. Aunt Branwell

ABOUT a year after Mrs. Brontë's death an elder sister, as I have before mentioned, came from Penzance to superintend her brother-in-law's household and look after his children. Miss Branwell[1] was,

[1] Miss Ellen Nussey's descriptions of the aunt and of 'Tabby' the servant are the best that I have seen:

'Miss Branwell was a very small, antiquated little lady; she wore caps large enough for half a dozen of the present fashion, and a front of light auburn curls over her forehead. She always dressed in silk. She talked a great deal of her younger days, the gaieties of her native town, Penzance in Cornwall, the soft, warm climate etc. She very probably had been a belle among her acquaintances; the social life of her younger days she

I believe, a kindly and conscientious woman, with a good deal of character, but with the somewhat narrow ideas natural to one who had spent nearly all her life in the same place. She had strong prejudices, and soon took a distaste to Yorkshire. From Penzance, where plants which we in the north call greenhouse flowers grow in great profusion and without any shelter even in the winter, and where the soft, warm climate allows the inhabitants, if so disposed, to live pretty constantly in the open air, it was a great change for a lady considerably past forty to come and take up her abode in a place where neither flowers nor vegetables would flourish, and where a tree of even moderate dimensions might be hunted for far and wide; where the snow lay long and late on the moors, stretching bleakly and barely far up from the dwelling which was henceforward to be her home; and where often, on autumnal or winter nights, the four winds of heaven seemed to meet and rage together, tearing round the house as if they were wild beasts striving to find an entrance. She missed the small round of cheerful social visiting perpetually going on in a country town; she missed the friends she had known from her childhood, some of whom had been her parents' friends before they were hers; she disliked many of the customs of the place, and particularly dreaded the cold arising from the flag floors in the passages and parlours of Haworth Parsonage. ... Miss Branwell was unaware of the fermentation of unoccupied talent going on around her.

MRS. GASKELL, *Life of Charlotte Brontë*

---

appeared to recall with regret. She took snuff out of a very pretty little gold snuff-box, which she sometimes presented with a little laugh, as if she enjoyed the slight shock and astonishment visible in your countenance. In summer she spent most of her afternoons in reading aloud to Mr. Brontë, and in the winter evenings she must have enjoyed this, for she and Mr. Brontë had sometimes to finish their discussions on what she had read when we all met for tea; she would be very lively and intelligent in her talk, and tilted argument without fear against Mr. Brontë.'

32. Matthew Arnold's Family

MISS ARNOLD, of Fox How,—Dr. Arnold's last surviving child—said that her mother had often told her of the deep affection *her* mother (Mrs. Penrose) had for her home in Cornwall.[1] When the carriage in which she and her husband drove away crossed the border of Cornwall and Devon, she made it stop, got out and stooped down and kissed the dust on the road, saying that it was her tender farewell to the land she loved.

A. B. BALDWIN, *The Penroses of Fledborough Parsonage*

*   *   *

Matthew Arnold to his Mother: I could not but think of you in Brittany, with Cranics and Trevenecs all about me, and the peasantry with their expressive, rather mournful faces, long noses and dark eyes, reminding me perpetually of dear Tom and Uncle Trevenen.

The Letters of Matthew Arnold, ed. G. W. E. Russell

33. Coleridges at Helston

OCTOBER 15, 1835.—Papa and I spent the evening at the Derwent Coleridges' at Helston. It left a beautiful impression on us, and we visited the lovely little sleepers, Derwent and Lily, saw the library, and the silver salver presented by his boys, and, best of all, listened to his reading of passages from 'Christabel' and other of his father's poems, with his own rare felicity. He talked of architecture with reference to George Wightwick's designs for the Falmouth Polytechnic, and mentioned a double cube as the handsomest of all

[1] Dr. Arnold married her daughter; so that Mrs. Penrose, whose maiden name was Trevenen—hence the name carried on in the Arnold family—was Matthew Arnold's grandmother.

forms for a room. Mary Coleridge was in all her beauty, and ministered to a bevy of schoolboys at supper with characteristic energy.

CAROLINE FOX, *Journals and Letters*

34. *Evening at Enys*

FALMOUTH, October 5, 1837.—Went to Enys; found them with the addition of Davies Gilbert; he looks well, and they have all excessively enjoyed their time on the Continent. Read us some of his new book, in which he speaks very handsomely of Papa and his doings. Drove on to Carclew; found Sir Charles Lemon and Lady de Dunstanville. Sir Charles told us that Professor Airy (whom he has invited to Carclew) was so shy that he never looked a person in the face. A friend remarked to him, 'Have you ever observed Miss ——'s eyes? They have the principle of double refraction.' 'Dear me, that is very odd', said the philosopher. 'I should like to see that; do you think I might call?' He did so, and at the end of the visit begged permission to call again to see her eyes in a better light. He, however, found it a problem which would take a lifetime to study, and he married her. Lady de Dunstanville was in the House of Peers when the Queen first appeared. It was a most imposing sight. Her voice was full, clear, and sweet, and distinctly heard. We drove home to a quiet afternoon. W. E. Forster[1] has come to stay a little, and looks taller than ever.

CAROLINE FOX, *Journals and Letters*

[1] The Right Hon. William Edward Forster, M.P., Chief Secretary of State for Ireland.

35. Mill on Sir William Molesworth

Kensington
23d Decr 1840

... I am glad you have seen Molesworth. He is genuine, & *is
perfectly* the thing he is; complete within his limited sphere. One
ought to be satisfied with that; so few are as much & so very, very
few are more. A man of Molesworth's sort of limitation has a
natural tendency to be intolerant, because unappreciative of ideas &
persons unlike him & his ideas—I knew how to excuse all that
because I have been just like him myself & I believe knowing me
keeps him out of much intolerance & prejudice because he sees that
many things which are nothing to him are much to one whom he
allows to be fully a match for him in the things in which his
strength lies. I believe if I have done any good a large share of it
lies in the example of a professed logician & political economist
who believes there are other things besides logic & political economy.
Molesworth in spite of his bluster, at least half believes it too, on
trust from me.

JOHN STUART MILL, *Letters*

36. Molesworths

Two Moles there were, of equal Worth,
But not, alas, of equal birth:
The one who said his blood was blue
Was far the bloodier of the two.

37. George Borrow Visits his Kinsfolk

I must tell you a bit of our distinguished visitor, George Borrow. I will first try to describe his personal appearance, though it will be but faintly. He is a fine tall man of about six feet three, well-proportioned and not stout; able to walk five miles an hour successively; rather florid face without any hirsute appendages; hair white and soft; eyes and eyebrows dark; good nose and very nice mouth; well-shaped hands—altogether a person you would notice in a crowd. His character is not so easy to portray. The more I see of him, the less I know of him. He is very enthusiastic and eccentric, very proud and unyielding. He says very little of himself, and one cannot ask him if inclined to.... His mother is still living and is said to be a fine woman at her age [eighty-two]. On his arrival at Plymouth he stopped at the Royal Hotel. The next day he could not get a seat on the coach, so he threw his cloak on his arm (a very old friend which has seen some thirty years' service, the constant companion of his travels), left his carpet bag for the mail, and walked off for Liskeard.

He reached here on Christmas Eve. The following morning he trudged off to St. Cleer and saw about as much as the snow would permit. He was enraptured with Trevethy Stone and Cheese Wring; altogether he is much pleased with neighbourhood and people. At Trethinnick he was much affected, on being taken upstairs, at the remembrance of his father, and shed tears. He remained with us sixteen days, and then walked off for the Land's End. He was absent sixteen days, returning on Wednesday eve [Jan. 25th]. Yesterday Robert took him to Kilmarth and home by North Hill. He is thinking of going across the moors to see Tintagell. He seems to have a desire to visit King Arthur's Castle. I should not wonder if he went into Wales before he returns. He is a marvel in himself. There is no one here to draw him out. He has an astonishing memory as to dates when great events have taken place, no matter in what part of the world. He seems to know everything. He has lived years in Russia and Moldavia and Wallachia, and has been in Turkey, Greece, and Egypt, all over Germany and Italy, and I can-

not tell where. To Spain of course he took his wife (!) Two or
three people at Liskeard have asked him for his autograph, but it is
a thing he will not give to anybody.

W. I. KNAPP, *Life, Writings and Correspondence*
of George Borrow

38. *Jonathan Couch the Naturalist*

HE was a born naturalist, by habit of mind as by local circumstance sealed, if I may put it so, of the tribe of Gilbert White of
Selborne; which is to say that he kept a speculative mind under
strictest discipline of minutely recorded fact. A list of his pamphlets
and contributions to various learned Societies would fill some pages,
and his correspondence with Yarrell, Bewick and other naturalists
many more. He kept accurate journals of his observations in the
geology, the fauna, the flora, of his district, and trained many
disciples up and down the coast. One of them, the late William
Pengelly, F.R.S., famous for his exploration of Kent's Hole by
Torquay with its relics of primitive man, once shook my childish
hand with 'My boy, I learned more of your grandfather than of any
man or book'. But his main line of research lay in ichthyology,
material for which would come almost daily to his door, often to the
dismay of a household as scrupulously clean as its master in his
person. For, instructed by him, the fishermen of Polperro would
bring anything unusual taken by their nets, and he kept a small
apparatus of his invention—a stand which held the specimen while
a jet of salt water played upon it and he with rapid brush, being a
competent water-colourist, transferred to paper the evanescent
brilliance of the creature before proceeding to dissect it under the
magnifying glass. These drawings illustrate his *magnum opus*, the
History of the Fishes of the British Islands (in four volumes,
1862–5), which continues a classic. In an old folio intermixed with

87

the original water-colours are hundreds of small drawings, minutely executed, of almost every bone, joint, or section of marine fish and birds. Among various other relics I possess of his activities I may mention here a short pioneer book *Illustration of Animal Instinct*, a manuscript treatise *On Dreams*, and some scattered papers—all these indicating a range of speculation, from star to flower, which, as a servant of knowledge, pending exact evidence he kept to himself. Also I have in three volumes a translation by him, for the 'Wernerian Club', of Pliny's *Natural History*, based on the old version by Philemon Holland but pruned by my grandfather's more rigid Latinity.

He married, in early middle age, Jane Quiller, daughter of a race of seamen who, although said to be of French extraction, had been residents in Polperro for at least five generations. All her male kinsmen had been lost at sea. Her own father, Richard Quiller, had sailed with his elder brother John in command of an armed merchant ship under Government orders, and had perished with the whole crew, homeward bound, in a gale off Teneriffe. This befell in 1812. The widows survived but a short while, and my grandfather, on his marriage with Jane, moved into the deserted home of the Quillers—a huddled house of all contrariwise roofs and chimneys at an angle of the bridge. Often threatened with demolition, it survives to this day as 'Couch's house'. From its front door patients would be turned to a narrow backway because a garden spider had chosen to spin in the porch and the female must not be disturbed in her questionable career. Indoors by various levels past the living rooms and the doctor's study one climbed to a largish bedroom fitted with a wig-cupboard; in the floor were removable boards revealing a hole, in the past equally convenient (it was rumoured) for a fugitive from the press-gang or for storing a few kegs of smuggled brandy. On a beam of the old house hung a key which no one dared to touch, since Richard Quiller, Jane's father, had hung it there, the key of his quadrant, before starting on his last voyage, with strong injunctions that no one should take it off the nail until his return; and there it hung until by some later tenant, not of our family, it was taken down, swept away, or lost.

A proud man, stiff in his Methodist ancestry, he strode his domain as its unchallengeable great man, in top-hat, high white stock, long black coat, and until past middle age, black breeches and silver-buckled shoes—a costume which forfeited no dignity as he would sit, after his wont, on an inverted fish-basket by the quay, with brush and paint-box ready and the eye of an osprey on the nets, should perchance they discharge something rare, however minute.

As a doctor his care for the sick was exemplary and taken for granted by all (often without reward), as his efforts to improve the conditions of his people and to safeguard the fishermen's lives never ceased. For a single instance, it was he who conceived the building of the 'Duke of Cornwall's' pier on the east side of the little haven, prepared plans, made one of his infrequent visits to London to convince the Government, and after a long fight as Chairman of Committee saw its foundation laid on September 5th, 1861. Amid these local concerns he kept the even tenor of his chosen seclusion, gratified, no doubt, by many medals received from learned Societies, more by a constant exchange of correspondence with English and foreign naturalists and the entertainment of some eminent man who found his way down into Cornwall (then beyond railways) to visit him.

Q, *Memories and Opinions*

39. Burnard the Sculptor

OCTOBER 4, 1847. Burnard, our Cornish sculptor, dined with us. He is a great powerful, pugilistic-looking fellow of twenty-nine; a great deal of face, with all the features massed in the centre; mouth open, and all sorts of simplicities flowing out of it. He liked talking of himself and his early and late experiences. His father, a stone-mason, once allowed him to carve the letters on a little cousin's tombstone which would be hidden in the grass; this was his first attempt, and instead of digging in the letters, he dug around them, and made each stand out in relief. His stories of Chantrey very odd: on his death Lady Chantrey came into the studio with a hammer and knocked off the noses of many completed busts, so that they might not be too common—a singular attention to her departed lord. Described his own distress when waiting for Sir Charles Lemon to take him to Court; he felt very warm, and went into a shop for some ginger-beer; the woman pointed the bottle at him, and he was drenched! After wiping himself as well as he could, he went out to dry in the sun. He went first to London without his parents knowing anything about it, because he wished to spare them anxiety, and let them know nothing until he could announce that he was regularly engaged by Mr. Weekes. He showed us his bust of the Prince of Wales—a beautiful thing, very intellectual, with a strong likeness to the Queen—which he was exhibiting at the Polytechnic, where it will remain.

CAROLINE FOX, *Journals and Letters*

40. *Billy Bray: Miner, Evangelist*

His grandfather had been one of Wesley's earliest followers in Cornwall; and his parents, too, were devout Methodists. Billy's schooling was as scanty as that of other children of his day; and at seventeen—a seasoned miner by that time—he went off to Devonshire. His seven years there were marked by degradation and hard drinking. Night after night his young wife had to bring him home from the ale-house—and sometimes wheel home the coal he had gone to fetch. When he came back to Cornwall he was a 'proper wild-de-go', using swear words that his fellow miners declared 'must a come from hell, for they smelt o' sulphur.'

Then, one November day when Billy was twenty-nine and had long been wrestling with his Bible and Wesley's hymnbook, he became a new man—having found God as his Father. Thereafter, he was Billy Bray, the King's son. In place of fiery oaths, ribald jests, and witty, wounding repartee, new words and a new song were put into his mouth. Not that Billy was much of a singer! 'I can't sing so well as some', he readily admitted, 'but my Feyther do like for to hear me sing so well as they that can sing better'n I can. My Feyther do like to hear the crow so well as the nightingale—for He made both on 'em.'

Well, for forty years and more Billy Bray sang, and shouted, and preached from one end of Cornwall to the other. In a time of emotional revivals, he was a most individual and successful evangelist. Thousands of miles he must have walked and ridden to his appointments; and wherever he went he sang—and danced.

He called the dancing 'catchin' up his heels.' On one occasion he went to Truro to buy a new frock for his 'l'il maid', and on the way back one of those upsurgings of happiness which he often felt led him to 'catch up his heels a bit.' On his return home he handed over the basket to his wife who quickly asked, 'William, where's the cheel's frock?' 'I dun knaw,' said Billy, 'ed 'na in the basket?' It wasn't. 'Glory be to God,' exclaimed Billy, 'I bin an danced the frock out of the basket.' For poor people that was a serious loss, but next day Billy's friends at the class-meeting made it good, and not very long afterwards somebody picked up the lost frock and returned it. 'So the l'il maid had two frocks 'stead o' one,' said Billy. 'Glory!' Not everybody approved of his dancing, but Billy always had a reply to the critics. Why shouldn't he dance, like David? 'Ah, you say, but David was a king—well, bless the Lord, I'm a King's son; and I've got just so much right to dance as David had!'

So the wiry little man in black went dancing through the Cornish lanes and over the rolling downs.

CLAUDE BERRY

41. The Death of Cheelie

CHEELIE was a regular card, and to judge from the stories told of him and the impression he made on all who knew him—there are still people about who remember him—he was a born actor. He was 'so full o' fun as ever 'ee could be', says my mother, 'up to any wickedness'. After the day's work was over he would change, 'take his music and go over to the village, playin' as he went'. He was a great hand at dressing up and frightening people and all the regular amusements of the village—only he was the ringleader and chief performer in them all. 'Now look 'ere', said my mother, who used not to encourage him, 'you ent goi' to 'ave my things to put up, so go on'. But nothing daunted him, nothing would stop him. Old Betsy Hicks, who lived in a cottage at the top of Back Lane, was a preordained victim for his games and pranks. My father used to tell how one dark winter's night Cheelie made a turnip-lantern, placed a lighted candle in it, fixed it on to a clothes-post and bobbed it up and down outside Betsy's bedroom window. Betsy had gone to bed by eight o'clock and, wakened by these unwonted flickering gleams, could be heard trying to rouse her sleeping partner: 'Cusn't tha see the lightnin'?' But Mary Jane had her head safe under the bed-clothes. All to Cheelie's great glee outside and for ever after. The question, 'Cusn't tha see the lightnin'?' would bring a flicker of amusement into my father's grey eyes years afterwards—and perhaps something else: the memory of that gay, unquenchable spirit, the perpetrator of those harmless little jokes.

Little enough as I have in common with the old village folk, I do share their quite irrational pleasure in this kind of simple joke, playing a prank on people, some turn or other, giving them a fright, keeping up All Fools' Day.

Cheelie was very devoted to children, himself remaining always a child at heart. He won my mother's favour, when she was apt to look on father's family with no very friendly eye, by his devotion to the baby, Hilda. She was a querulous infant, always ready to cry, but was seduced by Cheelie's attentions. He would dandle her up and down on his knee singing:

Daisy, Daisy, give me your answer, do;
I'm half crazy all for the love of you.

This was well received. He was very good at minding the baby. Once when mother wanted to go to Charlestown Church—it was harvest festival, and father could never get away from Sunday work: he had to milk the cows—Cheelie looked after this difficult infant the whole evening, took her out to show her proudly round the village, brought her back, gave her her bottle of milk and put her off to sleep in her cradle. This was counted unto him for righteousness, as against his 'wickednesses', by the womenfolk. He had, for instance, a way of making up songs about people he did not like, and then singing them, performing them to the village. There was one about 'Ole Rebecca Rhubarb an' Ole Joe Oogly', two sour-faced, prim persons of the next village, Lane End: very much appreciated by our village.

Then Tom sent for him to come out to South Africa. For three weeks before going he stayed with my father; mother had the job of putting his clothes in order, making green-baize cases for the beloved musical instruments he was taking with him. One day he said to her: 'By the time I come home again there'll be a cheel lookin' out of every one of they bars', pointing to the staircase. 'Iss, I reckon', said she. During the seven months he was out there he was doing well, 'poor l'il fellow'—so she told me to-night, nearly fifty years after. He made enough money to pay back Tom's wife the advance she made him for his fare, some £20, and sent home £40 for her to bank for him. My father, after an unfortunate experience with his brother Bill, refused to have anything to do with the money side of their affairs. Cheelie wanted him to look after his money for him. My father said, with his strict sense of justice: 'The ones that trust you, you must trust they. I'm not havin' anything to do with it.'

During the weeks Cheelie was at home, he was for ever fiddling with an old worn-out clock that had stopped working, yet hung in the kitchen over the table. One morning about eight o'clock, some months after he had gone away, while mother and father were sitting at breakfast, the clock suddenly struck 'one' out loud. 'That's funny', said my father, 'there must be a mouse in 'n.' He got up and looked; there was no mouse there. Three weeks later they got the news that Cheelie had been killed on that day, about that time. They ever afterwards took it as a 'token', a signal of his death: there are many such stories in Cornish families. When the poor boy was brought up to the surface dying—he was almost cut in two by the crashed skip—he said these last words: 'I've neither father nor mother to grieve for me, so it's all right.' I have always taken those last words of an unknown Cornish lad as equal to any of the famous last words uttered by the great. He was a brave spirit, Cheelie, and has left a fragrant and beautiful memory in my family and among all that knew him. My father didn't trust himself to talk about him much, and I have noticed that there came a little pause, a silence upon the lips of these simple folk after a while, when they talked about him. I suppose they saw a glimpse in the mind's eye of that gay, dancing personality, the years roll away from them and themselves young again with him, who was for ever young. He must have been about twenty-two when he died. To think that he would have been seventy now if he were alive! Though he was dead long before I was born, I have often thought of him about the fields at Tregonissey, roaming about the village in the evening, the day's work over; but it is only to-night that I see myself in his words as one of the children 'lookin' out of they bars' by the time Cheelie came home again.

A. L. ROWSE, *A Cornish Childhood*

42. The Squire of Lanarth

P. D. WILLIAMS lived at Lanarth amidst remote pine plantations and rhododendrons. He owned seventy-five per cent. of St. Keverne farms and was proud of it. 'One is nothing without land', he had confided to my father, much to his disgust, when refusing his offer for Pengerrick. Lanarth and the Williams were always mentioned with bated breath, and I cannot avoid the conclusion that our people were afraid of them. Their respect conjured up in my mind an exaggerated image of the house and family, so that when I actually met both I was disappointed to find them perhaps rather ordinary. Or were they? In my imagination, however, they certainly loom larger than life even still.

P.D. and his family always managed their public appearances with maximum effect. I might be sitting on the milestone up by the beacon, chatting to our roadsweeper, when the man would suddenly stiffen and glance back. Along the road from St. Keverne a large car was coming at speed, with that purposive look which the vehicles of important people always have. 'P.D.', the man whispered to me as he stood up cap in hand; and the car swept by with splendid *éclat*, hardly deigning to touch the road in its progress; just a muted hum like the faint whiff of an exotic perfume, all dove-grey upholstery and impeccable black. The chauffeur looked neither to right nor left, but had his eyes fixed upon some far horizon, upon some impossibly lofty goal. His white-gloved hands rested upon the steering-wheel like the hands of the Lord Buddha in the immutable lap. Within, P.D., wearing a bowler hat and a grey tweed overcoat with the collar turned up, was lost in ineffable contemplations. Neither minion nor master acknowledged my companion's greeting; I don't think they had even seen it. P.D.'s car never sounded its horn. It relied on a sort of psychic projection to warn people of its approach. I have hardly ever known this method fail it. When the car was half a mile away and quite out of sight, people would begin to get restless and fidgety, stand up, walk about, and eventually start staring down the road. Soon everyone would be lining the verge as if for a royal progress, necks craning and mouths agape. And, sure enough, that damned car would materialise round a bend and come rushing towards them with its special muted moan. If I had ever had a bomb I should have thrown it.

Only once did I really manage to master this car and its occupant, and that by taking a gamble on P.D.'s driver. P.D.'s driver was a nice man, and after the incident we became friends.

Our party was off badger-hunting in the Trelowarren woods. We had stopped at Mawgan to offload and get the men a drink before starting on the serious business. We were a large party. My father and mother were there in the big Packard, driven by John. Then there was the incredibly old Straker Squire, with the huge brass bonnet like a Rolls-Royce, and the massive headlamps, fitted up now as a travelling dog-kennel specially for badger-hunting. Behind this, parked at the roadside, was our lorry with the picks and shovels, crowbars, badger tongs, sacks, the lunch and the beer, together with Tommy and John'o, Penner, Bosestoe and several others. The dogs were just out of the Straker, jumping and yapping; the bull terrier was sniffing excitedly at the badger sacks, just beginning to realise why he had come, always five minutes later than the others to catch on. Penner and Bosestoe were lifting down the beer from the lorry. We were as merry as crickets. Then I had a horrible feeling that P.D.'s car was coming along. You can't mistake this feeling once you know it; it cripples everything. And sure enough I noticed symptoms among the men. They began glancing down the road furtively at first, and then with increasing frankness until I was certain they would soon be standing along the edges, caps in hand, ready to do reverence to our enemy. I was determined to prevent this. And with my father and mother present it would have been a mortal insult. Working against time, and with an eye on the distance, I started to distract their attention, cracked jokes, danced around, played with the dogs, got in everybody's way, talked about prospects for the day's sport, demanded some of Penner's beer, and played the fool to such an extent that the tension really relaxed and I had everybody at ease, noses inside beer mugs and minds on the twelve badgers of Trelowarren which we were going to capture and release in the Three Tuns at St. Keverne just before closing time, when the bar would be crowded and everybody pretty full.

At this moment P.D.'s car rounded the distant bend and wooshed towards us with its eccentric sound. Nobody paid it the slightest attention. But I watched it like a lynx. When it was about two hundred yards distant and going well, I detached myself from the men and stood at the roadside, contemplating something. Thirty or forty yards off I strolled slowly and unconcernedly across, looking in the wrong direction, and stopped dead. There was a screech of brakes and a smell of scorched rubber. Everybody looked up. I saw my mother, out of the corner of my eye, start towards me and my father restrain her with a pressure of his hand. The car stood, smoking slightly, about five yards off and a bit askew. The chauffeur was looking awfully surprised. P.D. had been thrown forward; neither of them saw the nature of the trap. Then P.D. looked around at the beer drinkers, at the badger dogs and the two cars. He recognised my father. A deep flush mantled his face, starting from below his starched collar and disappearing up under his hat. He leant back on the cushions as if to hide himself. The chauffeur, too, had caught on. He looked mildly amused. I walked up to him. 'Sorry', I said, 'but you should have sounded your horn', and I waved him on. The car was started with a jerk, disarranging P.D.'s hat.

FRANK BAINES, *Look Towards the Sea*

43. *The Perpetual Curate of Cury-with-Gunwalloe*

THERE are few men living round whom so many legends have grown up as round Father Wason. Many of these stories have little foundation; but the fact that they exist and are believed give him distinction in an age when so few achieve a personality to which it would be possible to attach any legend. I can picture him as 'The White Knight' in *Through the Looking-Glass*, for ever falling off his horse with the setting sun illuminating his white face, or better still as a Confessor of Gnomes, bending down and listening with interest to the little sins of those small people, or even as a certain medieval saint who caused great inconvenience to his Bishop by refusing to be parted from a crucifix and image of Our Lady which it was his custom to carry in either hand when he walked abroad. I can picture him in any or all of these guises, so unpractical is he and so aloof from ordinary affairs. But for me his charm lies in a tenderness that expressed itself in a telegram when he first heard of my illness:

Saying Mass for your intention tomorrow 10.30 a.m.,

followed by another telegram the next morning:

Too late overslept—To-morrow without fail,

and the arrival by post of a relic of St. Teresa of the Child Jesus, his most treasured possession.

After knowing him for many years I find his whimsical nature too difficult to describe, except by saying that his scale of values is different from ours and often disconcerting to his friends. I remember a luncheon party he once gave at Cury to which we and Dod and Ernest Proctor were invited. We arrived tired after a long bicycle ride from St. Hilary, and found a notice pinned to the door, 'No one to enter'. After a time of waiting Father Wason came from the garden with his cassock tucked up round his waist and his arms full of iris blossoms. He made no attempt to welcome us but hurried by, murmuring as he passed, 'Colour scheme of the table all wrong. Must get it right for Dod Proctor'. After a further time of waiting and knocking on the door, an upstairs window was thrown open and Father Wason shouted down, 'Table all wrong without a black centre. Am looking for my tall hat'. After a further delay the door was opened and we were greeted by Father Wason, as if we had at that moment arrived, and were led to the dining-room where in the centre of the table was the tall hat filled with flowers. There was no hint of eccentricity in the tall hat as a table decoration, its shape and glossy blackness supplied a note that would otherwise have been lacking, so that one began to wonder why people had never thought of using tall hats as table centres before, although possibly it was not the tall hat that pleased us so much as the subtle compliment that had been paid us.

BERNARD WALKE, *Twenty Years at St. Hilary*

44. *The Vicar of Poughill*

De mortuis nil nisi bonum, 'tis said;
And so, since the vicar of Poughill is dead,
If truth and this maxim are both to be served,
Then silence on him must now be preserved.

45. *'Atky'*

ELSPETH did not have her husband to herself for long. Three days
of the honeymoon were spent at St. Ives; but when the coast was
clear of relatives the Grahames soon returned to Fowey, and the
congenial company of the Quiller-Couches. Once again Elspeth
became a martyr to tides, but this time in a more physical sense.
Nothing—not even marriage—could keep Grahame for long from
his beloved boats, or the uninvolved male companionship, free of
emotional stress, which he came more and more to rely upon. Q was
a great yachtsman, and the rest of July was spent afloat, in yawl or
dinghy. It was not, we may surmise, Elspeth's kind of world;
Fowey and Onslow Square had little in common, and the London
hostess probably felt somewhat out of things in this bracing atmo-
sphere.

From the start she and Q failed to hit it off: each saw the other
as a dangerous influence, and Q, one suspects, made short work of
her literary pretentiousness. Nor did she feel any natural sympathy
with Grahame's other great Fowey friend, Edward Atkinson.
'Atky', as he was universally known, represented the extreme of all
those characteristics which Elspeth learnt to distrust in her husband.
He was a sixty-two-year-old bachelor of private means, who owned
thirty boats and—though an indifferent sailor—was Commodore of
the Fowey Yacht Club. He was also an obsessional collector of
objets d'art, and his beautiful riverside house up the Fowey estuary

was filled to overflowing with knick-knacks of every description: the surplus went into forming a Fowey art gallery. He had drawer-fuls of mechanical toys (which delighted Grahame) and a rope-ladder in lieu of a staircase. His neat grey beard and aquiline features were a familiar sight in the Fowey streets—generally crowned by an exquisite and idiosyncratic hat ordered specially from Paris. He lived alone with his devoted housekeeper, Miss Marsden, but occasionally took undergraduate friends on canoeing trips in the South of France. Grahame found him highly congenial; Elspeth saw him as a subtle menace to her marriage. It probably never occurred to her, then or later, that Atky's influence would play a large part in the crystallization of *The Wind in the Willows*.

*　　*　　*

In September an unhappy tragedy occurred. 'Atky' was drowned while out yachting with Bevil Quiller-Couch, despite the younger man's gallant attempts to rescue him. Grahame wrote to Purves:

Again and again in imagination I get into my boat at Whitehouse Steps and scull up the river by the grey old sea-wall, under the screaming gulls, past the tall Russian and Norwegian ships at their moorings, and so into Mixton Pill, and find Atky waiting in the steps, thin, in blue serge, with his Elizabethan head; and stroll up the pathway you know, to the little house above it, and be talking all the time and always some fresh whimsicality ... I feel as if we had all suddenly grown much older. All, that is, except Atky. He couldn't do it; he didn't know how.

PETER GREEN, *Kenneth Grahame*

46. Charles Henderson

A passionate loss to his friends—and they were many—for all serious students of Cornwall and Cornish history the untimely death of Charles Henderson cropped the most confident hope of a generation. *Tu Marcellus eris . . .*, and what his countrymen feel all who knew him at Oxford will understand.

There was no one like him, nor can be none in my lifetime. He began as a precocious child intent on many things that, surrounding his elders' daily life, were taken for granted by them, and on questions for which his juvenile companions had no immediate use. To him, even thus early, this native ancient world in which he found himself, with its fields, demesnes, 'properties', roads, streams, bridges, was a palimpsest to be conned, and a family tree offered all the enchantment of birds'-nesting. It might have been feared of so singular a boy that translation to undergraduate Oxford would either contract him into a recluse or 'force' him into a prig. But in Oxford Charles Henderson not only enlarged his chest as a scholar: he also grew into one of the best of talkers and easiest of private companions. Yet I would not overstress Oxford's play in his development: it seemed that he belonged there as a country person with a town house belongs to London: he had the freedom of the City, but the native acres held his heart.

In the interval before his return as Fellow of Corpus Christi I 'assisted' at some lectures he gave as a missionary-teacher for Exeter University College. Having some experience of lecturers, I came (if unconsciously) in a mental attitude which he at once defeated. For his talk shed away from the start all that self-consciousness which is a lecturer's first bane. As if confident that his hearers were already—or would presently find themselves—as eager as he in his subject, he would dash into it and carry our attention and a weight of detail along with a kind of conversational enthusiasm. I do not say it was perfect accomplishment, but it was almost perfect promise.

And he carried this same boyish ardour into his researches. No jealous or suspicious inheritor of family documents could resist him. He came to see, he conquered, he saw. Once (I remember) when the luncheon-bell had twice sounded in a house not previously visited by him, I had to dig him out of a neglected muniment-room and wash and dress him, so to speak, for table: from which, the meal over, he plunged again into the vault, to emerge two hours later with armfuls of deeds and dangling seals and carry off the trove in a borrowed wash-basket. If either of us blushed for the assault it was not he. He neither blushed nor wheedled. He just wanted those documents to examine them, and the rest was fated. They would come back to their rightful owner, duly, bearing enlightenment for interest on the loan.

In this and other ways of his own he had acquired in his short life a detailed knowledge of Cornwall which all confessed to be incomparable. Nor was the half of it confined to documents. If, for example, a question started upon one of our many streams, his talk would catch up and run with the stream itself, yet as the stream caressing every shore it passed and feeling into the very memory of every bridge on its way: and not only that: for it seemed to have caught up all the latest humorous gossip of every parish it had watered.

Looking back on what he did so feverishly yet so carefully in his short while, I have wondered if he did it under some overtaking shadow, some echo behind him of 'Time's winged chariot hurrying near'. For certain, he did it swiftly, neatly, as one ready to render account. For certain, too, when to his friends the whole promise of his life shone clear ahead, he took thought to bequeath his collection of documents and manuscripts to his native County. I met him for a minute or two after a marriage so radiantly happy in conjunction of heart and mind that no wiseacre could have planned—no, nor no friend wished—a happier. A few weeks later, in Italy, the blow fell.

I can only tell here how the news of it on the telephone fell on us at this distance. It stunned. So much of affectionate hope, so much of priceless knowledge dispersed; with that delicate apparatus of a brain born, trained, exquisitely adjusted to pursue knowledge further for man's benefit; all that finest web slit and gone down the wind. Many older hearts were heavy as we filed out from the memorial service in Truro Cathedral. Two or three of us walked away to the building where his legacy is to be stored, the artillery he was ever collecting for his great Parochial History.

Days, when the ball of our vision
    Had eagles that flew unabashed to sun;
When the grasp on the bow was decision,
    And arrow and hand and eye were one. . . .

There the artillery will lie. But who now can bend his bow?

    Q, Preface to Charles Henderson, *Essays in Cornish History*

47. *Christopher Wood*

The sea was permanent: its lyrical foam
washed the broken white
of houses that danced on the sky
or gathered round the so serious sailors
to the drum and pipe.

Briton and Breton were one,
the brown sails between.

There were the misty seines,
the inshore green,
the blue that never was.

But doom was darker.
Yellow man, what are you doing?
What are those sinister shapes on the sand?
The horse with its sea saddle
in the haunted moonlight?

Will the thunder move this way
over the indigo sea?

Why does life dangle
from the absurd parachute?

Death was land-locked; but the sea was permanent.

ROBIN ATTHILL

48. *The Voyages of Alfred Wallis*

Worldhauled, he's grounded on God's great bank,
Keelhauled to Heaven, waved into boatfilled arms,
Falls his homecoming leaving that old sea testament,
Watching the restless land sail rigged alongside
Townful of shallows, gulls on the sailing roofs.
And he's heaved once and for all a high dry packet
Pecked wide by curious years of a ferreting sea,
His poor house blessed by very poverty's religious
Breakwater, his past house hung in foreign galleries.
He's that stone sailor towering out of the cupboarding sea
To watch the black boats rigged by a question quietly
Ghost home and ask right out the jackets of oil
And standing white of the crew 'what hellward harbour
Bows down her seawalls to arriving home at last?'

Falls into home his prayerspray. He's there to lie
Seagreat and small, contrary and rare as sand.
Oils overcome and keep his inward voyage.
An Ararat shore, loud limpet stuck to its terror,
Drags home the bible keel from a returning sea
And four black, shouting steerers stationed on movement
Call out arrival over the landgreat houseboat.
The ship of land with birds on seven trees

Calls out farewell like Melville talking down on
Nightfall's devoted barque and the parable whale.
What shipcry falls? The holy families of foam
Fall into wilderness and 'over the jasper sea'.
The gulls wade into silence. What deep seasaint
Whispered this keel out of its element?

W. S. GRAHAM

IV. History and Events

1. Tumult over King Arthur

On a tour of the canons of Laon, collecting for their cathedral, in 1113 at Bodmin:

A certain man having a withered hand was watching before the Bier in the hope of being healed, but—as the Bretons are wont to contend with the French for King Arthur—so this man began to dispute with one of our servants, saying that Arthur was still alive. Whereupon no small tumult was made and so many people with arms rushed into the church that if Algar, the clerk, had not prevented it there would have been bloodshed in the end. We believe that this brawling in front of Her Bier was so displeasing to Our Lady that the man with the withered hand, who had made the tumult on behalf of Arthur, did not receive his cure.

> CHARLES HENDERSON, *Essays in Cornish History,*
> from Migne, *Patrologia*

2. Excommunication at St. Buryan

In 1328 the dean and his clergy tried to get rid of the obnoxious Beaupré whom Stapledon had appointed Prebendary of Trethyn, but he held his ground and secured a conviction for robbery against those persons who seized his tithes. Grandisson, the new bishop, replied by issuing no less than three sentences of denunciation and excommunication in the summer of 1328 against the inhabitants of Buryan who had assaulted Beaupré, and put the parish under an interdict. In November of that year the bishop came to the Mount and there with the prior, Richard Beaupré, and other clergy standing around him, their stoles put off and their lighted candles in their hands, fulminated a sentence of greater excommunication against John Kaer, calling himself a parochial priest of St. Buryan, excommunicate and schismatic, for presuming to celebrate mass in an interdicted place, against Richard Vyvyan, 'auctorem fautorem et incentorem multorum malorum et flagitiorum' in the said parish, against all those who had laid violent hands upon Beaupré, and against all those joining in the masses, services, and prayers held in the church which with its cemetery had been interdicted on account of the effusion of blood therein. Then the candles were suddenly extinguished with the words, 'As these lights are extinguished in our eyes so may your souls be put out in the presence of God, the Blessed Mary, and All Saints and handed over to the Devil and his Angels to be punished with fire, world without end, unless ye repent. Amen.' The sentence was published and on the morrow sixteen of the leading parishioners including four Boscawens and Thomas Trewoef appeared before the bishop as penitents and promised to obey him for the future. Still the dean and his clergy remained obstinate, and the bishop reports that he dared not send any of his servants to Buryan for fear of death or at least mutilation.

In 1333 Bishop Grandisson finally declared the dean excommunicate, and three years later decided to settle the matter once and for all. On July 12th, 1336, he proceeded from Alverton, where he had been staying several days, and accompanied by an imposing retinue took the road for Buryan. With him were three knights—Sir Edward de Monthermer, Sir John Dawnay, and Sir Ralph Bloyou, the Archdeacons of Exeter and Cornwall, the Chancellor of the Cathedral, two canons of Glasney College, and many other chaplains, familiars, and domestics *in multitudine populosa*.

On arrival at the church the bishop before holding his visitation desired to ascertain the sentiments of the majority of the parishioners, and since some of them only knew the *lingua Cornubica* he appointed Henry Massely the Vicar of St. Just to act as interpreter and put to them the question: 'Did they wish to return to the bosom of the Holy Church and to cease from being rebels against God?' At length, after discussing the matter among themselves, the parishioners unanimously promised that from that hour they would obey the bishop and his successors in all things as faithful Christian subjects. This the leading parishioners promised *in lingua Anglica et Gallica* and the rest in Cornish, one and all genuflecting at the bishop's feet, raising their hands. Whereupon the bishop, zealous for the safety of their souls, having first sung the hymn *Veni Creator Spiritus* with its versicles and having said certain prayers, absolved the parishioners from all the sentences of excommunication. He then preached a sermon on the text 'Ye were as sheep going astray but are now returned to the shepherd and bishop of your souls'. When the sermon was done the interpreter recited it in Cornish. Thereupon the bishop ordained many youthful parishioners to the first tonsure and confirmed innumerable children from the wide and scattered parish. He then received an oath of obedience from the clerical staff of the church and finally completed his visitation. This was on July 12th. On August 16th, 1336, the final triumph was achieved.

The bishop was seated in the hall of his manor house at Clyst, attended by Sir Ralph Bloyou and Canon Nassyngton, when a visitor was announced. It was John de Maunte, the Dean of Buryan, come of his own free will to ask for absolution. Laying his hand upon the sacred relics, he took an oath on behalf of himself and his parishioners to obey the bishop, and on promising to pay his share of the Papal subsidy was declared absolved from the sentence of excommunication.

CHARLES HENDERSON, *Essays in Cornish History*

3. St. Michael's Mount

STEPPING over to the south-sea (for the distance is in comparison but a step) S. Michael's Mount looketh so aloft, as it brooketh no concurrent for the highest place. Ptolemy termeth it Ocrinum, the Cornishmen, Cara Cowz in Clowze, that is, The hoar Rock in the Wood. The same is sundered from the main land by a sandy plain, of a flight shoot in breadth, passable at the ebb on foot, with boat on the flood. Your arrival on the farther side is entertained by an open green, of some largeness, which finishing where the hill beginneth, leaves you to the conduction of a winding and craggy path; and that, at the top, delivereth you into a little plain, occupied for the greatest part by a fort of the old making: it compriseth lodgings for the captain and his garrison, and a chapel for devotion: this latter builded by William Earl of Moreton, to whom William the Conqueror, his uncle, gave much lands in those quarters, and greatly haunted, while folk endured their merits, by far travelling. They have a tye-pit, not so much satisfying use as relieving necessity. A little without the castle there is a bad seat in a craggy place, called S. Michael's Chair, somewhat dangerous for access, and therefore holy for the adventure.

Until Richard the First's reign, the Mount seemeth to have served only for religion, and (during his imprisonment) to have been first fortified by Henry de la Pomeray, who surprised it, and expulsed the monks: howbeit, soon after, when he became ascertained of his Sovereign's enlargement, the very fear of ensuing harm wrought in him a present effect of the uttermost that any harm could bring, namely, his death: whereon, the old cell and new fort were surrendered to the Archbishop of Canterbury, in the King's behalf. Thus Hoveden reporteth. But the descendants from this Pomeray, alias Pomeroy, make a somewhat different relation of this accident; for they affirm, that a sergeant at arms of the King's came to their ancestor, at his castle of Berry Pomeroy in Devon, received kind entertainment for certain days together, and at his departure was gratified with a liberal reward: in counterchange whereof, he then, and no sooner, revealing his long-concealed errand, flatly arresteth his host, to make his appearance before the King, for answering a capital crime. Which unexpected and ill-carried message the gentleman took in such despite, as with his dagger he stabbed the messenger to the heart: and then well knowing, in so superlative an offence, all hope of pardon foreclosed, he abandons his home, gets to a sister of his, abiding in this Mount, bequeatheth a large portion of his land to the religious people there, for redeeming his soul: and lastly, causeth himself to be let blood unto death, for leaving the remainder to his heir: from which time forward, this place continued rather a school of Mars, than the temple of peace. For shortly after the discomfiture of Henry the Sixth's party, by Edward the Fourth at Barnet field, John Earl of Oxford, who had made one, and one of the principal on the weaker side, arrived here by shipping, disguised himself, with some of his followers, in pilgrims' habits, therethrough got entrance, mastered the garrison, and seized the place. Which, thus politickly won, he as valiantly kept, and kept a long time defended against the King's power, until reasonable conditions swayed him into a surrender.

A like surprise, but of later date, I read in Popeliniere, touching the like named and seated Mount in Normandy.

During the last Cornish commotion, divers gentlemen, with their wives and families, fled to the protection of this place, where the rebels besieged them, first winning the plain at the hill's foot by assault, when the water was out, and then the even ground on the top, by carrying up great trusses of hay before them, to blench the defendants' sight, and deaden their shot: after which, they could make but slender resistance; for no sooner should anyone within peep out his head over those enflanked walls, but he became an open mark to a whole shower of arrows. This disadvantage, together with the women's dismay, and decrease of victuals, forced a surrender to those rakehells' mercy, who, nothing guilty of that effeminate virtue, spoiled their goods, imprisoned their bodies, and were rather by God's gracious providence, than any want of will, purpose or attempt, restrained from murdering the principal persons.

Here also was the Lady Katherine Gordon (an unfit yoke-fellow for that counterfeit Prince, Perkin Warbeck) taken by the Lord Daubney, and conveyed to the King.

RICHARD CAREW, *Survey of Cornwall*

4. *Before Agincourt*

PISTOL: What is thy name?
KING HENRY (*in disguise as a common soldier*): Harry le Roy.
PISTOL: Le Roy! a Cornish name: art thou of Cornish crew?

WILLIAM SHAKESPEARE, *King Henry V*, IV I

*   *   *

OVER the south gate at Launceston was a portrait of Henry V with a couplet:

> He that will do aught for mee
> Let him love well Sir John Tirlawnee.[1]

R. and O. B. PETER, *Histories of Launceston and Dunheved*

5. *The Trevelyans*

THE Trevelyans are a very old family. All families, we must suppose, are equally old, whether we adopt the Darwinian or the Fundamentalist view of human origins; but 'an old family', I take it, can trace an ascent far back in the catalogue of gentry. That much the Trevelyans can do, as three volumes of their *Papers*, published by the Camden Society, bear witness.

[1] Sir John Trelawny fought at Agincourt under Henry V.

From time immemorial a water-mill has stood over a Cornish stream, where its sweet water falls into the estuary of the sea, in the parish of St. Veep, a few miles above Fowey town. The ancient Britons called the spot Trevelyan, which I am told means 'the place of the mill'. A farm near it was already called by that name in Doomsday Book. It is recorded that in the reign of Henry III, and it is probable that even earlier, Trevelyan was in the hands of the people who had taken their name from it. Thence they spread over Cornwall and the neighbouring counties. In the days of the rival Roses, a John Trevelyan, sometime Member of Parliament, dabbled in the muddy political waters of that period. Being staunch for Lancaster, he was satirised in Yorkish lampoons as 'the Cornish chough who oft with his train [tail feathers] hath made our eagle blind'—the 'eagle' being apparently the least aquiline of all our monarchs, the poor, draggled dove, Henry VI. One year, when the white rose was blooming, Trevelyan was arraigned for a piracy of which he had been guilty when his party was in the ascendant. It was such an act as any lusty gentleman of the coastwise counties would commit as a matter of course in that litigious but lawless age. It seems that his ship had seized a richly laden Catalan galley that lay at anchor off Plymouth. Not a very heroic exploit, but, in the language of so competent an authority as Mr. Kingsford, John Trevelyan belonged to the 'school of English seamen' and of 'west country piracy' which in the fullness of time produced Francis Drake. Even so, our ancestor has not won his way into the 'Dictionary of National Biography', nor has any other of his surname who flourished prior to the nineteenth century. Generation after generation went by, and neither the world of politics nor the world of letters heard talk of the Trevelyans. For five hundred years and more they went on, from father to son, pursuing the quiet life of country gentlemen in the remote south-west, farming, collecting rents and taking game, surviving in their middle station the storms that were sweeping away the great families, as the brushwood survives when the oak is rooted up.

G. M. TREVELYAN, *Memoirs of Sir G. O. Trevelyan*

Most dear Lady,—Of the best and worst that happens to us, your Majesty must receive account. I send this gentleman to inform your Majesty of the state of your Majesty's army, as far as I know myself. If I write shortly and confusedly by him, I humbly crave pardon; for, as my industry to overcome the difficulties in which I find myself, gives me no time to write, so my sad spirit is not fit to indite anything that your fair eyes should read. Receive, dear Lady, the devout and more than most affectionate wishes of your Majesty's humblest vassal,

Essex

Falmouth, this 19th July.

* * *

Most dear Lady,—After I had dispatched Sir Thomas Gates from Falmouth, I had news that Sir Walter Ralegh, with divers of your Majesty's ships, and others of the army, were in Plymouth; wherefore I came all night post over the rugged mountains of Cornwall. Here I find Sir W. Ralegh, Sir G. Carew, Sir Fras. Vere, with the *Warspight*, the *St. Matthew*, the *St. Andrew*, the *Mary Rose*, the *Bonaventure*, and many fly-boats, and other ships of the fleet. I met at Falmouth with Sir Ferdinando Gorges in the *Dreadnought*, and the *Foresight*, so as now I shall gather a fleet able to beat the Adelantado's vaunt-guard, if we meet them at sea. . . .

Essex

Plymouth, this 20th July.

DEVEREUX, *Lives and Letters of the Devereux Earls of Essex*

7. The Spanish Raid on Penzance

1595. 'Jenken Keigwin of Mousehole, being killed by the Spaniards, was buried ye 24 of Julii 1595.'

'Jacobus de Newlyn occisus fuit per inimicos et sepultus est 26 die Julii.'

PAUL PARISH REGISTER

8. Charles I on Sir John Eliot

LET Sir John Eliot be buried in the parish in which he died.[1]

9. Sir Bevil Grenville Goes to War

'I cannot contain myself within my doors, when the King of England's standard waves in the field upon so just occasion: the cause being such as must make all those that die in it little inferior to martyrs. And for mine own part, I desire to acquit an honest name or an honourable grave. I never loved my life or ease so much as to shun such an occasion, which if I should I were unworthy of the profession I have held as to succeed those Ancestors of mine who have so many of them sacrificed their life for their country.'

MARY COATE, Cornwall in the Great Civil War

[1] On the request of the family for his body. Sir John Eliot died in the Tower for his opposition to Charles I's misgovernment.

10. Inscription on St. Ives Loving Cup

If any discord twixt my friends arise
Within the borough of beloved St. Ies,[1]
It is desyred that this my cup of love
To everie one a peacemaker may prove,
Then am I blest, to have given a legacie
So like my hearte unto posteritie.

FRANCIS BASSET, 1640

11. Francis Basset Rejoices over a Royalist Victory

'DEAREST Soul, Oh dear soul, praise God everlastingly. Read the enclosed. Ring out your bells. Raise bonfires, publish these joyful tidings, believe these truths. Excuse my writing larger. I have not time. We march on to meet our victorious friends, and to seize all the rebels left if we can find such living. Your duteous prayers God has heard, and blessed us accordingly. Pray everlasting. So Jane and Betty and all you own. I will God willing it, hasten to thee all possibly I may. Truro, this 18th May, 1643. Thy own Francis Basset 6 o'clock ready to march. Pray love let my cousin Harris know these joyful blessings. Send word to the ports south, and north, to search narrowly for all strangers travelling for passage and seize them keeping them close and safe, off those rebels of the best, let it be duly commanded.'

MARY COATE, *Cornwall in the Great Civil War*

[1] The original spelling of St. Ives, the 'v' in which crept in by adoption from St. Ives in Huntingdonshire.

12. King Charles's Letter to the Inhabitants of Cornwall[1]

C.R.

To the inhabitants of the county of Cornwall.

We are so highly sensible of the merit of our county of Cornwall, and of their great zeal for the defence of our person and the just rights of our crown in a time when not only no reward appeared, but great probable dangers were threatened to obedience and loyalty, of their great and eminent courage and patience, in their indefatigable prosecution of their great work against so potent an enemy, backed with so strong, rich, and populous cities, and so plentifully furnished and supplied with men, arms, money, ammunition, and provisions of all kinds, and of the wonderful success with which it pleased Almighty God (though with the loss of some eminent persons, who shall never be forgotten by us), to reward their loyalty and patience by many strange victories over their and our enemies, in despight of all human probability, and all imaginable disadvantages, that as we cannot be forgetful of so great desert, so we cannot but desire to publish it to all the world, and perpetuate to all time the memory of their merits and of our acceptance of the same, and to that end we do hereby render our royal thanks to that our county in the most public and lasting manner we can devise, commanding copies hereof to be printed and published, and one of them to be read in every church and chapel therein, and to be kept for ever as a record in the same, that as long as the history of these times and of this nation shall continue, the memory of how much that county hath merited from us and our crown, may be derived with it to posterity.

Given at our camp at Sudely Castle, the 10th of September, 1643.

[1] Still preserved, painted on wood, in many Cornish churches.

13. *The Surrender of Pendennis Castle*

THIS was the case of Raglan and Pendennis castles, which endured the longest sieges and held out the last of any forts or castles in England; being bravely defended by two persons of very great age; but were at length delivered up within a day or two of each other. Raglan was maintained, with extraordinary resolution and courage, by the old marquis of Worcester against Fairfax himself, till it was reduced to the utmost necessity. Pendennis refused all summons, admitting no treaty till all their provisions were so far consumed that they had not victual left for four and twenty hours; and then they treated, and carried themselves in the treaty with such resolution and unconcernedness that the enemy concluded they were in no straits, and so gave them the conditions they proposed, which were as good as any garrison in England had accepted. This castle was defended by the governor thereof, John Arundell of Trerice in Cornwall, an old gentleman of near fourscore years of age, and of one of the best estates and interest in that county; who, with the assistance of his son Richard Arundell (who was then a colonel in the army, a stout and diligent officer, and was by the king after his return made a baron, lord Arundell of Trerice, in memory of his father's service and his own eminent behaviour throughout the war), maintained and defended the same to the last extremity.

CLARENDON, *History of the Rebellion*

14. *Prince Charles Escapes via Scilly*

BECAUSE Jersey was so near to France, and so might give the greater umbrage, and that Scilly was a part of Cornwall, and was by them all conceived a place of unquestionable strength, the public resolution was for Scilly, it being in their power, when they were at sea, to go to Jersey, if the wind was fair for one and cross to the other. So the resolution being imparted to no more that night than was of absolute necessity (for we apprehended clamour from the army, from the country, and from that garrison in whose power the prince was), the next morning, being Monday the second of March, after the news was come that the army was retiring from Bodmin, and the enemy marching furiously after, and thereby men were sufficiently awakened with the apprehension of the prince's safety; the governor and his son were called into the council and made acquainted with the prince's resolution, 'that night to embark himself for Scilly, being a part of Cornwall, from whence, by such aids and relief as he hoped he should procure from France and foreign parts, he should be best able to relieve them.' And accordingly that night about ten of the clock he put himself on board; and on Wednesday in the afternoon arrived safe in Scilly.

... The prince stayed in the Isle of Scilly from Wednesday the 4th of March till Thursday the 16th of April, the wind having continued so contrary that the Lords Capel and Hopton came not to him from Cornwall till the Saturday before; at which time likewise arrived a trumpeter from Sir Thomas Fairfax, with such a message from the parliament to the prince as might well be called a summons, rather than an invitation; yet it was well it came not to Pendennis, where it would have found a party among the prince's servants. The next morning, being Sunday, a fleet of about twenty-seven or twenty-eight sail of ships encompassed the island; but within three or four hours, by a very notable tempest which continued two days, they were dispersed. Upon this, and a clear determination of the weakness of the place if it should be attacked by any considerable strength (which both by the message and the attendants of it they had reason to apprehend), together with the extreme scarcity of provisions in that island, which had not been, in the six weeks the prince stayed there, supplied with victual for two days out of Cornwall, neither had there been any returns from France upon the Lord Colepepper's application to the Queen, which returns would every day grow more difficult by the season of the year, his highness inclined to remove to Jersey.

... After consideration of the probability that the rebels would make some attempt upon his highness there, and the impossibility of resisting such an attempt in the condition the island then stood, it was by his highness with great earnestness proposed, and by the whole council (except the Earl of Berkshire) unanimously advised, that the opportunity should be then laid hold on, whilst the rebels' ships were scattered, and that his highness should embark for Jersey; which he did accordingly on Thursday; and on the next day, being the 17th of April, with a prosperous wind, landed at Jersey.

CLARENDON, *History of the Rebellion*

15. *A Brief Narration of the Town of Fowey's sufferings and services both for his late Majestie of Blessed Memory [Charles I] and our Present Soveraigne [Charles II]*

IN the first place, wee did mount twenty guns in the beginning of the late Rebellion [1642] in our owne costs and charges, which wee did make use of to defend your Royal Father's and your Majestie's right to our utmost power and ability under the government of John Treffry Esquire and others deceased, Commissioned by your Royall Father, and in particular by defending your Majesty's Port against the Earle of Warwick's Fleet. And wee always continued our Garrison for his Majestie in our owne charge up till we were overrun by the power of the Earle of Essex [August 1644] and then not willingly, but by constraint, we were forced to give way to a common evil. And most men of any considerable estate did largely suffer in the losse of what they had, being plundered by the said Earle for their loyalty. When he was gone, wee did rally our power again for his Majesties' interest, maintaining garrison at our owne cost, and replanted 10 guns, and we still continued stedfast until wee were again overpowered by Sir Thomas Fairfax [winter, 1645–6].

Several Inhabitants can testifie that almost for 5 years they were in actual service for his Majestie. In the late Dutch Warre [1667] wee did receive into our Port the whole Virginia Fleet which wee did defend against De Ruyter and all his Forces by fighting them from our Fortifications (which put us your Majesties' subjects to a considerable expence) without any consideration from the publique. Our harbour which is very good and commodious for the greatest ships is strongly defended both by nature and art having a Fort with two Blockhouses which together with our towne are becoming very ruinous through the damage of the late warrs and other shocks of evil fortune it might bee made Impregnable and a safe Receptacle for his Majesties' ships upon any occasion. The Truth of this Narrative, wee the abovesaid Inhabitants, are ready to attest.

CHARLES HENDERSON, *Essays in Cornish History*

16. *Restoration Amenities*

A gift given by John Seyntawbynn of ye Mount Esqr. unto John Vyvyan of St. Collumb Esq. Mr Vyvyan sent Mr Seyntawbyn an outlandish goose and gander, about the gander's neck were these verses:

> I send this goose and gander
> Unto ye Mount's Comander.

Mr Seyntawbyn returned him this answeare:

> If that your gander were a gelder
> T'would make a Presbyterian elder.

17. George Fox in Doomsdale

THE assize being over, and we settled in prison upon such a commitment, that we were not likely to be soon released, we discontinued giving the jailer seven shillings a week each for our horses, and seven for ourselves; and sent our horses out into the country. Upon which he grew very wicked and devilish; and put us down into Doomsdale, a nasty, stinking place, where they put murderers, after they were condemned. The place was so noisome, that it was observed few that went in ever came out again in health. There was no house of office in it; and the excrements of the prisoners that from time to time had been left there, had not been carried out (as we were told) for many years. So that it was all like mire and in some places to the top of the shoes in water and piss; and he would not let us cleanse it, nor suffer us to have beds or straw to lie on. At night some friendly people of the town brought us a candle and a little straw, and we burnt some of it to take away the stink. The thieves lay over our heads, and the head jailer in a room by them, over us also. It seems the smoke went up into the jailer's room; which put him into such a rage, that he took the pots of excrements of the thieves, and poured them through a hole upon our heads in Doomsdale; whereby we were so bespattered, that we could not touch ourselves or one another. And the stink increased upon us, so that what with that, and what with smoke, we had nearly been choked and smothered. We had the stink under our feet before, but now we had it on our heads and backs also; and he having quenched our straw with the filth he poured down, had made a great smother in the place. Moreover he railed at us most hideously, calling us hatchet-faced dogs, and such strange names as we had never heard. In this manner were we fain to stand all night, for we could not sit down, the place was so full of filthy excrements....

This head-jailer, we were informed, had been a thief, and was branded in the hand and in the shoulder: his wife, too, had been branded in the hand. The under-jailer had been branded in the hand and shoulder; and his wife in the hand also. Colonel Bennet,[1] who

[1] Colonel Bennet was a Cromwellian officer.

was a Baptist teacher, having purchased the jail and lands belonging to the castle, had placed this head-jailer therein. The prisoners, and some wild people, talked of spirits that haunted Doomsdale, and how many had died in it; thinking perhaps to terrify us therewith.

GEORGE FOX, *Journal*

18. *The Funeral of Margaret Godolphin*

17TH SEPTEMBER. She was, accordingly, carried to Godolphin, in Cornwall, in a hearse with six horses, attended by two coaches of as many, with about thirty of her relations and servants. There accompanied the hearse her husband's brother, Sir William, two more of his brothers, and three sisters: her husband was so overcome with grief, that he was wholly unfit to travel so long a journey, till he was more composed. I went as far as Hounslow with a sad heart; but was obliged to return upon some indispensable affairs. The corpse was ordered to be taken out of the hearse every night, and decently placed in the house, with tapers about it, and her servants attending, to Cornwall; and then was honourably interred to the parish church of Godolphin. This funeral cost not much less than £1000.

JOHN EVELYN, *The Life of Mrs. Godolphin*

19. *A Sea-Fight Off the Lizard*

FROM the tops of the hills, on this extremity of the land, you may see out into that they call the Chops of the Channel, which, as it is the greatest inlet of commerce, and the most frequented by merchant-ships of any place in the world; so one seldom looks out to seaward, but something new presents; that is to say, of ships passing, or re-passing, either on the great or lesser channel.

Upon a former accidental journey into this part of the country, during the war with France, it was with a mixture of pleasure and horror that we saw from the hills at the Lizard, which is the southernmost point of this land, an obstinate fight between three French-men of war, and two English, with a privateer, and three merchant-ships in their company; the English had the misfortune, not only to be fewer ships of war in number, but of less force; so that while the two biggest French ships engaged the English, the third in the meantime took the two merchant-ships, and went off with them; as to the piccaroon, or privateer, she was able to do little in the matter, not daring to come so near the men of war, as to take a broadside, which her thin sides would not have been able to bear, but would have sent her to the bottom at once; so that the English men of war had no assistance from her, nor could she prevent the taking the two merchant-ships; yet we observ'd that the English captains manag'd their fight so well, and their seamen behav'd so briskly, that in about three hours both the French-men stood off, and being sufficiently bang'd, let us see that they had no more stomach to fight; after which the English, having damage enough too no doubt, stood away to the eastward, as we suppos'd, to refit.

DANIEL DEFOE, *A Tour Through England*

20. *Planting the Tree of Liberty*

To George Hunt, Esquire—23rd March 1795

I am sorry to observe an alarming spirit of disorder to influence a great number of Tinners at this time, owing chiefly to the high price of corn and other provisions. Those from Ding Dong, Wheal Malkin and some mines in St. Just have more than once broke out, within the last fortnight, and rushed into Penzance where they have hitherto been checked by the principal inhabitants, aided by the Independents of that and the neighbouring villages—but a desperate disposition seems to have taken hold of many of them. I am told that in St. Just they went so far, in imitation of our Gallic neighbours, as to plant the 'Tree of Liberty'—and am sorry to hear several cant words among the Tinners, much in use among the French. Last Friday morning a great number of them marched off from a neighbouring parish (called St. Agnes) for Padstow, under pretence that there were several vessels there loading Corn to be sent to France.

WILLIAM JENKIN, in A. K. H. JENKIN, *News From Cornwall*

21. *Trevithick's Steam Locomotive*

THE Travelling Engine took its departure from Camborne Church Town for Tehidy on 28 December 1801, where I was waiting to receive it. The carriage, however, broke down after travelling very well and up an ascent, in all about three or four hundred yards. The carriage was forced under some shelter, and the Parties adjourned to the Hotel, and comforted their Hearts with a Roast Goose and proper drinks: when, forgetfull of the Engine, its Water boiled away, the Iron became red hot, and nothing that was combustible remained either of the Engine or the house.

DAVIES GILBERT's account, in H. W. Dickinson and A. Titley,
Richard Trevithick

22. Up Camborne 'ill, Comin' Down[1]

Goin' up Camborne 'ill, Comin' down,
Goin' up Camborne 'ill, Comin' down,
The 'osses stood still, the wheels turned aroun',
Goin' up Camborne 'ill, Comin' down.

White stockins, white stockins she wore,
White stockins, white stockins she wore,
White stockins she wore, the saame as before,
Goin' up Camborne 'ill, Comin' down.

23. Napoleon's Curiosity about Cornwall

THE evening of the 26th being appointed for our presentation to the Emperor, we attired ourselves in our Local Militia uniform, and having taken coffee with Count Bertrand, at a little after eight o'clock we proceeded from his apartments to the Imperial residence, amidst a flood of rain. From the entrance, which was situated in the left wing, we passed into an anti-chamber containing two windows, and the walls of which were hung with a number of good prints. Here we remained whilst the Count went to announce our arrival, and we were shortly after ushered into the presence of Napoleon, without any form or ceremony whatever. We found him standing by the fire, at the further end of a room adjoining the

[1] This traditional song, sung in Camborne on all popular occasions—feasts and football matches—refers to the celebrated occasion when Richard Trevithick first tried out a steam road-carriage up Beacon Hill at Camborne, 28 December 1801. It got up the hill on the way to Tehidy —home of the Bassets, where Lord De Dunstanville was awaiting the outcome of the trial—and then broke down. The white stockings refer to Lady De Dunstanville, who had on a previous occasion started up the engine.

anti-chamber, and into which he had come, on being informed of our arrival. This room was about the size of what we had left, and was fitted up with old yellow furniture, brought, as we understood, from the palace of his sister, at Piombino. On our entrance, he advanced towards us, and we took our station with our backs against a table that stood between the windows. Whilst he was advancing he began the conversation:—[1]

'What uniform is that you are wearing?'—'That of the Militia.'

'Of what county?'—'Cornwall.'

'It is a very hilly country?'—'Yes, rather.'

'How high are the hills? Like these here?'—'They are rather higher and less isolated.'

'Are they as high as those of the Principality of Wales?'—'Not quite.'

'What is the capital of Cornwall?'—'Truro is one of the chief towns.'

'What, Truro, quite near Falmouth? How many times a year are you assembled?'—'One month each year.'

'Who pays you—the government?'—'Yes, but the Prince Regent provides our uniforms.'

'What rank are you—Colonel?'—'No, Major.'

'Ah, Major.'—'We are the Cornish Miners' Militia.'

'Ah, are there tin mines there?'—'Yes, and copper mines.'

'Has the Prince Regent rights over the mines?'—'Yes, over the tin, but not over copper.'

'How much a year does he receive from them?'—'From £9,000 to £10,000.'

I. H. Vivian, *Minutes of a Conversation with Napoleon Bonaparte at Elba in January 1815*

[1] The notes of this conversation were written immediately after it had taken place, and, therefore, their accuracy may be entirely relied on. (I have translated the dialogue from the French.—A.L.R.)

24. Saltash Bridge: The First Span

THE day fixed for the floating, September 1st 1857, was brilliantly fine and the whole neighbourhood was en fête. Church bells pealed, flags hung from every house in Saltash, a general holiday was declared and from all over the country round the people flocked to see the wonder performed, until every field and vantage point on both banks of the Tamar was crowded to capacity. Out in the river the five naval vessels under the command of Captain Claxton lay ready at their moorings. Beyond their field of operations the water was packed with crowded, flag-bedecked craft. In the morning the expectant throng watched the pontoons being manœuvred into position, two in each dock, and the cables attached. As the tide rose the water was pumped out of the pontoons and at a quarter past one there sounded a murmur like the sudden sighing of a wind as the great truss lifted slightly and the thousands of awestruck spectators whispered 'she floats'.

At this moment, like the conductor of an orchestra, Brunel moved to his place upon a platform mounted high in the centre of the truss. Directly above him were his signallers, standing ready with their numbers and flags. He had insisted that the whole operation must be carried out in complete silence and his wishes had been widely publicised. Consequently, no sooner had he taken up his position than there fell a dramatic stillness like that which follows the tap of a conductor's baton, and every eye in the vast crowd was strained towards the distant figure of the engineer. Numbers whose purport was unintelligible to the crowd were displayed; flags flickered and then the huge truss swung slowly and majestically out into the Tamar. 'Not a voice was heard', wrote an eye-witness, '... as by some mysterious agency, the tube and rail, borne on the pontoons, travelled to their resting place, and with such quietude as marked the building of Solomon's temple. With the impressive silence which is the highest evidence of power, it *slid*, as it were, into its position without an accident, without any extraordinary mechanical effort, without a "misfit", to the eighth of an inch.'

Just as the time of high water came at three o'clock, the ends of the tube were secured in their positions on the piers from which they would be raised by hydraulic presses as the masonry was built up beneath them. As soon as the truss was safely in place the tension was broken. A band of the Royal Marines struck up 'See the conquering hero comes' and Brunel stepped down from the platform to the accompaniment of a storm of cheering. It was a moment of triumph which must have sweetened the bitter memory of the atmospheric disaster. But not one of the thousands of west-countrymen who cheered themselves hoarse that day realised that their tribute was also a valediction, that their hail was also a farewell.

It was Brunel's chief assistant, Brereton, who superintended the floating of the second Saltash span in July 1858 and who saw the work through to its successful completion in the following spring. When Prince Albert, as Lord Warden of the Stannaries, travelled down from Paddington to open the Royal Albert Bridge in May 1859 amid fresh scenes of wild enthusiasm, the last link in the broad gauge route to the west was completed. Wrote the ballad monger:

> From Saltash to St Germans, Liskeard and St Austell,
> The County of Cornwall was all in a bustle,
> Prince Albert is coming the people did say
> To open the Bridge and the Cornish Railway.
> From Redruth, and Cambourne, St Just in the west
> The people did flock all dressed in their best.
> From all parts of England you'll now have a chance
> To travel by steam right down to Penzance.

But the engineer was not there. No flags flew, no bands played, no crowds cheered when he took his first and last look at the completed bridge. He lay on a specially prepared platform truck, while one of Gooch's locomotives drew him very slowly beneath the pier arches and over the great girders. For his railway career was ended. Broken by the last and the most ambitious of all his schemes—his great ship—Brunel was dying.

L. T. C. ROLT, *I. K. Brunel*

25. *The Duchy of Cornwall*

(Written after the Abdication of Edward VIII, in 1936)

RECENT events have brought the Duchy of Cornwall, or rather its revenues, very much to the fore. There has been much coming and going of its officers; never have they occupied so prominent a position in the public eye. Indeed, the public may well have wondered at this sudden importance the Duchy has attained; it has served to call to mind the existence of a peculiarly interesting institution, with a constitutional status and characteristics all its own, of which few people are aware and with which only a few lawyers are competent to deal.

It is first necessary to clear out of the way the popular confusion between the Duchy and the county of Cornwall. They are, of course, two entirely separate entities, utterly differing in character. The one is an ordinary—or to a Cornishman, a not so very ordinary—English shire, as it might be Devonshire or Dorset; whereas the Duchy is an institution, a great landed estate vested in the eldest son of the Sovereign (or, in the absence of a son, lying dormant in the Crown), an estate which has been based from time immemorial upon extensive lands in Cornwall, and which has existed as a duchy, save for the interregnum of the Commonwealth period, since 1337. So that we are just on the threshold of celebrating its sexcentenary.

The habit of referring to the 'Duchy' when people mean the county of Cornwall is no doubt due more than anything to one of Q.'s early books, *The Delectable Duchy*, the title of which caught on and has become popularised over the last forty years—in itself a tribute to that charming volume of stories.

I remember, when my name was entered in the register as a Fellow of my college at Oxford, I was entered as having been born in the 'Duchy' of Cornwall. It was intended as a compliment, and, for sentimental reasons, taken as such, without protest. But it was inaccurate. The popular habit of referring to Cornwall as the 'Duchy'—in the sixteenth century they called it a 'shire' like any other English shire—is a modern error; it may be compared to what grammarians call the 'transferred epithet'.

For all that, the Duchy, in the exact sense—the appanage of the Duke when there is one, and when there is not, lying dormant in the Crown—is no less interesting and curious historically than it is on legal and constitutional grounds. For one thing, it goes back direct as an institution to the reign of Edward III, who created it for the support of his eldest son, the Black Prince; and indirectly to the Norman earldom of Cornwall, and perhaps further than that to the conquests of the House of Wessex upon Cornish soil. For it is worth noting that two of the Duchy castles, Launceston and Trematon, were at places with names ending in 'ton', indicating Saxon settlement; and their positions guarded entries into or exits from Cornwall across the Tamar—the one in the north, the other in the south.

A. L. ROWSE, *West Country Stories*

26. *Mylor in War-Time*

So here we were at Hoopers Hill, with our gas masks, identity cards and ration books. Howard joined the Home Guard, and was the liaison officer between them and the regulars—the Worcesters were stationed quite close to our bungalow, just by the Mylor jetty, where the old *Ganges* training-ship used to be. Howard slept just inside the front door, so that the Home Guards could walk in and report to him before and after their spell of duty along the coast-line.

At first we carried our gas masks, but gradually we left off doing so, except when we went to Falmouth to do our shopping.

I joined the Women's Institute, and listened to lectures on all sorts of dodges to make our meagre rations go round. I also bought a dozen Rhode Island Reds, and fed them on all sorts of unlikely odds and ends which we boiled up and mixed with their ration of bran, or whatever it was. Rude people called it shop sweepings! Anyhow, they were splendid hens and behaved in a most patriotic way. I was able to give three eggs a day to an invalid who lived up the creek and who was unable to eat normal food. Each autumn after the harvest we used to go over the stubble and glean every bit of corn we could find, and I grew giant sunflowers, as my Rhode Island Reds loved the seeds.

One day I saw an aeroplane over our raspberry cage with little puffs of smoke all round it, and that was the first of our German visitors. After that they came often, in ones, twos or threes, dropping casual bombs here and there—nuisance raids they were called. If they came close we would go into our concrete cellar, where we should be safe from anything but a direct hit. It was very tiring and nerve-racking, and one day, when the siren had gone for the fifth time, I said out aloud in the hearing of a farmer neighbour of ours: 'I can't stand it!' Then he went for me hammer and tongs, and said I had jolly well got to stand it like everybody else. That did me a lot of good and I learned to control my words and my face, but my heart always fluttered when I heard the bombs whistling down. The coolness of those around me helped considerably. I used to say to Mrs. Ashwin: 'Now you must not go home until the All Clear has sounded,' and she would answer: 'Oh, it's all right. I'll just keep under the trees.'

MARION HOWARD SPRING, *Memories and Gardens*

27. *Fighting Gunboats*

PAST the Eddystone Lighthouse, always to my mind like an enormous candle surrounded by a sea of its own grease, the latest droppings of which show white and foaming at the foot, until we could see the sheer black outline of the Dodman, tremendously impressive against the watery sinking sun. Where was the entrance to Fowey? As ever there seemed to be no opening in those grey Cornish cliffs. Ah, there was the Gribben day mark, like a man, a giant, silhouetted against the skyline. The cliffs closed in on us and we slowed to a crawl to pass the boom gates, a strange reminder in these, to me, intensely familiar surroundings.

I shall pass very quickly over our brief stay at Fowey. We thrashed about in the open waters off the Udder Rock, doing shoots and manoeuvres and learning to keep station, the most necessary qualification in a gunboat officer. Looking back on it the thing that strikes me most is the fact that we had no idea of what out fighting would be like, so that our preparation was mostly wrong; we had to learn our correct tactics in the hard school of night actions at sea.

Fowey was a brief bright interlude, chiefly memorable for the glorious story of the old man who was quietly rowing close to the Town Quay at high tide; an over-zealous young officer proceeded up the river in his gunboat, strictly against orders, at over 20 knots, and the next stroke the old man took was on dry land: he had been lifted neatly upon the wash and deposited on the quay!

Then one evening, after we had been there for ten days, there came the whispered rumour of a job:

'All available gunboats to sail the following evening on a special job.'

I shall never forget our get-away that evening. We were the only boat of the three tied up to the jetty, the others having fuelled and moored to a buoy in mid-stream. We were slipping at dusk, and being T.A.C. ('Tail arse Charley' as the junior boat was called) I was to follow in behind the others as they sailed down the river. In good time I gave the order to start up. The self-starters ground. Nothing happened. This went on and on. Presently the first lieutenant and others were delivering short and concise messages to the engine room. Still nothing happened.

The others burst into throbbing life and let go. I could see them begin to slide slowly down past the town. I had no means of explaining my predicament; my feelings can be imagined. My very first operation, and unable to join because the engines wouldn't start, a thing that had never happened before. Nothing worse could occur to an untried C.O.; they might think anything of one. At the last moment by the grace of God one engine started.

'Let go!'

They would be out of sight in a minute. I had to risk manoeuvring on one engine.

Turning hard a-port with the starboard engine running we just managed to get round inside the line of ships moored the length of the harbour, the engines picked up and accelerating rapidly took up our station as though nothing had happened. It is hard to define the reason, but it remains one of the most anxious moments of my life.

Our job for the night was to act as a covering force for another operation. We achieved this without incident, but how we managed to keep together as a unit I do not know. We had had no night experience, and it came on to blow from the south-west force 3 to 4 with driving rain. Howes had not yet learnt the tips we subsequently practised of getting a unit off in difficult conditions and of giving warning of a turn; nor did we have a shaded stern light in the rain, which later would have been installed. We did 30 knots under way the whole time. I can still remember vividly the anxiety we went through in the blinding rain near the French coast when we seemed to have lost the leader at the turn. We hung on somehow and we had our compensations in the morning. There was the impressive high land behind the Start with a bright, clear dawn and a rapidly freshening wind, very beautiful to behold; and had we not accomplished our first operation successfully? And did we not anxiously spell out a semaphore signal from the S.O., as the great hills of the river valley enclosed us once more, 'Well done'? We had only achieved the least that was expected of us, but we had been inexperienced and he knew what we had been through.

LIEUT-COMMANDER ROBERT HICHENS, D.S.O., D.S.C.
We Fought Them In Gunboats

V. Travellers and Travelling

1. Ralegh and Spenser Land at the Mount from Ireland

The first to which we nigh approchèd was
An high headland thrust far into the sea,
Like to an horne, whereof the name it has,[1]
Yet seemed to be a goodly pleasant lea:
There did a loftie mount at first us greet,
Which did a stately heape of stones upreare,
That seemd amid the surges for to fleet,
Much greater then that frame which us did beare:
There did our ship her fruitfull wombe unlade,
And put us all ashore on Cynthia's land.[2]

EDMUND SPENSER, *Colin Clouts Come Home Againe*

2. A Great Naturalist on Tour

THURSDAY, June the 26th 1662, we set out for Launceston, twenty miles. There we saw the castle, which is well delineated by Speed. This day we found, near Woodford Bridge, *Campanula cymbalariae*

[1] Cape Cornwall.   [2] Queen Elizabeth's = England.

foliis . . . :[1] near Launceston, in a shady lane, are two species of *mucus* . . . [which] grows in great plenty by the way sides; and near Holsworthy (a mean market-town in Devonshire) in the way to Launceston, we saw in the hedges great numbers of a kind of wild cherry-trees, with a long sharp-pointed leaf.

Friday, June the 27th, we passed on towards Padstow; but rode first to Tintagel, where we found Cornish diamonds on the rocks; but the fairest and largest are met with in the quarries, where they dig stone. Some there are, of the bigness and length of one's finger, very clear and pellucid; all of them have six sides, besides the ends. At Denbyboul [Delabole], about two miles from Tintagel, is the best quarry of slate in the country; it lies east and west, and deepens westward. They slit it with chisels into thin laminae: when it is first dug it slits easily, afterwards the sun hardens it so, that it will not slit at all. It is divided into several beds, both longways and broadways, by cracks and rifts, which they call junks; the out-side of the slate, where the junks go, is commonly of a red colour. At St. Elyn's we passed one Mr. Matthews' house,[2] riding on to Padstow, where is as pretty a quay as any I have seen. Mr. Prideaux has a seat here. This town is noted for strong beer. Great plenty of slate is dug up about this place, which they send into South Wales, and it is a good trade: they bring from thence pit-coal. Near Padstow we saw great flocks of Cornish choughs . . . The gannets . . . they told us were almost of the bigness of a goose, white, the tips only of their wings black; they have a strange way of catching them, by tying a pilchard . . . to a board, and fastening it so that the bird may see it, who comes down with so great swiftness for his prey that he breaks his neck against the board.

Saturday, June the 28th, we travelled on to Truro, sixteen miles. By the way we passed St. Columb, an old town. The churches in Cornwall, for the most part, have good tower-steeples of free-stone; the churches are made up of three rows or ridges of building, of an

[1] In this extract most of the Latin names of botanical and zoological species, noted by Ray, have been omitted.
[2] Tresunger, in the parish of St. Endellion, belonged to the Mathews family.

equal height, and sometimes length too and covered with slate. Near St. Columb, by the way side, are found in several places *Euphrasia pratensis lutea....* Between St. Columb and St. Michael[1] (and in several other places), a plant, which we guess to be *Alsine palustris minor serpilli folia*. It hath long, weak trailing branches; the stalk is round and red, the leaves of a pale green, growing by pairs, the flowers grow *verticillatim* about the stalk, at every joint; each particular flower is compounded of five, as it were tubuli, in figure like the seed-vessel of larkspur; it grows in watery places near springs. Nothing more common than *Osmunda regalis* about springs and rivulets in this country. Camomile ... grows in such plenty along the way side, that one may scent it as one rides. Truro is a pretty town, the second in Cornwall, and is governed by a mayor and four aldermen, with their four assistants; the lord Roberts hath an house there, but it is a small one; the church is handsome and large, and hath two monuments in it, one of them of the three children of the Michells, the other of the present lord Roberts's grandfather. Here is an indifferent good quay. They dredge up from the bottom of the sea abundance of a sort of white coral, among the sand wherewith they manure their land, and an infinite number of small turbines or buccinae. I suppose the bottom of the sea is thereabout, where they take up this sand, all over covered with this coral. They find also on this coast the shells of the *Echini marini*.

Monday, June 30th, we rode over the sands to St. Ives. There we saw a church almost quite covered with sand, blown up by the wind; the name is Uny Lelant. Here is a pretty little fortification which they call the castle. We saw also here some of the young murres, a bird black on the head and back, white under the breast and belly, and hath a black and sharp bill, black feet, whole footed. We were assured that the Cornish murre ... is nothing else but the razor-bill. All along the cliffs, as we rode upon the sand toward St. Ives, grew *Foeniculum vulgare* ... in great plenty. St. Ives is a borough town, governed by a mayor and aldermen. There are a great many houses to the north of the town, which (as well as the

[1] i.e. Mitchell.

church) are almost buried or overwhelmed with sand, blown up there by the wind in stormy weather. On a rock, a little above the town, to the north, stands a little chapel dedicated to St. Ia, as they say. The people of Brittany drive a great trade here for *Raiae* [rays] ... which they dry in the sun, and then carry away. In exchange for this, they bring salt. The inhabitants of this town are of opinion, that their fish are better and more daintily tasted than those taken about Penzance, or anywhere on the other side of the country, because theirs lie and feed on the sand, and the others on ooze or mud. The fish taken about St. Ives, are salmon-peal, ling, codfish, mullet, bass, hake (*sed rarius*), bream, and whiting, plaice, soles, turbot in plenty, as also gurnards, red and grey, mackerel, but not many, herrings, pilchards, and for this fish it is the best place in Cornwall; of these have been taken 1,500 barrels in a day, some say 1,800. Here are also taken lobsters, crabs, which they call pollacks ... dogfish dranicks (as they call them), tomlins ... which are nothing but a young codfish, shads ... dories ... sand eels, launces ... etc. We passed over to Godrevy Island, which is nothing but a rock, about one league distant from St. Ives, to the north-east near the land, upon which, in time of year, build great store of birds, viz., gulls, cormorants, razor-bills, guillems ... and puffins. The razor-bills are not so numerous on this island as the guillems, or kiddaws, of which many scores of young ones lie dead here. Here they call the puffins, popes; and the guillems, kiddaws. We saw many of those birds which they call gannets, flying about on the water. This bird hath long wings, and a long neck, and flieth strongly. Possibly it may be the *Catarreactes*. He preys upon pilchards ... the shoals whereof, great multitudes of these fowls constantly pursue. Another bird they told us of here, called wagell ... which pursues and strikes at the small gull so long, till out of fear it mutes, and what it voids, the wagell follows, and greedily devours, catching it sometimes before it is fallen down to the water. This several seamen affirmed themselves to have oftentimes seen.

Tuesday, July the 1st, we rode to the Land's End. Near St. Ives, in the way to Penzance, we found a kind of plant, whose leaf is somewhat like to *Saxifraga aurea*; it runs out in long wires like to

Campanula cymbalariae fol.; at each leaf it bears one small purplish-coloured flower. We found another plant on a boggy ground, which had small grassy leaves, but very few; it was almost all stalk; it grew not above an hand high, had a yellow flower, but not open in any when we were there, it being a close day; the seed-vessel was somewhat large, *pro ratione*, round, biggest in the middle, smaller at both ends, like some rolls wherewith they roll corn. At the Land's End we saw nothing remarkable. Here they give names to some of the rocks; for instance, one they call the Longship, another the Armed Knight, which they told us fell down about the time the king was beheaded; and a third they call the Spanish Lady, etc. Cornish diamonds are found hereabout, and indeed in all this country. Mr. Dicken Gwyn lives not far off, in St. Just's parish, who is the only man we could hear of that can now write the Cornish language. We met with none here but what could speak English; few of the children could speak Cornish; so that language is like, in a short time, to be quite lost.

Memorials of John Ray, ed. E. Lankester (1846), 184–90

3. *Apple Pie at St. Austell*

WELL, to pass on, I went over some little heath ground but mostly lanes, and those stony and dirty, three miles and half to Par; here I ferried over again, not but when the tide is out you may ford it. Thence I went over to the heath to St. Austell, which is a little market town where I lay, but their houses are like barns up to the top of the house. Here was a pretty good dining room and chamber within it, and very neat country women. My landlady brought me one of the West-country tarts; this was the first I met with, though I had asked for them in many places in Somerset and Devonshire. It is an apple pie with a custard all on the top. It is the most acceptable entertainment that could be made me. They scald their cream and milk in most parts of these countries, and so it is a sort of clouted cream as we call it, with a little sugar, and so put on the top of the apple pie. I was much pleased with my supper, though not with the custom of the country, which is a universal smoking, men, women, and children have all their pipes of tobacco in their mouths and so sit round the fire smoking, which was not delightful to me when I went down to talk with my landlady for information of any matter and customs among them. I must say they are as comely sort of women as I have seen anywhere, though in ordinary dress—good black eyes and crafty enough and very neat.

CELIA FIENNES, *Through England on a Side-Saddle*

4. *Wesley in West Cornwall*

JULY 2, 1745, *Tues.*—I preached in the evening at St. Just. I observed not only several gentlemen there, who, I suppose, never came before, but a large body of tinners, who stood at a distance from the rest; and a great multitude of men, women, and children beside, who seemed not well to know why they came. Almost as soon as we had done singing a kind of gentlewoman began. I have seldom seen a poor creature take so much pains. She scolded, and screamed, and spit, and stamped, and wrung her hands, and distorted her face and body all manner of ways. I took no notice of her at all, good or bad; nor did almost any one else. Afterwards I heard she was one that had been bred a Papist; and when she heard we were so, rejoiced greatly. No wonder she should be proportionately angry when she was disappointed of her hope.

Mr. Eustick, a neighbouring gentleman, came just as I was concluding my sermon. The people opening to the right and left, he came up to me, and said, 'Sir, I have a warrant from Dr. Borlase, and you must go with me.' Then turning round, he said, 'Sir, are you Mr. Shepherd? If so, you are mentioned in the warrant, too. Be pleased, sir, to come with me.' We walked with him to a public-house, near the end of the town. Here he asked me if I was willing to go with him to the doctor. I told him just then, if he pleased. 'Sir,' said he, 'I must wait upon you to your inn; and in the morning, if you will be so good as to go with me, I will show you the way.' So he handed me back to my inn, and retired.

Wed. 3.—I waited till nine; but no Mr. Eustick came. I then desired Mr. Shepherd to go and inquire for him at the house where-in he had lodged; *si forte edormisset hoc villi.*[1] He met him coming, as he thought, to our inn. But after waiting some time we inquired again, and learned he had turned aside to another house in the town. I went thither, and asked, 'Is Mr. Eustick here?' After some pause, one said, 'Yes'; and showed me into the parlour. When he came down he said, 'Oh sir, will you be so good as to go with me to the doctor's?' I answered, 'Sir, I came for that purpose'. 'Are you ready, sir?' I answered, 'Yes'. 'Sir, I am not quite ready. In a little time, sir, in a quarter of an hour, I will wait upon you. I will come to William Chenhalls'.' In about three-quarters of an hour he came, and, finding there was no remedy, he called for his horse and put forward towards Dr. Borlase's house; but he was in no haste, so that we were an hour and a quarter riding three or four measured miles. As soon as we came into the yard, he asked a servant, 'Is the doctor at home?' Upon whose answering, 'No, sir, he is gone to church', he presently said, 'Well, sir, I have executed my commission. I have done, sir; I have no more to say'.

About noon Mr. Shepherd and I reached St. Ives. After a few hours' rest we rode to Gwennap. Finding the house would not contain one-fourth of the people, I stood before the door. I was reading my text when a man came, raging as if just broke out of the tombs; and, riding into the thickest of the people, seized three or four, one after another, none lifting up a hand against him. A second (gentleman, so called) soon came after, if possible, more furious than he; and ordered his men to seize on some others, Mr. Shepherd in particular. Most of the people, however, stood still as

[1] 'If possibly he might have slept off this drop of wine' (Terence, *Adelphi*, v ii 11).

they were before, and began singing a hymn. Upon this Mr. B.[1] lost all patience, and cried out with all his might, 'Seize him, seize him! I say, seize the preacher for his Majesty's service'. But no one stirring, he rode up and struck several of his attendants, cursing them bitterly for not doing as they were bid. Perceiving still that they would not move, he leaped off his horse, and caught hold of my cassock, crying, 'I take you to serve his Majesty'. A servant taking his horse, he took me by the arm, and we walked arm-in-arm for about three-quarters of a mile. He entertained me all the time with the 'wickedness of the fellows belonging to the society'. When he was taking breath I said, 'Sir, be they what they will, I apprehend it will not justify you in seizing me in this manner, and violently carrying me away, as you said, to serve his Majesty'. He replied, *'I seize you! And violently carry you away!* No, sir; no. Nothing like it. I asked you to go with me to my house, and you said you was willing; and if so, you are welcome; and if not, you are welcome to go where you please'. I answered, 'Sir, I know not if it would be safe for me to go back through this rabble'. 'Sir,' said he, 'I will go with you myself'. He then called for his horse, and another for me, and rode back with me to the place from whence he took me.

JOHN WESLEY, *Journal*

5. *Dr. Borlase Disapproves*

THE person who comes to it (St. Just) should have a due sense of the irregularity and ill tendency of Mr. Wesley's principles and practice, because this parish being populous, and few people of figure or knowledge, is one of this quack's constant stages.

DR. BORLASE, in P. A. S. Pool, 'William Borlase', in
Journal of the Royal Institution of Cornwall (1966)

[1] Francis Beauchamp, of Pengreep, Sheriff of Cornwall in 1755.

6. Riot at Falmouth

THUR. July 4, 1745.—I rode to Falmouth. About three in the afternoon I went to see a gentlewoman who had been long indisposed. Almost as soon as I was set down, the house was beset on all sides by an innumerable multitude of people. A louder or more confused noise could hardly be at the taking of a city by storm.[1] At first Mrs. B. and her daughter endeavoured to quiet them; but it was labour lost. They might as well have attempted to still the raging of the sea. They were soon glad to shift for themselves, and leave K.E. and me to do as well as we could. The rabble roared with all their throats, 'Bring out the Canorum! Where is the Canorum?'[2] (an unmeaning word which the Cornish generally use instead of Methodist). No answer being given, they quickly forced open the outer door and filled the passage. Only a wainscot-partition was between us, which was not likely to stand long. I immediately took down a large looking-glass which hung against it, supposing the whole side would fall in at once.

When they began their work, with abundance of bitter imprecations, poor Kitty was utterly astonished, and cried out, 'O sir, what must we do?' I said, 'We must pray.' Indeed at that time, to all appearance, our lives were not worth an hour's purchase. She asked, 'But, sir, is it not better for you to hide yourself? To get into the closet?' I answered, 'No. It is best for me to stand just where I am.' Among those without were the crews of some privateers, which were lately come into the harbour. Some of these, being angry at the slowness of the rest, thrust them away, and, coming up all together, set their shoulders to the inner door, and cried out, 'Avast, lads, avast!' Away went all the hinges at once, and the door fell back into the room. I stepped forward at once into the midst of them, and said, 'Here I am. Which of you has anything to say to

[1] The scene of this disturbance was almost certainly near Greenbank Terrace.
[2] 'Canorum'. This 'unmeaning word' is perhaps derived from the Cornish *Canor* (Welsh *canwr*), a singer: an allusion to the love of singing among the Methodists. (*Lexicon Cornu-Britannicum*, by Rev. R. Williams, p. 44.)

me? To which of you have I done any wrong? To you? Or you? Or you?' I continued speaking till I came, bare-headed as I was (for I purposely left my hat, that they might all see my face), into the middle of the street, and then, raising my voice, said, 'Neighbours, countrymen! Do you desire to hear me speak?' They cried vehemently, 'Yes, yes. He shall speak. He shall. Nobody shall hinder him.' But having nothing to stand on, and no advantage of ground, I could be heard by few only. However, I spoke without intermission, and, as far as the sound reached, the people were still; till one or two of their captains turned about and swore not a man should touch him. Mr. Thomas, a clergyman, then came up, and asked, 'Are you not ashamed to use a stranger thus?' He was soon seconded by two or three gentlemen of the town and one of the aldermen, with whom I walked down the town, speaking all the time, till I came to Mrs. Maddern's house.[1] The gentlemen proposed sending for my horse to the door, and desired me to step in and rest the meantime; but, on second thoughts, they judged it not advisable to let me go out among the people again: so they chose to send my horse before me to Penryn, and to send me thither by water; the sea running close by the back-door of the house in which we were.[2]

I never saw before, no, not at Walsall itself, the hand of God so plainly shown as here. There I had many companions who were willing to die with me; here, not a friend, but one simple girl, who likewise was hurried away from me in an instant, as soon as ever she came out of Mrs. B.'s door. There I received some blows, lost part of my clothes, and was covered over with dirt; here, although the hands of perhaps some hundreds of people were lifted up to strike or throw, yet they were one and all stopped in the mid-way; so that not a man touched me with one of his fingers: neither was anything thrown from first to last; so that I had not even a speck of

[1] 'The house into which he was assisted has been removed, but I am told that in the village of Buck's Head, near Truro, the door is still preserved, indented with stones which were hurled against it.' (H. Arthur Smith, *Cornish Magazine*, October 1898.)
[2] *Methodist Recorder*, 20 Nov. 1902.

dirt on my clothes. Who can deny that God heareth the prayer, or that He hath all power in heaven and earth?

I took boat at about half an hour past five. Many of the mob waited at the end of the town, who, seeing me escaped out of their hands, could only revenge themselves with their tongues; but a few of the fiercest ran along the shore, to receive me at my landing. I walked up the steep, narrow passage from the sea, at the top of which the foremost man stood. I looked him in the face, and said, 'I wish you a good night'. He spake not, nor moved hand or foot till I was on horseback. Then he said, 'I wish you was in hell,' and turned back to his companions.

JOHN WESLEY, Journal

7. Georgian Tour

IN the summer of 1752 Dr. Lyttelton went for a tour in Cornwall, accompanied by Dr. Borlase, an eminent antiquary. They went on horseback, and among the places they visited was Trelowarren, belonging to an old Lady Vyvyan, 'where the situation was so bad' and the country round so wild and dreary that, wrote the Dean to his eldest brother:

Nothing would have carried me thither, but the prospect of finding a *sweet* bed to sleep in, which is seldom to be found at the inns in Cornwall, for both the houses and the beds stink worse than a pigstye. [Trelowarren not only provided this, but] what must please an antiquary, both the house and its inhabitants are an exact picture of the old style of living in Good Queen Bess's days. You pass thro' a pair of gates into a quadrangle; the left side consisting of a handsome chapel and large eating room, the right, a huge kitchen and other offices; in front is the mansion house, the entrance of which leads you directly into a spacious hall furnished with calivers, hunting poles, militia drums, and stags' horns. The furniture of the old parlour and bedchamber are in the same style;

especially the latter where you see the labours of the female Vyvyans in workt cloth hangings, point lace beds, etc., for several generations past. But the greatest curiosity of all is the old lady herself, with her children and grandchildren all around her. After the ceremony of kissing both old and young was performed, for this is Cornish custom, we were refreshed with a cup of sack, (it should have been *hippocras* to have suited the rest of the entertainment) and then proceeded in great form to chapel, (where prayers are regularly said twice a day) and in like form returned back to the parlour to supper, an hour before candle light. The old lady eat a pound of Scotch collops for supper, and wondered I could not do the like. Next morning Mr. Borlase and myself set out after breakfast and returned back to Trelowarren to our dinner, though the old lady's supper.

Dr. Borlase and the Dean went to see Lord Godolphin's house; after describing the scenery and all they had seen on their way, Dr. Lyttelton said:

Godolphin is not near so good a house as Lady Vyvyan's and is situate in worse country, if worse can be found; and I cannot, therefore, but honour my Lord Godolphin's taste for rejecting such a horrid spot, tho' it has been the seat of his ancestors for ages, and at the same time keeping a constant family of servants and a table for the exercise of hospitality and relief to the poor. There remain some good family pictures by Cornelius Johnson and Lely. Miller would have been pleased with a sight of the old wardrobe, where I unmasked some curious old pinked silk waistcoats and petticoats which are not to be matched even in the Green Room at Drury Lane Playhouse.

Tho' all this tract has an appearance of great poverty, and the houses in general miserable cottages, yet they differ I believe from all other cottages in Europe; scarce one in twenty minutes wanting a *sash window*; such is the fondness these people have for this kind of ornament in their houses. I would forgive them if they confined it only to their houses (tho' it looks very odd in thatched low mansions) but they have sashed all their churches in these parts, which ill suits the Gothick simplicity of these antient buildings. The winters are so mild in this part of Cornwall that *aloes, winter cherry,* and other greenhouse plants thrive well here in the open air.

MAUD WYNDHAM, *Chronicles of the Eighteenth Century*

8. A Summer Jaunt

TUESDAY *13th August, 1782.* Set out with my wife on a little tour. Rode to Heligan, Mr. Tremayne's, to dinner 20 miles. Found there Mr. Bettesworth and Nathan Garrick and their wives and a Mr. Williams, vicar of the parish, nicknamed Truth. Staid all night, but the weather was so rainy had no opportunity of viewing the grounds. Next morning in spite of the weather proceeded to Lostwithiel 14 miles, to the Revd. Mr. Baron, Vicar of the town. We met there at dinner Mr. Forster and Mr. Dixon of Boconnoc and Mr. Harris, Mr. Macgilvray and Mr. Elliott. The afternoon passed pleasantly enough.

15 Wednesday. Mr. Baron and I took a ride to Lanhydrock, a seat of Mr. Hunts. The house is Gothick, but mutilated. There is a curious old gateway, formerly united to the mansion and leading to it, but now detached and standing by itself. There is too much roughness and wildness in the park, but in some places it is well wooded. Mr. Hunt had made some new plantations forming a sort of belt round the park; but generally the walk instead of being in the middle is on the outside of the plantation or belt, so that you have a constant glare and no variety. This almost joins with Glyn, the seat of the family of that name. It is chiefly composed of an extensive valley finely wooded with a fine stream winding through it. Thursday in the evening Mr. Forster came to conduct us to Boconnoc, whither we accompanied him.

Friday. The weather was unfavourable. We took various views of the park and grounds. The stile of this place is highly picturesque. It is a beautiful assemblage of wood, waters, lawn, bank and valley. Its most beautiful feature is a valley the Banks on each side finely wood(ed) with sometimes meadow, sometimes corn fields interspersed, a clear rivulet called the Lerryn running at bottom. The Parsonage stands in this valley, with a charming view both above and below. The site of Boconnoc house is higher on a fine open lawn which opens to an extensive prospect.

Saturday. Rode to Bodithiel bridge. This is a most striking scene. The Banks are bolder and more highly wooded, a noble stream.

Sunday. Before prayers rode in the parish of Boconnoc. Fine points of view, the grounds charmingly broken.

Monday. Rowed up the Lerryn till its confluence with Lostwithiel river then down the river to Fowey. Still nobler and loftier banks and woods strikingly irregular in their appearance, one while opening, another contracting themselves; the river forms itself into three lakes, which till you come near seem to have no communication. This row of five miles terminated all of a sudden by a noble view of the sea and the town of Fowey. Tor walk, though made in Elizabeth's time, pleasingly irregular. Rowed back again to St. Winnow the vicarage of Mr. Walker where we all dined. On the opposite side Penquoit Mr. Rashleigh's, an ugly house, the lawn too much crowded with trees. Rowed past St. Winnow in sight of Lostwithiel and its tower, which had a fine effect. Returned to Lostwithiel.

Tuesday. Rode with Mr. Baron to Luxulyan Valley, a very singular appearance running from Luxulyan to St. Blazey. The country around wild and savage, the valley scattered over with immense stones or rather rocks, a rapid stream at bottom. The banks boldly advancing or retiring, sometimes thickly wooded, sometimes bare. The same day Prideaux wood, consisting of lofty and richly wooded banks, our ride was terminated by a beautiful range of sweetly swelling hills ending in the sea.

Thursday evening. Returned to Gluvias. All this neighbourhood is the Arcadia of Cornwall abounding in finely broken grounds, wood, water, and all the materials of Landskip, infinitely diversified. There is much intercourse among the Gentry, they are liberal and sociable.

Diaries of W. J. Temple, ed. Lewis Bettany

9. *William Beckford at Falmouth*

Falmouth, March 6, 1787

THE glass is sinking; the west wind gently breathing upon the water, the smoke softly descending into the room, and sailors yawning dismally at the door of every ale-house.

Navigation seems at a full stop. The captains lounging about with their hands in their pockets, and passengers idling at billiards. Dr. V— has scraped acquaintance with a quaker, and went last night to one of their assemblies, where he kept jingling his fine Genevan watch-chains to their sober and silent dismay.

In the intervals of the mild showers with which we are blessed, I ramble about some fields already springing with fresh herbage, which slope down to the harbour: the immediate environs of Falmouth are not unpleasant upon better acquaintance. Just out of the town, in a sheltered recess of the bay, lies a grove of tall elms, forming several avenues carpeted with turf. In the central point rises a stone pyramid about thirty feet high, well designed and constructed, but quite plain without any inscription; between the stems of the trees one discovers a low, white house, built in and out in a very capricious manner, with oriel windows and porches, shaded by bushes of prosperous bay. Several rose-coloured cabbages, with leaves as crisped and curled as those of the acanthus, decorate a little grass-plat, neatly swept, before the door. Over the roof of this snug habitation, I spied the skeleton of a gothic mansion, so completely robed with the thick ivy, as to appear like one of those castles of clipped box, I have often seen in a Dutch garden.

Yesterday evening, the winds being still, and the sun gleaming warm for a moment or two, I visited this spot to examine the ruin, hear birds chirp, and scent wall-flowers.

Two young girls, beautifully shaped, and dressed with a sort of romantic provincial elegance, were walking up and down the grove by the pyramid. There was something so lovelorn in their gestures, that I have no doubt they were sighing out their souls to each other.

As a decided amateur of this sort of promenade, I would have given my ears to have heard their confessions.

The Travel Diaries of William Beckford, ed. Guy Chapman

10. *Southey Arrives by Packet*

W E passed in sight of St. Mawes, a little fishing-town on the east of the bay, and anchored about noon at Falmouth. There is a man always on the lookout for the Packets; he makes a signal as soon as one is seen, and every woman who has a husband on board gives him a shilling for the intelligence....

The perpetual stir and bustle in this inn is as surprising as it is wearisome. Doors opening and shutting, bells ringing, voices calling to the waiter from every quarter, while he cries 'Coming', to one room, and hurries away to another. Everybody is in a hurry here; either they are going off in Packets, and are hastening their preparations to embark; or they have just arrived, and are impatient to be on the road homeward. Every now and then a carriage rattles up to the door with a rapidity which makes the very house shake. The man who cleans the boots is running in one direction, the barber with his powder-bag in another; here goes the barber's boy with his hot water and razors; there comes the clean linen with the washer-woman; and the hall is full of porters and sailors bringing in luggage, or bearing it away; now you hear a horn blow because the post is coming in, and in the middle of the night you are awakened by another because it is going out. Nothing is done in England without a noise, and yet noise is the only thing they forget in the bill!

Thursday, April 22 (1802)

Early in the morning our chaise was at the door, a four-wheeled carriage which conveniently carries three persons. It has glass in front and at the sides, instead of being closed with curtains, so that you at once see the country and are sheltered from the weather. Two horses drew us at the rate of a league and a half in the hour; such is the rapidity with which the English travel. Half a league from Falmouth is the little town of Penryn, whose ill-built and narrow streets seem to have been contrived to make as many acute angles in the road, and take the traveller up and down as many steep declivities as possible in a given distance. In two hours we reached Truro, where we breakfasted: this meal is completely spoilt by the abominable bitterness of the bread, to which I shall not soon be able to reconcile myself. The town is clean and opulent; its main street broad, with superb shops, and a little gutter stream running through it. All the shops have windows to them; the climate is so inclement that it would be impossible to live without them. J— showed me where some traveller had left the expression of his impatience written upon the wainscot with a pencil—'Thanks to the Gods another stage is past'—for all travellers are in haste here, either on their way home, or to be in time for the Packet.

DON MANUEL ALVAREZ ESPRIELLA (Robert Southey),
Letters from England

11. *A Fight with an American Privateer*

JOHN NANKEVELL, late Master of H.M. Packet *Princess Amelia*, was unfortunately killed after fifteen minutes' engagement with an American Privateer of superior force in defence of his King and country on his homeward voyage from the West Indies on the 15th September, 1812, aged 34 years.

In Mylor Church

12. *An American Ally*

In memory of J. M. Macomb, Esqr., of New York, who was mortally wounded on board of H.M. *Princess Charlotte*, whilst gallantly assisting in her defence in an action with a French privateer off Scilly, on the 9th day of November 1810, and died the same day in Falmouth harbour, aged 36 years. This tablet is placed here by a few friends to commemorate his bravery and their regret.

In Falmouth Parish Church

13. *Byron Departs by Packet*

My Dear Hodgson,—Before this reaches you, Hobhouse, two officers' wives, three children, two waiting-maids, ditto subalterns for the troops, three Portuguese esquires and domestics, in all nineteen souls, will have sailed in the Lisbon packet, with the noble Captain Kidd, a gallant commander as ever smuggled an anker of right Nantz.

We are going to Lisbon first, because the Malta packet has sailed, d'ye see?—from Lisbon to Gibraltar, Malta, Constantinople, and 'all that', as Orator Henley said, when he put the Church, and 'all that', in danger.

This town of Falmouth, as you will partly conjecture, is no great ways from the sea. It is defended on the sea-side by twin castles, St. Mawes and Pendennis, extremely well calculated for annoying every body except an enemy. St. Mawes is garrisoned by an able-bodied person of fourscore, a widower. He has the whole command and sole management of six most unmanageable pieces of ordnance, admirably adapted for the destruction of Pendennis, a like tower of strength on the opposite side of the Channel. We have seen St. Mawes, but Pendennis they will not let us behold, save at a distance, because Hobhouse and I are suspected of having already taken St. Mawes by a coup de main.

The town contains many Quakers and salt fish—the oysters have a taste of copper, owing to the soil of a mining country—the women (blessed be the Corporation therefor!) are flogged at the cart's tail when they pick and steal, as happened to one of the fair sex yesterday noon. She was pertinacious in her behaviour, and damned the mayor.

This is all I know of Falmouth.

I don't know when I can write again, because it depends on that experienced navigator, Captain Kidd, and the 'stormy winds that (don't) blow' at this season. I leave England without regret—I shall return to it without pleasure. I am like Adam, the first convict sentenced to transportation, but I have no Eve, and have eaten no apple but what was sour as a crab;—and thus ends my first chapter. Adieu.

BYRON, *Letters*

14. *Byron's Farewell*

Falmouth Roads, June 30, 1809

'Huzza! Hodgson, we are going,
    Our embargo's off at last;
Favourable breezes blowing
    Bend the canvass o'er the mast.
From aloft the signal's streaming,
    Hark! the farewell gun is fired,
Women screeching, tars blaspheming,
    Tell us that our time's expired.

Here's a rascal
Come to task all,
Prying from the Custom-house;
Trunks unpacking,
Cases cracking,
Not a corner for a mouse
'Scapes unsearch'd amid the racket,
Ere we sail on board the Packet.

'Now our boatmen quit their mooring,
And all hands must ply the oar;
Baggage from the quay is lowering,
We're impatient—push from shore.
"Have a care! that case holds liquor—
Stop the boat—I'm sick—oh Lord!"
"Sick, ma'am, damme, you'll be sicker
Ere you've been an hour on board."
Thus are screaming
Men and women,
Gemmen, ladies, servants, Jacks;
Here entangling,
All are wrangling,
Stuck together close as wax.—
Such the general noise and racket,
Ere we reach the Lisbon Packet.

'Now we've reach'd her, lo! the captain,
Gallant Kidd, commands the crew;
Passengers their berths are clapt in,
Some to grumble, some to spew.
"Hey day! call you that a cabin?
Why 'tis hardly three feet square;
Not enough to stow Queen Mab in—
Who the deuce can harbour there?"
"Who, sir? plenty—
Nobles twenty—

Did at once my vessel fill"—
    "Did they?" Jesus,
        How you squeeze us!
Would to God they did so still:
Then I'd 'scape the heat and racket,
Of the good ship, Lisbon Packet.

'Fletcher! Murray! Bob! where are you?
    Stretch'd along the deck like logs—
Bear a hand, you jolly tar you!
    Here's a rope's end for the dogs.
Hobhouse muttering fearful curses,
    As the hatchway down he rolls;
Now his breakfast, now his verses,
    Vomits forth—and damns our souls.
            "Here's a stanza
            On Braganza—
    Help!"—"A couplet?"—"No, a cup
        Of warm water."—
        "What's the matter?"
    "Zounds! my liver's coming up;
I shall not survive the racket
Of this brutal Lisbon Packet."

'Now at length we're off for Turkey,
    Lord knows when we shall come back!
Breezes foul and tempests murky
    May unship us in a crack.
But, since life at most a jest is,
    As philosophers allow,
Still to laugh by far the best is,
    Then laugh on—as I do now.
            Laugh at all things,
            Great and small things,
    Sick or well, at sea or shore;

While we're quaffing,
Let's have laughing—
Who the devil cares for more?—
Some good wine! and who would lack it,
Ev'n on board the Lisbon Packet?'

Lord Byron, Poems

15. The Picturesque Tamar

As we sailed farther up the river, we came in view of the rocks and woods of Cotehele, which are still on the Cornish side, and afford some beautiful scenery. Here we had grand sweeping hills, covered with wood. At the bottom of one of them stands a noble limekiln-castle, which is relieved by a lofty background.

Near the bottom of another stands a small Gothic ruin, situated, with much picturesque beauty, in a woody recess. It was formerly a votive chapel, built by a chief of the Cotehele family; though some say by one of the Edgcumbes. Its founder had engaged on the unsuccessful side, during one of the periods of the dubious wars of York and Lancaster. His party being beaten, he fled for his life; and as he was a man of consequence, was closely pursued. The Tamar opposed his flight. He made a short vow to the Virgin Mary, threw himself into the river, and swam safe to the promontory, before which we now lay on our oars. His upper garment, which he had thrown off, floated down the stream; and giving occasion to believe he had perished, checked the ardour of the pursuit. In the mean time Edgcumbe lurked in his own woods, till a happier moment; and in the day of security raised this chapel to the holy Virgin, his protectress, who had the full honour of his escape.

At Cotehele House we landed, which is entirely surrounded with wood, and shut out from the river. If it were a little opened, it might both see and be seen to advantage. To the river particularly it would present a good object; as it stands on a bold knoll, and is built in the form of a castle. But it is a deserted mansion, and occupied only as a farmhouse. Here we refreshed ourselves with tea, and larded our bread, after the fashion of the country, with clouted cream.

Round this old mansion grew some noble trees, and among them the Spanish chestnut, full grown and spread out in huge massy limbs. We thought these chestnuts scarce inferior to the proudest oaks. The chestnut on which Salvator Rosa has hung Edipus is exactly one of them.

We had now sailed a considerable way up the Tamar, and during the whole voyage had been almost solely obliged to the Cornish shores for amusement. But the Devonshire coast, as if only collecting its stretch, burst out upon us at Calstock, in a grander display of lofty banks, adorned with wood and rock, than any we had yet seen, and continued without interruption through the space of a league.

But it is impossible to describe scenes which, though *strongly marked*, have no *peculiar* features. In Nature these lofty banks are infinitely varied. The face of each rock is different; it projects differently: it is naked, or it is adorned; or, if adorned, its ornaments are of different kinds. In short, Nature's variations are as infinite on the face of a rock as in the face of a man. Each requires a distinct portrait to characterise it justly; while language can no more give you a full idea of one than it can of the other.

W. S. GILPIN, *Observations on the Western Parts of England*

16. Travelling

'Peckham Rye, Loughborough, Elephant, St. Paul's,'
Every morning the porter bawls.
The train grinds out ... and I gaze on lots
Of sad back gardens and chimney-pots,

Factory stacks and smoky haze
Showering smuts on the close-packed ways.
And the train jolts on and twists and crawls . . .
'Peckham Rye, Loughborough, Elephant, St. Paul's.'

But, trapped and prisoned as I may be,
I lift a latch and my thoughts go free,
And once again I am running down
On a winding track from a Cornish town
And I dream the names of the stations through—
'Moorswater, Causeland, Sandplace, Looe.'

An ancient engine with puff nigh gone,
Drags a couple of coaches on
Close where a stream runs all the way
Muttering music night and day;
There isn't a porter about at all
To spoil the peace with a raucous bawl,
But a kind old guard to see me through,
Give me a ticket and take it too.
The line twists down through patches sweet
Of soft green pasture and waving wheat
And the stream spreads out to a river wide
Where ships creep up at the turn of tide,
Till a tangle of spars on a blue sky spun
Gives me the sign of the journey done,
And I stand contented on the quay
And hear the surging song of the sea.

So runs the dreamlike journey through,
'Moorswater, Causeland, Sandplace, Looe';—
But every morning the porter bawls,
'Peckham Rye, Loughborough, Elephant, St. Paul's.'

BERNARD MOORE, *A Cornish Collection*

VI. Occupations and Callings

1. A Dream of a Tinwork

SOME have found tin works of great value through means no less strange than extraordinary, to wit, by dreams; as in Edward the Sixth's time, a gentlewoman, heir to one Trescuiierd, and wife to Lanine, dreamed that a man of seemly personage told her how in such a tenement of her land she should find so great store of tin, as would serve to enrich both herself and her posterity. This she revealed to her husband; and he, putting the same in trial, found a work, which in four years was worth him well near so many thousand pounds. Moreover, one Taprel, lately living, and dwelling in the parish of the hundred of West, called St. Neot, by a like dream of his daughter (see the luck of women) made the like essay, met with the effect, farmed the work of the unwitting lord of the soil, and grew thereby to good state of wealth. The same report passeth as current, touching sundry others; but I will not bind any man's credit, though that of the authors have herein swayed mine; and yet he that will afford his ear to astrologers and natural philosophers, shall have it filled with many discourses of the constellation of the heavens, and the constitution of men's bodies, fitting to this purpose.

RICHARD CAREW, *Survey of Cornwall*

2. Tinners' Finds

TINNERS do also find little hopps of Gold amongst their ore, which they keep in quills, and sell to the goldsmiths oftentimes with little better gain than Glaucus' exchange.

RICHARD CAREW, *Survey of Cornwall*

3. Early Tin Mining

HALF a mile from thence they blow their tin, which I went to see. They take the ore and pound it in a stamping mill which resembles the paper mills, and when it is as fine as the finest sand—some of which I saw and took—this they fling into a furnace and with it coal to make the fire. So it burns together and makes a violent heat and fierce flame; the metal by the fire being separated from the coal and its own dross, being very heavy falls down to a trench made to receive it at the furnace hole below. This liquid metal I saw them shovel up with an iron shovel, and so pour it into moulds, in which it cools, and so they take it thence in sort of wedges, or pigs I think they call them. It is a fine metal in its first melting—looks like silver; I had a piece poured out and made cold for to take with me. The ore as it is just dug looks like the thunderstones, a greenish hue full of pendust—this seems to contain its full description—the shining part is white.

I went a mile farther on the hills, and so came where they were digging in the tin mines. There were at least twenty mines all in sight, which employ a great many people at work almost night and day, but constantly all and every day, including the Lord's Day, which they are forced to prevent their mines being overflowed with water. More than 1,000 men are taken up about them; few mines but had then almost twenty men and boys attending it, either down in the mines digging and carrying the ore to the little bucket which conveys it up, or else others are draining the water and looking to the engines that are draining it, and those above are attending the drawing up the ore in a sort of windlass as it is to a well. Two men keep turning, bringing one up and letting down another. They are much like the leather buckets they use in London to put out fire, which hang up in churches and great men's halls. They have a great labour and great expense to drain the mines of the water with mills that horses turn, and now they have the mills or water engines that are turned by the water which is conveyed on frames of timber and trunks to hold the water, which falls down on the wheels as an overshot mill, and these are the sort that turns the water into the several towns I have seen about London, Derby, and Exeter, and many places more. They do five times more good than the mills they use to turn with horses, but then they are much more chargeable.

Those mines do require a great deal of timber to support them and to make all those engines and mills, which makes fuel very scarce here. They burn mostly turves, which is an unpleasant smell; it makes one smell as if smoked like bacon. This ore, as said, is made fine powder in a stamping mill which is like the paper mills, only these are pounded dry and no water let into them as it is to the rags, to work them into a paste. The mills are all turned with a little stream or channel of water you may step over; indeed they have no other mills but such in all the country. I saw not a windmill all over Cornwall or Devonshire, though they have wind and hills enough, and it may be it is too bleak for them. In the tin mines there is stone dug out and a sort of spar something like what I have seen in the lead mines at Darbyshire, but it seemed more solid and hard; it shines and looks like mother of pearl. They also dig out stones as clear as crystal, which are called Cornish diamonds. I saw one as big as my two fists, very clear and like some pieces of crystal my father brought from the Alps in Italy. I got one of those pieces of their Cornish diamonds as long as half my finger, which had three or four flat sides with edges; the top was sharp and so hard as it would cut a letter on glass.

CELIA FIENNES, *Through England on a Side-Saddle*

4. Dr. Borlase's Occupations

As for my part, I am preparing for old age, that is, laying in a fund of amusements, such as may inable me to spend my time within doors to my satisfaction, since rambling abroad and good fellowship are become tiresome, and the severity of the seasons become more sensible. I read a little, I write a little, I paint a little, I collect a little, I think a little unless it be upon my friends and them I hope I shall never forgett, in short betwixt a little of one and a little of the other I find the days short enough in the midst of summer, and endeavour to lengthen them in the winter by rising early that I may fill every portion of time somehow or other, although the marks and traces I shall leave may be none of the most important, nor at all interesting to the rest of mankind.

DR. BORLASE, in P. A. S. Pool, 'William Borlase', in *Journal of the Royal Institution of Cornwall* (1966)

5. The Mines of Gwennap

Falmouth, March, 1787

SCOTT came this morning and took me to see the consolidated mines in the parish of Gwynnap; they are situated in a bleak desert, rendered still more doleful by the unhealthy appearance of its inhabitants. At every step one stumbles upon ladders that lead into utter darkness, or funnels that exhale warm copperous vapours. All around these openings the ore is piled up in heaps waiting for purchasers. I saw it drawn reeking out of the mine by the help of a machine called a whim, put in motion by mules, which in their turn are stimulated by impish children hanging over the poor brutes, and flogging them round without respite. This dismal scene of *whims*, suffering mules, and hillocks of cinders, extends for miles. Huge iron engines creaking and groaning, invented by Watt, and tall chimneys smoking and flaming, that seem to belong to old Nicholas's abode, diversify the prospect.

Two strange-looking Cornish beings, dressed in ghostly white, conducted me about, and very kindly proposed a descent into the bowels of the earth, but I declined initiation. These mystagogues occupy a tolerable house, with fair sash windows, where the inspectors of the mine hold their meetings, and regale upon beef, pudding, and brandy.

While I was standing at the door of this habitation, several woful figures in tattered garments, with pickaxes on their shoulders, crawled out of a dark fissure and repaired to a hovel, which I learnt was a gin-shop. There they pass the few hours allotted them above ground, and drink, it is to be hoped, an oblivion of their subterraneous existence. Piety as well as gin helps to fill up their leisure moments, and I was told that Wesley, who came apostolising into Cornwall a few years ago, preached on this very spot to above seven thousand followers.

Since this period Methodism has made a very rapid progress, and has been of no trifling service in diverting the attention of these sons of darkness from their present condition to the glories of the life to come. However, some people inform me their actual state is not so much to be lamented, and that, notwithstanding their pale looks and tattered raiment, they are far from being poor or unhealthy. Fortune often throws a considerable sum into their laps when they least expect it, and many a common miner has been known to gain a hundred pounds in the space of a month or two. Like sailors in the first effusion of prize-money, they have no notion of turning their good-luck to advantage; but squander the fruits of their toil in the silliest species of extravagance. Their wives are dressed out in tawdry silks, and flaunt away in ale-houses between rows of obedient fiddlers. The money spent, down they sink again into damps and darkness.

Having passed about an hour in collecting minerals, flopping engines with my finger, and performing all the functions of a diligent young man desirous of information, I turned my back on smokes, flames, and coal-holes, with great pleasure.

Travel Diaries of William Beckford, ed. Guy Chapman

6. A Rich Mine

At Poldice the men are like mice,
    The tin is very plenty;
Captain Teague is one of Breague,
    And he'll give ten for twenty.[1]

7. A Young Sailor

BY the smallness of this table judge not, Reader, of that loss which
it deplores. Christopher Borlase, a youth of sweet and amiable
disposition, chusing the life of a sailor, and making quick advances
to deserve the honours of his profession, died, neither by the fury of
war in which he was engaged about four years, nor by the dangerous element on which he served his king and country, but by a
fever; like a fair flower that had survived the winter's hail and
storms, reserved to be gathered, not torn off, in time of peace. He
was taken by God to himself on the coast of Guinea, February 21,
1749. His affectionate parents, deprived of a most hopeful son, and
unable to pay him the proper funeral duties, engrave their remembrance of him in this plate; contented, because such was the will of
God.

                                                    In Ludgvan Church

8. Wedgwood and China Clay

WEDGWOOD, as we have seen, whilst attending his sick wife at
Bath in 1772, was studying Borlase's 'History of Cornwall', and

[1] i.e. the value of 10 cwt of white tin for 20 cwt of tin ore.

from that date we find him more or less occupied in the business relative to the supplies of native clay. Cookworthy's Patent, which had been taken out in 1768, virtually confined the China clay and China stone of Cornwall to one monopolist, or to such as the monopolist might license to use them; and this fell hard upon the general body of manufacturers, all of whom were more or less interested in improving their wares; and upon Wedgwood in especial, who just at this date was engaged with his jasper composition, as also in making experiments for a whiter ware, and to him therefore finer and whiter clays were a desideratum. The fashionable world were getting tired of cream colour, and enquiring for other; and Wedgwood, though much against his inclination, saw that he must ultimately obey.

In 1774 Cookworthy assigned over his patent to Champion of Bristol, who soon after applied to Parliament for its extension for a further period of fourteen years, when the original term should have expired. This desire of a further monopoly excited the warmest opposition; and we find Wedgwood as early as March 1775 bidding Bentley 'mount his chariot' and wait upon the county members and others who, in addition to Earl Gower, were likely to use their influence in behalf of the Potters. An explanatory pamphlet from Wedgwood's pen was also published and widely dispersed; and two months later we find him and his friend Mr. Turner, the eminent potter of Lane End, on their way to Cornwall to view for themselves its mineral treasures. They were accompanied by a Mr. Tolcher and by Thomas Griffiths, Wedgwood's former clay agent in Carolina, by a guide and two servants, and for several days they explored the clay-producing districts.

This appears to have been Wedgwood's first visit to the southern shore of our island, and he was singularly delighted with its beautiful scenery. He kept a journal of his tour for Bentley, and therefore wrote briefly. But he says in a letter dated from Plymouth —'We were upon the waters several hours yesterday afternoon. Have you seen Mount Edgecombe? If you have not seen Mount Edgecombe you have seen nothing. We sailed twice past this terrestrial paradise, and such a sun setting I never beheld.' The result of this visit was, that Turner and Wedgwood became joint lessees of certain clay mines at St. Stephen's, a place between St. Austell and Redruth, and that Griffiths remained as their agent.

* * *

From the date of the settlement of the question relative to Champion's patent, Wedgwood had become lessee, in conjunction with a Mr. Carthew, of certain clay mines near St. Austell in Cornwall; and as his knowledge of the mineral resources of the county extended—both through his own agents, and from information derived from Boulton and Watt, whose mining business was at this period on an extensive scale—he seems to have entered into arrangements for working others, of which the products were not entirely clay. To look after his interests in this direction he again visited Cornwall in the spring of 1782, this time accompanied by Baron Beda. Of the products of one mine he was about to visit, Watt had given him intimation, and when about to set out on his journey, the latter wrote and asked to share in them. He cheerfully promised 'half the produce of the mine or vein on the terms mentioned and whenever you shall make the claim . . . for it would be unreasonable indeed in me to wish to preclude you from a share of the materials of which I should have been ignorant without your information'. It was also at this date that he wanted 'a mine captain to look after some workmen, to pay my rents, and other matters'. And he asked Watt if he could think of such a person on the spot. About the same date Wedgwood became a shareholder in the Polgooth mine, and somewhat later in the Cornish Metal Company, by both of which he was unfortunately a considerable loser.

E. METEYARD, *Life of Josiah Wedgwood*

9. Carclaze Tin Mine

SEPTEMBER 4, 1810.—At 9 I went to Carclaze tin mine, two miles distant, and made a sketch of the interior of the mine, it being an open mine, a vast chasm, in which mining is carried on, and the machinery used adds to the interest and to the variety of the scene. The depth of the chasm is very considerable; but the walk to the bottom is made easy by forming the path in an angular manner. When arrived there the view upwards on every side is sublime. The mine has an awful feeling of the vastness of the whole, and contemplating immensity, admires the singularity of many of the parts, which, in spiral forms, shoot up like the much reported glaciers in Switzerland, those pointed masses of Ice which excite in the traveller surprise and admiration. The resemblance is brought nearer by the rocks of this mine being of the colour of chalk, and wanting only transparency to make the similitude complete.—

This was my second visit to this mine, in which I made a drawing in October last. Having fixed upon another situation for the same purpose I sat down and commenced a sketch under very unfavourable circumstances. I had to endure a cold North wind, with the apprehension of rain. In this predicament I experienced great kindness and respect from those of the miners who were working near me. One of them threw his thick waistcoat over me to protect me against the cold; another held my umbrella over me, and thus I was enabled to remain a considerable time, but at last my fear of the cold which had chilled me much got the better of my desire to proceed, and I took my leave of my kind assistants sooner than I would willingly have done.—

Carclaze tin mine may be viewed without the least difficulty by those who being at St. Austell may be disposed to ride or walk the short distance of two miles. A horse may advance to almost the edge of the mine, and the length, and width, and depth of this excavation may be fully seen, with the machinery, and the miners who appear like spots below.—Carclaze tin mine is the largest *open* mine in Cornwall.

JOSEPH FARINGTON, *The Farington Diary*

10. Georgian Head-Master

On his (Mr. Conon's) successor, Dr. Cardew, the praises that candour, or even indifference, would bestow, may as coming from his pupil, and his friend, be attributed to partial affection. But to be suspected of an amiable prepossession shall not silence my gratitude which, though perhaps too lively in its perception of merit, can never be mistaken where merit is universally acknowledged. A native of Liskeard and educated under the care of the Rev. Richard Haydon, M.A., Rector of Oakford and of Zeal-Monachorum in Devon, and of Mr. John Lyne, Rector of St. Ives, Mr. Cardew carried with him to Exeter college, Oxford, those promises of a useful life which I am sure have been amply fulfilled in the discharge of his professional duties. At first an usher under Mr. Marshall at Exeter school, he came to Truro with high recommendations from persons of respectability both in Oxford and at Exeter. And with classical abilities and taste (to which Mr. Conon though an excellent linguest had no pretentions) he succeeded to the care of no more than 27 boys.

That the situation of a schoolmaster requires all the philosophy of an enlightened mind, will be readily allowed. Such philosophy was here constantly exerted. With that cultivated and refined understanding which naturally gives the preference to genius, he never remitted his attention to the dullest boys; and though quick and susceptible he had the full command of his temper. That he has acted as a magistrate with equal credit to himself and his connections is not so decided an opinion. But if, in some instances, his conduct as a member of the corporation of Truro incurred disapprobation, it was the disapprobation of those who viewed the transactions of the borough with an eye of prejudice. And chiefly to this circumstance has been owing the decline of Truro School. Yet those who thought differently from himself never accused him of inconsistency. His first living, that of Uni-Lelant was a sufficient proof of the favour of his diocesan, and the rectory of St. Erme to which he was lately presented by Dr. Wynne in the most liberal manner, does equal honour to them both. The father of a numerous family, a great part of whom he has placed in respectable situations, and possessor of a considerable fortune, for the acquisition of which he has to thank himself only, he has now retired to his rectory. It was on the 16th July, 1805, that Dr. Cardew resigned his school. In gratitude to their old master his scholars have entered into a unanimous resolution to present him with a silver urn or turin.

R. POLWHELE, *History of Cornwall*

11. *A Cornish Fellow of All Souls*

UPON his entering that foundation and ever since I took every opportunity of cautioning him against setting his mind on the high living which people of rank and fortune there might well afford but would not suit him, but that if he minded his studies (as he did not want capacity) he would be level to most of them in literature and esteem, and though of inferiour fortune would with the credit of that fellowship appear in the world on a very decent footing until he were better provided for. . . . I writ him about a month since that at Ladyday next my cure of St. Just should be vacant, and I would make it worth his while if he would come and serve it, but I am very apprehensive that he will make some frivolous objection to such a retired situation, without considering that all people were not born to live in Oxfordshire or London.

DR. BORLASE on his son, George, in P. A. S. Pool,
'William Borlase', in *Journal of the Royal Institution
of Cornwall* (1966)

12. *Dr. Cardew Makes Good*

IN the aforesaid period from Xmas, 1790 to Xmas, 1795, I had received:

from the living of St. Erme		£256	7	3
„ that of Feock		28	17	6
„ Lelant		1000	0	0

From the School at Truro:

for entrances	£78 15 0			
„ schoolings	1169 5 6			
„ gratuities	17 6 6			
„ stipend	125 0 0			
		£1390	7	0
from Board		1614	1	0
„ interest of monies		1182	13	6
„ Seal-hole mine ...		743	19	4
„ sale of houses in Liskeard		506	10	0
		£6722	15	7

Out of the said receipts I had expended:

in general disbursements		3545	10	5
in housekeeping ...		1001	9	6
		£4546	19	11

At Truro to the end of the year 1790:

in general disbursements and housekeeping ...		9077	9	10
At Exeter ...		111	1	6
At Oxford ...		275	13	0
		£14,011	4	3

Total disbursements to the end of the year 1795		14011	4	3
Total receipts to that time		19028	6	3
Total savings to that time		£5017	2	0

SIR ALEXANDER CARDEW, *Memoirs of Dr. Cornelius Cardew*

13. Mining under the Sea

WE were impatient to see the Wherry Mine, situated in the bay, about half a mile beyond Penzance. The opening of this mine was an astonishingly adventurous undertaking. I have never heard of one similar to it in any other part of the world. Imagine the descent into a mine through the sea; the miners working at the depth of seventeen fathoms only below the waves; the rod of a steam-engine extending from the shore to the shaft,—a distance of nearly one hundred and twenty fathoms; and a great number of men momentarily menaced with an inundation of the sea, which continually drains in no small quantity through the roof of the mine, and roars loud enough to be distinctly heard in it! The descent is by means of a rope tied round the thighs, and you are let down in a manner exactly the same as a bucket is into a well; a well indeed it is, for the water is more than knee-deep in many parts of the mine. The upper part of the shaft resembles an immense iron chimney, elevated about twelve feet above the level of the sea, and a narrow platform leads to it from the beach: close to this is the engine-shaft, through which the water is brought up from below. Tin is the principal produce of the Wherry Mine; it is found dispersed (in small, indurated, glass-like lumps, of a blackish colour) in a substance resembling the elvan of Polgooth, but much more compact in texture, and of the nature of a porphyry. The ore is extremely rich.

W. G. MATON, *Observations on the Western Counties*
of England

14. Iron Casting

FEBRUARY 13, 1840.—To Perran Foundry under Aunt Charles's guidance; met there Derwent Coleridge, and Barclay brought John Sterling to see them cast fourteen tons of iron for the beam of a steam-engine. This was indeed a magnificent spectacle, and induced sundry allusions to Vulcan's forge and other classical subjects. The absolute agony of excitement displayed by R. Cloke, the foreman, was quite beautiful. John Sterling admired his energetic countenance amazingly, and thought it quite the type of the characteristic Cornish physiognomy, which he considers Celtic. This beam was the largest they had ever cast, and its fame had attracted almost the whole population of Perran, who looked highly picturesque by the light of the liquid iron. My regretting that we had no chestnuts to employ so much heat which was now running to waste induced a very interesting discourse from Sterling, first, on the difference between utilitarianism and utility, then on the sympathy of great minds with each other, however different may be the tracks they select. It is folly to say that a man of genius, or one in whom moral philosophy has lighted her torch, cannot, if he would, understand any object of human science. As an extreme demonstration, you might as well assert that a poet could not learn the multiplication table. Plato and Pythagoras held all philosophy to be included in the properties of numbers; on the other hand, Watt was a great novel-reader, and many others had similarly involved gifts. D. Coleridge joined us, and we continued a most delectable chat, to which poetry was added by the last-comer. The triumph of machinery is when man wonders at his own works; thus, says Coleridge—all science begins in wonder, but the first is the wonder of ignorance, the last that of adoration. Plato calls God the great Geometrician. Sterling exceedingly admires our Hostess's face, fancying himself in company with a Grecian statue, and in reference to the mind evolved in her countenance, quoted those beautiful lines from the opening of 'Comus'—

> Bright aerial spirits live insphered
> Above the smoke and stir of this dim spot,
> Which men call Earth!

Surveyed the Foundry, almost everything eliciting something worth hearing from one of our genii.

CAROLINE FOX, *Journals and Letters*

15. *A Shipwright*

In memory of Joseph Crapp ship wright who died ye 26th of Nov. 1770, aged 43 years.

> Alass friend Joseph
> His end was almost sudden
> As though the mandate came
> Express from Heaven
> His foot did slip and he did fall
> Help, help he cries and that was all.

In Mylor Churchyard

16. *'Datur Hora Quieti'*

To the MS. of this Poem is the following note:—'Why do you wish the burial to be at five o'clock?' 'Because it was the time at which he used to leave work.'

> 'At eve should be the time', they said,
> To close their brother's narrow bed:
> 'Tis at that pleasant hour of day
> The labourer treads his homeward way.
>
> His work was o'er, his toil was done,
> And therefore with the set of sun,
> To wait the wages of the dead,
> We laid our hireling in his bed.

R. S. Hawker, *Cornish Ballads*

179

'So when even was come, the Lord of the Vineyard saith unto his steward, call the labourers, and give them their hire.'—Saint Matthew, xx. 8.

Among the rural inhabitants of Cornwall the burial of the dead usually takes place in the evening, because the bearers have then 'left work'.

Saving from the Sea

Save a stranger from the sea,
And he'll turn your enemy

17. *The Wreck of the 'Caledonia'*

IT was not long after my arrival in my new abode that I was plunged all at once into the midst of a fearful scene of the terrors of the sea. About daybreak of an autumn day I was aroused by a knock at my bedroom-door; it was followed by the agitated voice of a boy, a member of my household, 'Oh, sir, there are dead men on vicarage rocks!' In a moment I was up, and in my dressing-gown and slippers rushed out. I ran across my glebe, a quarter of a mile, to the cliffs, and down a frightful descent of three hundred feet to the beach.

It was indeed a scene to be looked on only once in a human life. On a ridge of rock, just left bare by the falling tide, stood a man, my own servant; he had come out to see my flock of ewes, and had found the awful wreck. There he stood, with two dead sailors at his feet, whom he had just drawn out of the water stiff and stark. The bay was tossing and seething with a tangled mass of rigging, sails, and broken fragments of a ship; the billows rolled up yellow with corn, for the cargo of the vessel had been foreign wheat; and ever and anon there came up out of the water, as though stretched out with life, a human hand and arm. It was the corpse of another sailor drifting out to sea. 'Is there no one alive?' was my first question to my man. 'I think there is, sir,' he said, 'for just now I thought I heard a cry.' I made haste in the direction he pointed out, and, on turning a rock, just where a brook of fresh water fell towards the sea, there lay the body of a man in a seaman's garb. He had reached the water faint with thirst, but was too much exhausted to swallow or drink. He opened his eyes at our voices, and as he saw me leaning over him in my cassock-shaped dressing-gown, he sobbed, with a piteous cry, 'O mon père, mon père!' Gradually he revived, and when he had fully come to himself with the help of cordials and food, we gathered from him the mournful tale of his vessel and her wreck. He was a Jersey man by birth, and had been shipped at Malta, on the homeward voyage of the vessel from the port of Odessa with corn.

I returned to the scene of death and danger, where my man awaited me. He had found, in addition to the two corpses, another dead body jammed under a rock. By this time a crowd of people had arrived from the land, and at my request they began to search anxiously for the dead. It was, indeed, a terrible scene. The vessel, a brig of five hundred tons, had struck, as we afterwards found, at three o'clock that morning, and by the time the wreck was discovered she had been shattered into broken pieces by the fury of the sea. The rocks and the water bristled with fragments of mast and spar and rent timbers; the cordage lay about in tangled masses. The rollers tumbled in volumes of corn, the wheaten cargo; and amidst it all the bodies of the helpless dead—that a few brief hours before had walked the deck the stalwart masters of their ship—turned their poor disfigured faces toward the sky, pleading for sepulture. We made a temporary bier of the broken planks, and laid thereon the corpses, decently arranged. As the vicar, I led the way, and my people followed with ready zeal as bearers, and in sad procession we carried our dead up the steep cliff, by a difficult path, to await, in a room at my vicarage which I allotted them, the inquest. The ship and her cargo were, as to any tangible value, utterly lost. . . .

The coroner arrived, held his 'quest, and the usual verdict of

'Wrecked and cast ashore' empowered me to inter the dead sailors, found and future, from the same vessel, with the service in the Prayer-Book for the Burial of the Dead. This decency of sepulture is the result of a somewhat recent statute, passed in the reign of George III. Before that time it was the common usage of the coast to dig, just above high-water mark, a pit on the shore, and therein to cast, without inquest or religious rite, the carcasses of shipwrecked men. My first funeral of these lost mariners was a touching and striking scene. The three bodies first found were buried at the same time. Behind the coffins, as they were solemnly borne along the aisle, walked the solitary mourner, Le Daine, weeping bitterly and aloud. Other eyes were moist, for who could hear unsoftened the greeting of the Church to these strangers from the sea, and the 'touch that makes the whole earth kin,' in the hope we breathed that we, too, might one day 'rest as these our brothers did'? It was well-nigh too much for those who served that day. Nor was the interest subdued when, on the Sunday after the wreck, at the appointed place in the service, just before the General Thanksgiving, Le Daine rose up from his place, approached the altar, and uttered, in an audible but broken voice, his thanksgiving for his singular and safe deliverance from the perils of the sea.

R. S. HAWKER, *Footprints of Former Men in Far Cornwall*

The North Coast

From Pentire Point to Lundy Light
Is a watery grave by day or night

18. The Smuggler's Song

On, through the ground-sea, shove!
Light on the larboard bow!
There's a nine-knot breeze above,
And a sucking tide below.

Hush! for the beacon fails,
　　The skulking gauger's by;
Down with your studding-sails,
　　Let jib and fore-sail fly!

Hurray! for the light once more!
　　Point her for Shark's-nose Head;
Our friends can keep the shore;
　　Or the skulking gauger's dead!

On! through the ground-sea, shove!
　　Light on the larboard bow!
There's a nine-knot breeze above
　　And a sucking tide below!

R. S. HAWKER, *Cornish Ballads*

19. *The Last of the Smugglers*

POOR old Tristram Pentire! How he comes up before me as I pronounce his name! That light, active, half-stooping form, bent as though he had a brace of kegs upon his shoulders still; those thin, grey, rusty locks that fell upon a forehead seamed with the wrinkles of threescore years and five; the cunning glance that questioned in his eye, and that nose carried always at half-cock, with a red blaze along its ridge, scorched by the departing footstep of the fierce fiend Alcohol, when he fled before the reinforcements of the coast-guard.

He was the last of the smugglers; and when I took possession of the glebe, I hired him as my servant-of-all-work, or rather no-work, about the house, and there he rollicked away the last few years of his careless existence, in all the pomp and idleness of 'The parson's man.' He had taken a bold part in every landing on the coast, man and boy, full forty years; throughout which time all kinds of men had largely trusted him with their brandy and their lives, and true and faithful had he been to them, as sheath to steel.

Gradually he grew attached to me, and I could but take an interest in him. I endeavoured to work some softening change in him, and to awaken a certain sense of the errors of his former life. Sometimes, as a sort of condescension on his part, he brought himself to concede and to acknowledge, in his own quaint, rambling way—

'Well, sir, I do think, when I come to look back, and to consider what lives we used to live,—drunk all night and idle abed all day, cursing, swearing, fighting, gambling, lying, and always prepared to shet (shoot) the gauger,—I do really believe, sir, we surely was in sin!'

But, whatever contrite admissions to this extent were extorted from old Tristram by misty glimpses of a moral sense and by his desire to gratify his master, there were two points on which he was inexorably firm. The one was, that it was a very guilty practice in the authorities to demand taxes for what he called run goods; and the other settled dogma of his creed was, that it never could be a sin to make away with an exciseman. Battles between Tristram and myself on these themes were frequent and fierce; but I am bound to confess that he always managed, somehow or other, to remain master of the field. Indeed, what Chancellor of the Exchequer could be prepared to encounter the triumphant demand with which Tristram smashed to atoms my suggestions of morality, political economy, and finance? He would listen with apparent patience to all my solemn and secular pleas for the revenue, and then down he came upon me with the unanswerable argument—

'But why should the king tax good liquor? If they *must* have taxes, why can't they tax something else?'

My efforts, however, to soften and remove his doctrinal prejudice as to the unimportance, in a moral point of view, of putting the officers of his Majesty's revenue to death, were equally unavailing. Indeed, to my infinite chagrin, I found that I had lowered myself exceedingly in his estimation by what he called standing up for the exciseman.

'There had been divers passons,' he assured me, 'in his time in the parish, and very learned clergy they were, and some very strict; and some would preach one doctrine and some another; and there was one that had very mean notions about running goods, and said 'twas a wrong thing to do; but even he, and the rest, never took part with the gauger—never! And besides,' said old Trim, with another demolishing appeal, 'wasn't the exciseman always ready to put *us* to death when he could?'

R. S. HAWKER, *Footprints of Former Men in Far Cornwall*

20. *Officious Zeal*

'We have not a moment we can call our own.'

In memory of Thomas James, aged 35 years, who on the evening of the 7th Dec. 1814, on his returning to Flushing from St. Mawes in a boat was shot by a Customs house officer and expired a few days after.

'Officious zeal in luckless hour laid wait
And wilful sent the murderous ball of fate:
James to his home which late in health he left
Wounded returned—of life is soon bereft.'

In Mylor Churchyard

21. *Thackeray Electioneers at Liskeard*

MONDAY, July 9, 1832. arrived by mail at 10 o'clock at Liskeard & found all the town in an uproar with flags processions & triumphal arches to celebrate C Buller's arrival. rode out to meet him & had the honour with some 1/2 dozen others to be dragged in with him. The gun was fired the people shouted & pulled us through all parts of the town. C Buller made a good speech enough then we adjourned to Mr. Austen's where we lunched & then to submit again to be pulled about for the pleasure of his constituents—This business speaking pulling & luncheon lasted from 12 to 4 during wh. time I was 3 times gratified by hearing my song about Jope sung to a tune I suppose by some of the choristers—arrived at Polvellan at 6 & was glad to see it again for certainly they have been very kind—

Fare	6
Coachman Guard &c	2.6.

Tuesday 10. Nothing happened today—read Wallenstein in the morning dined at 2 rode with Mr. Buller after dinner & got wet through drew pictures all the evening, & came to bed at eleven.

Wednesday 11. At Polvellan all day eating sleeping & dawdling; there arrived Mrs. & Miss Hillier of the Caledonia & Sir Wm. Molesworth who is standing for the county—the first 2 strike me as being fools, the last a sensible fellow enough. read some of the robbers with C Buller & wrote to Father.

Trowsers.   14.

Thursday 12. Set off with Mrs. Hillyar her daughter & Miss A. Buller to Liskeard where we found young women in waggons singing hymns charity children banners &c all awaiting the arrival of Sir W. Molesworth & C Buller who with Mr. & Mrs. Buller, were dragged into the town by the infuriated populace The day had set in fair & promised to smile on the 400 people who sat down to dinner at one o clock, but the rain began & lasted during the whole of dinner time—We adjourned to the town-Hall where the members the attorneys & a farmer called Greig made speeches, this latter was as fine an orator as ever I heard; came home at about eight & spent a pleasant evening laughing with Mrs. Hillyar who persisted in calling me by all names but my own, I in turn called her Villiers Pilliers &c. she gave rather an affecting account of her son's conversion to Catholicism—Sir W. Molesworth went away. he made a wretched speech as did everybody excepting CB & Greig—Mr. Buller returned thanks he is a dear old fellow the most good natured & amiable I ever saw.

Letters of Thackeray, ed. Gordon R. Ray

22. *Michael Verran the Miner*

ONE other little event dwells with me, out of those Falmouth times, exact date now forgotten; a pleasant little matter, in which Sterling, and principally the Misses Fox, bright cheery young creatures, were concerned; which, for the sake of its human interest, is worth mention. In a certain Cornish mine, said the Newspapers duly specifying it, two miners deep down in the shaft were engaged putting in a shot for blasting: they had completed their affair, and were about to give the signal for being hoisted up,—one at a time was all their coadjutor at the top could manage, and the second was to kindle the match, and then mount with all speed. Now it chanced while they were both still below, one of them thought the match too long; tried to break it shorter, took a couple of stones, a flat and a sharp, to cut it shorter; did cut it of the due length, but, horrible to relate, kindled it at the same time, and both were still below! Both shouted vehemently to the coadjutor at the windlass, both sprang at the basket; the windlass man could not move it with them both. Here was a moment for poor miner Jack and miner Will! Instant horrible death hangs over both,—when Will generously resigns himself: 'Go aloft, Jack,' and sits down; 'away; in one minute I shall be in Heaven!' Jack bounds aloft, the explosion instantly follows, bruises his face as he looks over; he is safe above ground: and poor Will? Descending eagerly they find Will too, as if by miracle, buried under rocks which had arched themselves over him, and little injured: he too is brought up safe, and all ends joyfully, say the Newspapers.

Such a piece of manful promptitude, and salutary human heroism, was worth investigating. It was investigated; found to be accurate to the letter,—with this addition and explanation, that Will, an honest, ignorant good man, entirely given up to Methodism, had been perfect in the 'faith of assurance', certain that *he* should get to Heaven if he died, certain that Jack would not, which had been the ground of his decision in that great moment;—for the rest, that he much wished to learn reading and writing, and find some way of life above ground instead of below. By aid of the Misses Fox and the rest of that family, a subscription (modest *Anti*-Hudson testimonial) was raised to this Methodist hero: he emerged into daylight with fifty pounds in his pocket; did strenuously try, for certain months, to learn reading and writing; found he could not learn those arts or either of them; took his money and bought cows with it, wedding at the same time some religious likely milkmaid; and is, last time I heard of him, a prosperous modest dairyman, thankful for the upper light and safety from the wrath to come. Sterling had some hand in this affair: but, as I said, it was the two young ladies of the family that mainly did it.

THOMAS CARLYLE, *John Sterling*

23. Early Train Services

UNTIL after 1876 all passenger trains stopped at all stations and took about an hour and twenty minutes to cover the 25¾ miles between Truro and Penzance. When through carriages from and to Paddington were inaugurated in 1867, the best train took twelve hours in each direction and the night mails over thirteen. Third-class passengers whiled away anything from thirteen to fifteen and a quarter hours on the journey till 1869, when they were admitted to the twelve-hour Down and to a twelve-and-a-quarter one Up. No noticeable improvement was made in the next seven years, save that from 1871 onwards the Down 'Flying Dutchman' was extended as a slow train through Cornwall to reach Penzance in ten hours and twenty minutes, but of course did not convey the 'proletariat'.

Originally the West Cornwall Company was unusually kind to the local third-class passengers, who formed the bulk of its patrons, welcoming them to all trains until the summer of 1862. For the second half of that year the Directors reported a decrease in the total number of passengers of no less than 39,105 with an increase of money received of £514, 'which arises from the discontinuance of the issue of Third-Class tickets by all trains. These tickets are now issued by two trains only.'

The Post Office awoke to the idea of using the railway for the carriage of Her Majesty's Mails in February 1855, and chartered a regular mail train between Truro and Penzance nine years later.

E. T. MacDermot, *History of the Great Western Railway*

24. *Wooden Viaducts on the G.W.R.*

Apart from the Royal Albert Bridge, the chief works were the timber viaducts, for which the Cornwall Railway was famous. There were thirty-four of them between Plymouth and Truro with a united length of just on four miles, the highest being St. Pinnock in the Glynn Valley with Liskeard a close second, and the longest Truro and next Weston Mill near Devonport. This last, together with Keyham and St. Germans, were entirely of timber owing to the depth of mud in the creeks they crossed; all the rest had masonry piers built up to 35 feet below rail level, supporting the timber superstructures. Otherwise they were all of uniform pattern with piers 66 feet apart.

These very high and fragile looking structures inspired many westcountrymen with awe, and made them reluctant to travel on the new railway. Most unfortunately too, on the 6th May, only two days after the opening, the engine and first two carriages of the evening train from Plymouth ran off the line just as it was entering on the Grove Viaduct near St. Germans and fell 30 feet into the creek. The engine (*Elk*) sank, wheels uppermost, in the mud; the driver and fireman and also the guard were killed, but the fourteen passengers in the two carriages escaped with bruises and cuts. Although the viaduct itself was in no way at fault, this mishap of course helped to frighten people.

E. T. MacDermot, *History of the Great Western Railway*

25. *Founding the Bishopric of Truro*

Benson had hardly set foot in Cornwall when he began raising funds for the building of a Cathedral, the first that had been erected in England since the Reformation. There was a church situated in the centre of Truro, mostly empty, for the place was a stronghold of Methodism, and just as, forty years before, he turned the empty room in his mother's house into an oratory, so he made this empty church into the nucleus of his cathedral. £100,000, he estimated, would be needed for the completion of this new oratory, and Cornwall, with the decline of its tin-mining industry, was a very poor county, but he never had a moment's doubt that this big sum would be raised. Old Lady Rolle of Bicton, daughter of a Cornish clergyman, and born in 1793, instantly lost her heart to him; she called him 'my bishop' and supported her claim to him by sending a cheque of £40,000 for the purposes of the See. She was an ancient and picturesque figure, she drove out in a chariot with four horses and postilions, she ruled her local kingdom with a rod of iron, and was herself terribly afraid of being left alone for a moment either by day or night. . . .

Railway communication was non-existent, except just down the spine of the county from Saltash to Penzance, and he drove over the whole of his diocese to visit and confirm, dictating letters to his chaplain on the way, and receiving from the warm-hearted folk such a welcome as was rarely accorded to 'a foreigner from England'. There was not a parish in the remotest coasts and fastnesses of the county which he did not periodically visit. Perhaps the church was in such disorder of repair that the sky showed through its gaping roof and the ivy penetrated through the walls of its aisles, and then he gave squires and landowners no peace till they had taken the necessary restoration in hand. There were queer pastors in many of these isolated hamlets; he arrived one morning, for instance, to preach and celebrate the Sacrament at one of these, and while he was talking to the Vicar before church-time, the parlour-maid came in to ask for the cellar-key that she might take a bottle of wine to the vestry for the Communion. 'We'll have a bottle of white wine to-day,' said the Vicar, 'just for a change.' . . . Another incumbent candidly acknowledged that he had little time for visiting his flock as his garden gave him so much pleasant occupation; but the most remarkable of all was a Vicar who never set foot in his church at all, far less held any kind of service there. Occasionally some neighbouring parson came over to minister to his unshepherded parishioners, but their rightful parson would not even consent to attend church as a member of his own congregation. It was in vain that the patron of his living pleaded with him. 'I don't ask you to do anything,' he said, 'but for the sake of example couldn't you just go to church yourself sometimes?' But it was no use: he preferred to stroll to the garden-gate of the vicarage which adjoined the church clad in a flowered dressing-gown and smoking a hookah, and when his parishioners came out he chatted with them very amiably. There he was, living in the vicarage, a beneficed priest performing no duties of any sort, and there was no ecclesiastical process by which he could possibly be deprived of his house and his income.

Many of the livings were miserably endowed, and their occupants had a hard struggle against poverty and Dissent. From one of these my father rented his vicarage for a month, so that the incumbent might get a holiday, and took the duty himself by way of enjoying his own. The Vicar's wife there played the organ, so my father deputed one of his sons to take her place in her absence. On a certain Sunday morning it was announced that the offertory would be devoted to the 'organist and choir fund', and that son still labours under the sense of injustice that was his, when he found that not one penny of the congregation's subscriptions was allotted to him. . . . Then one winter's day my father had a nasty accident when riding, straining his knee very badly, but next day there was a confirmation to be held ten miles away, so, strapped and bandaged, he was hoisted into his landau, and on arrival lifted on to a sofa and wheeled into church, where he took the service. There had been a fall of snow the night before: this had half melted during the morning, but in the afternoon a great frost such as had not been known for years in Cornwall set in, and turned the roads to ice. The Bishop's carriage came slewing and skidding down the steep street into Truro with him perfectly helpless inside, looking out of the window straight down the road, and wondering in what fashion he would arrive at the bottom.

E. F. BENSON, *As We Were*

26. *The Old Labourer*

His fourscore years have bent a back of oak,
His earth-brown cheeks are full of hollow pits;
His gnarled hands wander idly as he sits
Bending above the hearthstone's feeble smoke.
Threescore and ten slow years he tilled the land;
He wrung his bread out of the stubborn soil;
He saw his masters flourish through his toil;
He held their substance in his horny hand.

Now he is old: he asks for daily bread:
He who has sowed the bread he may not taste

Begs for the crumbs: he would do no man wrong.
The Parish Guardians, when his case is read,
Will grant him, yet with no unseemly haste,
Just seventeen pence to starve on, seven days long.

ARTHUR SYMONS, *Poems*

27. *Laying up the Boat*

THERE arrives a day towards the end of October—or with luck we may tide over into November—when the wind in the mainsail suddenly takes a winter force, and we begin to talk of laying up the boat. Hitherto we have kept a silent compact and ignored all change in the season. We have watched the blue afternoons shortening, fading through lilac into grey, and let pass their scarcely perceptible warnings. One afternoon a few kittiwakes appeared. A week later the swallows fell to stringing themselves like beads along the coast-guard's telephone-wire on the hill. They vanished, and we pretended not to miss them. When our hands grew chill with steering we rubbed them by stealth or stuck them nonchalantly in our pockets. But this vicious unmistakable winter gust breaks the spell. We take one look around the harbour, at the desolate buoys awash and tossing; we cast another seaward at the thick weather through which, in a week at latest, will come looming the earliest of the Baltic merchantmen, our November visitors—bluff vessels with red-painted channels, green deckhouses, white top-strakes, wooden davits overhanding astern, and the Danish flag fluttering aloft in the haze. Then we find speech; and with us, as with the swallows, the move into winter quarters is not long delayed when once it comes into discussion. We have dissembled too long; and know, as we go through the form of debating it, that our date must be the next spring-tides.

This ritual of laying up the boat is our way of bidding farewell to summer; and we go through it, when the day comes, in ceremonial silence. *Favete linguis!* The hour helps us, for the spring-tides at this season reach their height a little after night-fall, and it is on an already slackening flood that we cast off our moorings and head up the river with our backs to the waning sunset. Since we tow a dinghy astern and are ourselves towed by the silent yachtsman, you may call it a procession. She has been stripped, during the last two days, of sails, rigging, and all spars but the mainmast. Now we bring her alongside the town quay and beneath the shears—the abhorrèd shears—which lift this too out of its step, dislocated with a creak as poignant as the cry of Polydorus. We lower it, lay it along the deck, and resume our way; past quay doors and windows where already the townsfolk are beginning to light their lamps; and so by the jetties where foreign crews rest with elbows on bulwarks and stare down upon us idly through the dusk. She is after all but a little cutter of six tons, and we might well apologize, like the Athenian, for so diminutive a corpse. But she is our own; and they never saw her with jackyarder spread, or spinnaker or jib-topsail delicate as samite—those heavenly wings!—nor felt her gallant spirit straining to beat her own record before a tense northerly breeze. Yet even to them her form, in pure white with gilt fillet, might tell of no common obsequies.

So, as we near the beach where she is to lie, a sense of proud exclusiveness mingles with our high regret. Astern the jetty-men and stevedores are wrangling over their latest job; trains are shunting, cranes working, trucks discharging their cargoes amid clouds of dust. We and only we assist at the passing of a goddess. Euergetes rests on his oars, the tow-rope slackens, she glides into the deep shadow of the shore, and with a soft grating noise—ah, the eloquence of it!—takes ground. Silently we carry her chain out and noose it about a monster elm; silently we slip the legs under her channels, lift and make fast her stern moorings, lash the tiller for the last time, tie the coverings over cabin top and well; anxiously, with closed lips, praetermitting no due rite. An hour, perhaps, passes, and November darkness has settled on the river ere we push off our boat,

in a last farewell committing her—our treasure 'locked up, not lost'
—to a winter over which Jove shall reign genially

Et fratres Helenae, lucida sidera.

As we thread our dim way homeward among the riding-lights
flickering on the black water, the last pale vision of her alone and
lightless follows and reminds me of the dull winter ahead, the short
days, the long nights. She is haunting me yet as I land on the wet
slip strewn with dead leaves to the tide's edge. She follows me up the
hill, and even to my library door. I throw it open, and lo! a bright
fire burning, and, smiling over against the blaze of it, cheerful,
companionable, my books have been awaiting me.

Q, From a Cornish Window

28. Bathing

THE weather became so hot in July that I suggested the children
should celebrate it by learning to swim. The provision of bathing-
dresses was a problem for Gunwalloe. Mr. Wearne, Miss Gleig's
landlord, could afford to buy proper bathing-suits for his two boys,
striped affairs such as little visitors wore and as grand in their way
as the sailor suits they sported on Sundays. Leslie, too, would probably have been given a new equipment, if a girl visitor of two years
ago had not left behind a red bathing-dress which Mrs. Williams
declared it would be a sin and a shame not to use. Leslie might
have objected to the frills on the shoulders if all the rest of the
children had appeared in anything remotely like bathing-dresses;
but compared with theirs this was so clearly what it was intended to
be that he did not grumble at its having been originally designed for
a girl. Mrs. Francis cut up an old willow-pattern curtain for Lily
and Nellie, but made the dresses so much too baggy that the two

little girls looked like a couple of ginger-jars when they stood hugging themselves at the water's edge. The equipment of the Bolitho children taxed even their mother's optimistic extravagance. No doubt if she could have found a Helston tradesman to give her credit she would have indulged herself in a burst of sheerly luxurious shopping. In the end she bought a lot of fondants, which gratified her sense of colour but left her children clamorous and unclothed. At last Mrs. Bolitho applied herself seriously to the problem, and for a start took her husband's solitary pair of pyjama trousers, which had been washed ashore from a wreck eighteen months previously, and cut them down for Beatrice. For Bessie and her younger sister Lily a pair of poor Bolitho's underpants and a vest were cut about the stitches to provide two costumes, while for Alec, having robbed the males of the family for the females, she took Beatrice's only chemise and sent him into the water looking like a small clown. Of the other children I recall only Violet Bray's appearance in a confection of oilskin.

The first bathing expedition was one warm and misty Saturday morning in a sea of oxidized silver, but these children who had spent all their lives on the brink of the Atlantic were horribly frightened of entering it when the moment came. Each one urged the other to go in first; but nobody would advance beyond his or her knees. As far up as that their bodies were familiar with the sea when they went washing feet, which was what they called paddling; the moment the scarcely heaving water rose an inch higher all the children leapt back as if they were going to be bitten by a savage fish. No reproaches of mine for their timidity were of any avail until Alec Bolitho decided to set an example at Charlie Wearne's expense by suddenly giving him a push in the back which sent him face-downwards with a splash into the water. Fired by her brother's action Bessie did the same thing to her sister Beattie, and a moment later Charlie Wearne and Beatrice Bolitho were running back across the sands to the caves where they had undressed.

'Look out for red counters in your money-boxes when the day of judgment comes', I warned Alec and Bessie; so Alec and Bessie decided they must try to win whatever coloured counter was awarded for a brave action and agreed to pull each other down into the water. Leslie Williams let them pull him down too. When I teased them about not being true daughters of a sailor Lily and Nellie Francis sat down, and they were followed by the rest. On the way back to dress in the caves there was much bragging about their bravery, at the expense of Beatrice Bolitho and Charlie Wearne, who had refused to join the others in the water. . . . By the end of that summer most of them could swim.

SIR COMPTON MACKENZIE, My Life and Times

29. The Fisher's Widow

The boats go out and the boats come in
Under the wintry sky;
And the rain and foam are white in the wind,
And the white gulls cry.

She sees the sea when the wind is wild
Swept by the windy rain;
And her heart's a-weary of sea and land
As the long days wane.

She sees the torn sails fly in the foam,
Broad on the sky-line grey;
And the boats go out and the boats come in.
But there's one away.

ARTHUR SYMONS, Poems

30. Heva! Heva!

I look back to that August of 1908 and see John Freeman walking very slowly backwards and forwards along the road above the Helzephron cliffs, in his hand a large spray cut from a furze bush. He would be on duty like this every day from sunrise until noon; he was the 'huer' of the Gunwalloe Fishing Company. That means he was gifted with eyes that could detect the change in the appearance of the sea which marked the presence of a shoal of pilchards. The huer would then wave his branch of furze in the direction of the shoal, shouting as he did so 'Heva! Heva! Heva!' That meant fish in Cornish, a language which unlike Welsh or Breton had been a dead language for a century and a half. The cry of 'heva' was echoed all around by those working in the fields who would at once throw down spade or pick or whatever implement was in their hands and rush helter-skelter down to launch the boats and cast the net before the shoal moved out of Gunwalloe's territorial waters. An oar stuck up on the beach of Church Cove halfway between Church Cove and the Poldhu cliffs marked the boundary. Beyond that the territorial waters of the Gunwalloe Daws became those of the Mullion Gulls, and many a fight had there been in the past over the position of a shoal and the right to net it.

All through that summer there had been no sight of a shoal, but John Freeman had continued his watch until the end of October. We were lucky enough to be in Toy Cottage when on the very last day of his watch the huer was able to shout 'Heva!' and I with the rest of them ran to help in the launching of the boats. John Freeman himself was in the 'cock boat' whose job it was to direct the casting of the net; I was given a seat in it.

An echo of that excitement can be heard in an attempt by Leslie Williams to write a poem about it:

Heva
Pilchards again, Tom,
His yow a wacking great school,
Plenty of colour too.

Look out here comes the men
Jim is going some rate
There goes Bill down grunter.

I am at a loss to-day to understand that last word.

Hurah!!! Hurah!!! Hurah!!!
Get a jar of Beer put in the bow,
A launch a boat a launch,
Keep her going go-a-head-go-a-head

Out with the oars
Pull away pull away boys
No anchors on board!
Then the men started shouting
I wont say what it was too awful.

What the hitch was that caused so much bad language I have forgotten. The shoal was safely taken before it reached the territorial
waters of Mullion; the amount of money netted by the Gunwalloe
Fishing Company after they had taken that shoal and sold it in
Penzance was over £2000.

The farmers of to-day may have all sorts of mechanical improve-
ments and government subsidies, but none of them will share in the
profits of the Gunwalloe Fishing Company with its capital of £100.
No shoals of pilchards visit Mount's Bay any more; the huer with
his furze bush will never be seen again; the cry of 'heva!' is for ever
silent.

SIR COMPTON MACKENZIE, *My Life and Times*

31. *Holidays at Menabilly*

FOR our summer holiday in 1920 we went to Dr. Rashleigh's old
home, Menabilly, a few miles to the west of Fowey, and the child-

ren loved it so much that we returned there year after year till we had a home of our own. Menabilly was a well-proportioned rambling house. Up its walls climbed the loveliest creepers—flowering myrtles, *Camellia reticulata*, great clusters of clematis, pomegranate and fuchsias of the tenderest varieties. Its immense kitchen garden was in the sole charge of Mr. Tarr, an old man of the soil, who unearthed out of a wilderness of weeds his prize parsnips, leeks, potatoes and onions, which confounded all other vegetables at the local flower shows.

An open terrace, where we all slept out on hot nights, overlooked the sea, and to the right the Gribben headland formed the eastern boundary of St. Austell Bay. A precipitous path down which the boys careered on scooters and bicycles led through a tangle of exotic woodland—eucalyptus groves, Himalayan rhododendrons, blue hydrangeas, pittosporum and tree-ferns—to Pridmouth Cove, our early morning bathing place, and here many of their happiest hours were spent.

Most days we went sailing in the *Saucy Nell*, a five-ton cutter owned by Mikey Burns, the dearest blue-eyed weather-worn old mariner in Fowey Harbour, whom the boys adored. Embarking was a difficult operation, for Brindle had to be carried first into a row-boat and then trans-shipped, and we all took bundles of unnecessary books and food and clothes, not knowing how long it might be before we could regain the cove. Our favourite sails were across St. Austell Bay to Pentewan Sands or Gorran Haven beneath the Dodman, and coming home we would often watch the black sails of the Mevagissey fishing fleet slip out of their harbour into the bay which they starred all night with their lights. Once, hopelessly becalmed, we had to lug the boat back at midnight on heavy oars through tracks of phosphorescence.

From Pridmouth shore a smuggler's passage ran up the hill to the farm buildings, and round this centred many imaginary adventures during the boys' robber days.

In more enterprising moods we would go off exploring to the north coast, where surf-bathing on the open sands of Perranporth and Holywell Bay was the boys' great delight; or sometimes up the deep stretch of the Fowey River, where barges laden with china clay came floating down upon the tide; or to the ruined castle of Restormel, or Lostwithiel ('Swithel', as the natives say), or along Luxulyan Valley, or to Dozmary Pool, one of the many mysterious lakes which lay claim to the vanishing Excalibur. Or, best of all we would follow the upper waters of the Fowey River where it flows clear and golden through its borderland of meadowsweet and ivy-leaved campanula to its uncharted source at the foot of Brown Willy on the uplands of Bodmin Moor.

Shell hunts were a great excitement to the boys, and in the succession of little coves between the great rocky outcrops of the promontory different types of shells and various families of shore birds seemed to have segregated themselves in their own particular territory. First came the canary-shell beach inhabited by a lively family of water-wagtails: then the turks'-head cove with its cave fringed by *Asplenium marinum* and rock-pipits flitting to and fro: then, as the rocks grew sterner and the pools deepened, a limpet, sea-anemone and razor-shell region with its party of oyster-catchers, who would rise at one's approach with every display of alarm, circle once round the bay and return to their habitat. The last accessible cove was the cowrie beach, overlapped along the cliffs' foot by clumps of the sea-loving pea, *Lathyrus maritimus*, and echoing with wren-trills and fragments of robin-song. Here the boys would spend hours in competitive cowrie hunts, kneeling on the pebbles, skimming the tide line for its treasures, or, on less lucky days, delving below the dry stones into the shiny wet shingle, calling out the latest number at each fresh find. Coming home up the cliff-side, tangled with honeysuckle, figwort, centaurea, foxgloves, camomile, past the goldfinches' favourite thistle-grove, we never failed to see a pair of stonechats poised on the topmost curves of the brambles. 'Wheet, tick-tick', said one to the other as we passed them by. 'Wheet, tick-tick', said Mikey to them. At 7.20 p.m. all through August you could rely upon the Gribben buzzards to perform their spiral flight, sailing down the headland's mile length on one wing-beat and mounting up and up over the Gribben as the sun went down.

Michael loved to go up on to the Gribben alone and would spend hours there, stretched at full length on the fragrant turf, gazing down the cliff-side where gulls and jackdaws kept up a flying commentary, and far below where one special rock-ledge was always tenanted by a row of cormorants drying their wings in the wind. One day when he came back to the rest of us down in the cove below, he confided to me very secretly that it was on the Gribben when he was there alone that he saw visions.

(From *Michael*, a privately printed Memoir of Michael McKenna)

32. 'Bethlehem' at St. Hilary

I walked down to the belfry and waited. There were the six ringers with their coats off, with the bells set ready for ringing. The captain of the tower gave me a nod of his head, as if he would say, 'Don't be afeared, Parson, depend upon it, we'll ring a proper peal'. They were waiting for my signal, and as I raised my hand, 'She's gone', said the Captain of the tower, and the treble bell, followed by the other bells, proclaimed their message of the Nativity.

From that moment I had no feeling of anxiety, only a sense of exultation as I heard the bells ring out above the roaring of the gale. Never at any other time have I been so conscious of the wonder of the world. Over the High Altar burned a white light proclaiming the presence of the Incarnate God whose nativity we were celebrating, while above our heads was another light burning red, warning the players that any sounds within the church were at that moment being transmitted over the face of the earth.

The strangeness of the church with the batteries, engineers from London and overhead wires had gone. There remained the angel who was standing beneath the arch of the tower looking very lovely with gold and silver wings and uplifted hand waiting to proclaim the news of man's salvation, and Peter on his knees in the straw, with my cloak now fallen from his shoulders and his old hands uplifted in supplication. Time had fled and left me with the angel Gabriel and an old shepherd somewhere on the plains near Bethlehem.

The voices of the children returning home from Bethlehem, as they told of how they had met 'an old man and a maiden' and how the whole world was full of glory when they looked into the maiden's face, possessed a quality that no art could equal. Words were mumbled and never heard, inflections were often laid on the wrong syllables, but these things did not matter; this is the way that shepherds round Bethlehem would have told the news; it is the way men and women of all ages speak who come off the land.

I was there to prompt and direct them, but I did nothing that night but follow silently after them as they moved from the tower to the Chapel of the Sacred Heart and from there across the church to the crib in the Lady Chapel. They were children at their prayers whom none would venture to correct for their lack of diction. This is, I believe, the secret of the play 'Bethlehem', of which, after nine years, listeners are not tired.

BERNARD WALKE, *Twenty Years at St. Hilary*

33. *The Cinder-heap*

For twenty years they have lain,
Scorned by the sun and nudged by wind and rain,
Flaky and brittle scabs on mouldering sand.
The whole dune-face is wrinkled with the bruise
Where ash and gravel interfuse,
And the dim clay-land
Cowers in vague watchfulness and fear
As brambles straggle clear,
Pushing with live brown claws

From the hard refuse through the crust
Thrown out by fires long dead: thick rust
Lies on the furnace there
Where the sagging dune-top draws
Slowly around the roofless walls
Of the old engine-house which falls
More ruinous and bare
With every storm that batters. All that's left
Of purging and consuming fire now feeds
The rousing seeds;
And the world of refuse feels the alien sting
In the crumpled cleft,
In the warmth of Spring:
Sap forcing out through rubble, filming green
With soft coarse leaves the gritty silt
Which pit and engine-house have vainly spilt
To make the earth unclean.
And surly in its bafflement
The old black cinder-heap
Confronts the newer dunes on which no brambles creep,
Though they, too, just as bitterly are bent.
This clay-land of the cleansing jet,
The purging fire,
So fears the living sap, the flamy fret
Through stem and vein of earth's desire.

JACK CLEMO, *The Map of Clay*

34. China Clay

CHINA STONE (Cornish stone or pegmatite) is a variety of feldspathic rock closely resembling pure feldspar and melting at a slightly higher temperature. These two stones are extensively used as a basis for high-temperature glazes and together with china clay are the chief ingredients of true hard-paste porcelain. The natural decomposition of granite frees the feldspar of its alkaline content and the resulting *china clay*, or kaolin, is found in enormous deposits in various parts of the world, especially in Cornwall.[1] This primary clay is found near its mother rock. It is an invaluable material for potters because it withstands very high temperatures while retaining its colour. Without it the majority of our domestic wares could not be made. It is composed of silica, alumina and water, and is called by chemists alumino-silicic acid. In its theoretically pure form it has the formula $Al_2O_3,2SiO_2,H_2O$, the average composition of which is: alumina 39.45, silica 46.64, water 13.91. Most clays do not contain much more than 50 per cent. of this *pure clay* substance, but china clay may have as much as 95 per cent. As might be expected china clay is seldom plastic.

BERNARD LEACH, *A Potter's Book*

35. Glazing

MICHAEL CARDEW finds that the addition of seaweed (*Carrageen* or *Irish moss*) is necessary for raw glazing. He says, a small handful simmered for half an hour in a quart of water is enough for a pan of glaze (four gallons). Strain through a 30-mesh sieve, add to the glaze and stir. If the glaze contains much slip it will curdle, and it will become more difficult to judge its proper thickness, but it does prevent scaling. In winter the seaweed keeps its efficacy for about a fortnight or three weeks, but in hot summer weather it loses it in a few days. When seaweed is used the glazing is usually best done when the pots are hard but have not yet changed colour.

BERNARD LEACH, *A Potter's Book*

[1] The great white conical heaps to be seen in Cornwall, erroneously thought to be china clay, are actually composed of refuse—quartz, mica, and fragments of undecomposed feldspar.

36. Riches

Miss Tregear be a whisht poor woman,
    With her fine big house an' her carriage an' pair;
Her keeps four maids, not countin' the tweeny,
    An' another especial to do her hair.

Ruth Penwarne be a brave rich woman;
    Her lives in a cottage with a warpely door;
Her've got four childer, not countin' the baby,
    An' there b'aint no tellin' but her might have more.

Miss Tregear have a room for dinin',
    An' a room for drawin', where her doesn' draw,
An' a room where books be shut in cupboards,
    An' others us don't know what they'm for.

Ruth Penwarne have a little linhay,
    An' there her washes when the rain be nigh,
But when 'tis sunny her goes in the garden,
    An' spreads her clo'es on the fuzzen to dry.

Miss Tregear have a pile o' carpets;
    Her be frit of a moth or a speck o' dust;
Her be feared that the sun will spile her curtains,
    An' the damp will make her fire-irons rust.

Ruth Penwarne have a fine stone kitchen;
    An' two rooms aloft as be crammed with beds;
Her don't have carpets, so they can't get dirty,
    An' her soon clanes up where the childer treads.

Miss Tregear have a face that's lonely;
    Her be often sad, tho' her can't tell why;
Her be allays sayin' there's nothin' doin',
    An' thinks how slow all the days go by.

Ruth Penwarne haven't time for thinkin',
  With makin' an' mendin' an' scrubbin' too,
An' sartin sure, she'm a brave rich woman,
  With childer an' home an' her work to do.

BERNARD MOORE, *A Cornish Collection*

37. *Buying a Farm*

IT was the idlest fancy that made me write to Messrs. Button,
Menhenitt and Mutton, instead of to a hundred other local agents
in Cornwall. I had seen their advertisements in the *Farmer's Weekly*,
and I must violate the tiresome convention of anonymity in order to
give the real name of this charming firm, for it is more striking than
any fictitious substitute could ever be. And as I have nothing but
good to say of them, I may as well reveal it. Nothing more serious
than an impish delight in this comic trinity—for it is not the names
of the individual partners, but the combination of them in one firm
that is so irresistibly funny—that and nothing else, led me to the
farm where I now live and work; and on the whole I do not regret
it, for with our slender resources it was probably the best place we
could have got.

After so much actual and vivid contact with Trenoweth and its
problems, I cannot now remember how it looked to me when I first
beheld it in the week after Easter 1935. I only know that I liked it,
and that it appeared fair value for the money. Its special disadvantages—the lack of proper approach by road and the smallness of the
house—there were only two bedrooms—would to many have seemed
hopeless, but us they did not trouble greatly. We had no car and
did not expect many visitors. And, from the domestic point of
view, the servantless woman is better off in a small house. Of course,
there were other draw-backs: land on the granite at 700 feet above
sea-level tends to be cold and backward, and deficient in lime. For

several years the farm, like many another holding in these lean years, had been understocked and underfed. But the advantages were many. The place was secluded and private, without being isolated. For its size the buildings were spacious, dry, and in reasonable repair, and well placed in the middle of the farm. Half the fields had access to running water, and were well sheltered by trees and bushes. The hedges were in good order and there was comparatively little waste land. The farm extended to 44 acres enclosed, with unlimited grazing on the moor, at a rent of less than £40 a year.

To my mind, the moor grazing is of very great value, especially to the small farmer. With its aid he can keep a much larger head of stock than the man whose land is limited by enclosure. Hundreds, even thousands of acres are open at his door; pasture which is rough certainly, but in summer rich and succulent and at all seasons a useful outrun, on which questing beasts can always find water and a bite of grass, even at dead of winter. Turn out your cattle on the moor and shut up your home fields for hay or corn to feed them with in winter. But of this more later; it is enough here to say that the moor is the making of Trenoweth, and the moor led me to take it. And in the midst of all the tribulations (or shall I say damnalities) that have since overtaken us, I do not regret it.

MARGARET LEIGH, *Harvest of the Moor*

38. From the States

Jacky Trewhella came back from the States with a tidy bit put by,
An' he've settled hisself in a hansum house where he reckons to
　　live an' die;
An' often he'm tellin' o' folks he've met 'crost what he calls the
　　Ditch,
An' givin' advice o' the way to work if you want to be mortal rich.

He seems to have met with a Billins chap with some handy Texts
     to tell,
As gave him a motto he took to heart, for he found how it served
     him well,
An' Jacky Trewhella he sez to us, 'Josh Billins he sez to me—
"Don't you carry your wishbone where your backbone ought to be." '

Jacky Trewhella went out from here with only a miner's kit,
But he heerd o' money in Yankee land an' thought he could do
     with a bit,
An' he soon worked up to a Cap'n's job an' took a share in a mine,
An 'it turned out proper an' good, it did, an' Jacky was doin' fine;
But he worked away an' made for hisself a pocket without any
     holes,
An' picked up a bit on a railway line, an' pulled in a bit on coals;
An' Jacky Trewhella he sez to us, 'Josh Billins he sez to me—
"Don't you carry your wishbone where your backbone ought to be." '

Jacky Trewhella was doin' fine, but his thought would often come
Strayin' away to the Cornish shores an' his far-off Cornish home;
So he made up his mind to dollars enough to carry him over the sea,
An' settle him down in comfort like where his heart belonged to be.
So now he'm home in a hansum house with a tidy bit put by,
An' plenty o' time to strawl around an' look at the sea an' sky,
An' Jacky Trewhella he sez to us, 'Josh Billins he sez to me—
"Don't you carry your wishbone where your backbone ought to be." '

BERNARD MOORE, *A Cornish Collection*

VII. Folklore, Charms and Inscriptions

1. West Country Folk Song: Child's Verses for Winter

Devon was white,
But Cornwall was green:
The prettiest sight
That ever was seen.

When Cornwall was copper
Devon was gold:
On moorland and hilltop,
Pasture and fold.

When Devon was purple
Cornwall was brown,
With harvesting bracken
On ledra and down.

When Cornwall was grey
With sea-mist and spume,
Devon was greenest
With apples in bloom.

Devon was shrouded
With snow on each thing,
But Cornwall was verdant
With promise of spring.

A. L. ROWSE, *Poems of Cornwall and America*

2. A True Ballad of Sir Henry Trecarell

who in 1511 rebuilt the Parish Church of
St. Mary Magdalen at Launceston

Henry Trecarell sat up in bed
His face was white and his eyes were red,
I dreamed (he cried) *that our son was dead*
'Lie over, Sir Henry,' Her Ladyship said.

*I saw him sink in a silver fen
In the arms of a wicked white Magdalen.
I hope I'm imagining things!* Only then
Her Ladyship murmured, 'Amen! Amen!

'The moon walks west on the orchard wall,
Your daughters are dozing over the Hall
And your son sleeps as sound as a cannon-ball.
There is nothing the matter, Sir Henry, at all!'

But when the boy-baby, as naked as sin,
Stood up in a cold Cornish basin of tin
His nurse went away for a little napkin
And he fell on the water and breathed it all in.

The carpenters no longer whistled a carol.
Said Margaret to Henry (in mourning apparel):
'You'll finish the Manor, with roof like a barrel?'
I'm damned if I will, said Sir Henry Trecarell.

Sir Henry's and Margaret's tears fell hard
And their two Tudor faces were sorry as lard
As they built in the baby beneath the churchyard
In a parcel of linen and spikenard.

*   *   *

When Sir Henry descended one evening to dine
The Magdalen told him to build her a shrine,
But Her Ladyship said, as she poured out the wine,
'I'd hoped you'd forgotten that concubine.'

Sir Henry Trecarell stood at his ewer
And gazed at the granite among the manure.
He called out, *My grief I'll no longer endure!*
Send for the Mayor—John Bonaventure.

The limbers all lugged the stone in from Lezant
And the running-boys heard sad Sir Henry chant:
To the Glory of God this stone tree I now plant
For Mary, and Henry the Protestant.

For twelve years and one in Launceston town
The masons wore fifty flint fingers down
Carving an angel, a rose or a clown
On every inch of the Magdalen's crown.

While Flodden was fought and the Frenchmen fell low
And Cortes was conquering Mexico,
When Wolsey was Generalissimo
They hammered away at the holy château.

When the sun in the summer is spreading his hood
The beggar still sulks in the starving mud,
The pelican glides with a gift of blood
And the eagle ascends to the throne of good.

Where winter descends with her smudging snow
The nardus and pomegranate grow,
And through the forest the frozen doe,
The greyhound, the griffin and honey-bear go.

The immortal yew and the frigid oak
Stand about Martin slicing his cloak,
And George (on a pony) tries to invoke
The dragon, making crystal smoke.

Now the Magdalen lies on a mica strand
Spreading her hair with an idle hand,
And ready to play at her command
Is a sawing sixteenth-century band.

The ointment stands at the Magdalen's side,
St. Matthew's Gospel is open wide,
And round the wall the writings ride:
Behold! The Bridegroom loves the Bride!

*   *   *

Sir Henry Trecarell went up to bed
The pains all gone from his heart and head.
My life (he cried) *is newly-wed!*
'Praised be the Lord,' Her Ladyship said.

CHARLES CAUSLEY, Union Street

3. Constantine

CONSTANTINE church is now in ruins, and the parish, if it ever
was one, has long been merged in that of St. Merryn. The festival
of Constantine is still celebrated by an annual hurling match, on
which occasion the owner of Harlyn supplies—and has, according
to parish tradition, from time immemorial, supplied—the silver
ball.

Adjoining the church of Constantine was a cottage which a family of the name of Edwards held for generations under the proprietors of Harlyn by the annual render of a pie made of limpets, raisins, and various herbs, on the eve of the festival. This pie, as I have heard from my father, and from more ancient members of the family, and from old servants, was excellent. The Edwardses had pursued for centuries the occupation of shepherds on Harlyn and Constantine common. The last died about forty years ago, and the wreck of their cottage is almost buried in sand.

WILLIAM PETER of Harlyn, writing about 1837.
[J. Polsue], *Parochial History of Cornwall*

4. *Mevagissey*

Peter jumped up in the pulpit
His hands all smelling of fish,
His Guernsey was gay with the sparky spray
And white as an angel's wish.

The seagulls came in through the ceiling
The fish flew up through the floor,
Bartholomew laughed as he cast off aft
And Andrew cast off fore.

They charged the thundering churchyard
Like a lifeboat down the slip,
And the congregation in consternation
Prepared to abandon ship.

Overboard went the bonnets
Over went the bowlers
And, before the seas were up to their knees,
A hundred holy rollers.

'Draw your tots!' said Peter,
'Every man to his post!
It's not so far to heaven's bar
With the charts I've got of the coast!

Shoot the boom like Satan!
Prepare to take on boarders!
Send up your prayers like signal-flares!
I'll steam the secret orders!

Stoke up the engine-room boilers
With slices of heavenly toast!
The devil's a weasel and travels on Diesel
But I burn the Holy Ghost!'

What became of the vessel
Nobody dared enquire,
But the new church-room is tough as a tomb
And the walls are very much higher.

Its anchor is glittering granite,
Its cable is long as Lent,
But the winds won't reek, and refuse to speak
In a silent sail of cement.

Its mast is made of iron,
Its gunwales are made of lead,
Its cargo of bone is hard as the stone
That hangs about my head.

I walk all day in the dockyard
Looking for Captain Pete,
But there's not a marine or a brigantine
At the bottom of Harbour Street.

The boy-voiced boat, like summer,
Has sailed away over the hills
And I'm beached like a bride by the travelling tide
With a packet of seasick pills.

CHARLES CAUSLEY, *Union Street*

5. *To the Mermaid at Zennor*

Half fish, half fallen angel, none of you
Human at all—cease your lust's
Cold and insatiate crying from the tangled bay;
Nor, sea-hag, here
Stretch webbed and skinny fingers for your prey.

This is a hideous and a wicked country,
Sloping to hateful sunsets and the end of time,
Hollow with mine-shafts, naked with granite, fanatic
With sorrow. Abortions of the past
Hop through these bogs; black-faced, the villagers
Remember burnings by the hewn stones.

Only the saints,
Drifting on oak-leaves over the Irish Sea,
To sing like pipits from their crannied cells
With a thin stream of praise; who hear the Jennifer
Sob for her sins in a purgatory of foam—
Only these holy men
Can send you slithering from the chancel steps,
And wriggling back to your sunken paradise
Among the hollow-eyed and the capsized.

JOHN HEATH-STUBBS, *A Charm Against the Toothache*

6. 'Treade'

FALMOUTH, March 19, 1835.—Davies Gilbert[1] and others dined here. He was full of anecdote and interest, as usual. One on the definition of 'treade' was good.[2] It is really derived from 'trad' (Saxon), a thing. When he was on the bench a man was brought before one of the judges on some poisoning charge, and the examination of the witness proceeded thus: Q. 'Did you see anything in the loaf?' A. 'Yes; when I cut it open, I found it full of traed.' Q. 'Traed; why, what is that?' A. 'Oh, it's rope-ends, dead mice, and other combustibles.'

CAROLINE FOX, *Journals and Letters*

7. *Helston Furry Dance Song*

Robin Hood and Little John,
    They both are gone to the fair-O;
And we will to the merry green wood
    To see what they do there-O.
And for to chase-O,
    To chase the buck and doe.
        With Hal-an-tow,
        Jolly rumble-O.

And we were up as soon as any day-O,
    And for to fetch the summer home,
    The summer and the May-O.

[1] Gilbert (Davies), formerly named Giddy, born 1767, educated at Pembroke College, Oxford. M.P. successively for Helston and Bodmin, and President of the Royal Society. Celebrated as an antiquary and writer on Cornish topography, etc. He died in 1839.

[2] A Cornish term used by the lower classes as a synonym for trash. 'Doctor's treade', for instance, is a contemptuous phrase for medicine.

For the summer is a-come-O,
And winter is agone-O.

Whereas those Spaniards
    That make so great a boast-O,
They shall eat the grey goose feather,
    And we will eat the roast-O.
In every land-O,
    The land that ere we go.
            With Hal-an-tow, etc.
            And we were up, etc.

As for St. George-O,
    St. George he was a knight-O.
Of all the kings in Christendom
    King Georgy is the right-O.
In every land-O,
    The land that ere we go.
            With Hal-an-tow etc.

God bless Aunt Mary Moses
    With all her power and might-O;
And send us peace in merry England,
    Both day and night-O.

8. *The Furry Dance*

Jan said to me wan day
'Can you dance the Flora?'
'Iss, I can, with a nice young man.'
'Off we go to Trora.' [i.e. Truro]

9. Summercourt Fair

'Ere we'm off to Summercourt Fair;
  Me mother said 'Iss',
  Me faather said 'No',
And dash me buttons if I dunt go.

10. The Lezzard Lights

ON his death bed an old fisherman of the Lizard Point begged
the parson to read him the bit in the Bible about the Lizard lighthouse. 'The Lizard lighthouse?' echoed the vicar. 'Iss, Passon.
"The sun and the moon and all the Lezzard Lights".'

CHARLES HENDERSON, *Essays in Cornish History*

11. The Silent Tower of Bottreaux

Tintagel[1] bells ring o'er the tide,
  The boy leans on his vessel's side;
  He hears that sound, and dreams of home
Soothe the wild orphan of the foam.

[1] The rugged heights that line the seashore in the neighbourhood of
Tintagel Castle and Church are crested with towers. Among these, that
of Bottreaux, or, as it is now written, Boscastle, is without bells. The
silence of this wild and lonely churchyard on festive or solemn occasions
is not a little striking. On inquiry I was told that the bells were once
shipped for this church, but when the vessel was within sight of the tower
the blasphemy of her captain was punished in the manner related in the
poem. The bells, they told me, still lie in the bay, and announce by
strange sounds the approach of a storm.

'Come to thy God in time!'
Thus saith their pealing chime:
'Youth, manhood, old age past,
'Come to thy God at last.'

But why are Bottreaux' echoes still?
Her Tower stands proudly on the hill;
Yet the strange chough that home hath found,
The lamb lies sleeping on the ground.
'Come to thy God in time!'
Should be her answering chime:
'Come to thy God at last!'
Should echo on the blast.

The ship rode down with courses free,
The daughter of a distant sea:
Her sheet was loose, her anchor stored,
The merry Bottreaux bells on board.
'Come to thy God in time!'
Rung out Tintagel chime;
'Youth, manhood, old age past,
'Come to thy God at last!'

The pilot heard his native bells
Hang on the breeze in fitful swells;
'Thank God!' with reverent brow he cried.
'We'll make the shore with evening's tide.'
'Come to thy God in time!'
It was his marriage chime:
'Youth, manhood, old age past,'
His bell must ring at last.

'Thank God, thou whining knave! on land,
'But thank, at sea, the steersman's hand'—
The captain's voice above the gale—
'Thank the good ship and ready sail,'

'Come to thy God in time!'
Sad grew the boding chime:
'Come to thy God at last!'
Boom'd heavy on the blast.

Uprose the sea! as if it heard
The mighty Master's signal-word:
What thrills the captain's whitening lip?
The death-groans of his sinking ship.
    'Come to thy God in time!'
    Swung deep the funeral chime:
    'Grace, mercy, kindness past,
    'Come to thy God at last!'

Long did the rescued pilot tell—
When grey hairs o'er his forehead fell,
While those around him would hear and weep—
That fearful judgment of the deep,
    'Come to thy God in time!'
    He read his native chime:
    'Youth, manhood, old age past,'
    His bell rang out at last.

Still when the storm of Bottreaux' waves
Is wakening in his weedy caves:
Those bells, that sullen surges hide,
Peal their deep notes beneath the tide:
    'Come to thy God in time!'
    Thus saith the ocean chime:
    'Storm, billow, whirlwind past,
    'Come to thy God at last!'

R. S. HAWKER, *Cornish Ballads*

12. *Weather Rhyme: West Cornwall*

When Pons-an-dane calls to Larrigan river,
    There will be fine weather;
But when Larrigan calls to Pons-an-dane,
    There will be rain.[1]

13. *A Parish Rhyme against Mevagissey*

    Ye men of Porthilly,[2]
    Why were ye so silly,
    To have so little power,
    As Gorran men tell,
    To sell every bell
For money to pull down your tower?

Alternate Form:

Ye men of Mevagissey
O weren't you silly people
To sell every bell
For money to pull down the steeple?

[1] i.e. a wind from the sea, 'calling of the sea' was the old name for it.
[2] Porthilly is an old name for Mevagissey. Parish insults against a neighbouring parish were regular form. The point of this is that Mevagissey church has no tower, merely a saddle-back—the tower must have fallen at some time.

14. *Morwenstow Vicarage*

INSCRIPTION, carved in stone, over the porch door of the Vicarage House, Morwenstow.

> A House, a Glebe, a Pound a Day;[1]
> A Pleasant Place to Watch and Pray.
> Be True to Church—Be Kind to Poor,
> O Minister! For Evermore.

R. S. HAWKER, *Cornish Ballads and Other Poems*

15. *The Devil Takes Himself Off to Devon*

CORNISH traditions are very contradictory. On the one hand we have amid the rocks and hills numerous devil's coits, plenty of devil's footsteps, with devil's bellows, devil's frying-pans, devil's ovens and devil's caves in abundance. On the other hand we are told that the devil never came into Cornwall, 'because when he crossed the Tamar, and made Torpoint for a brief space his resting place, he could not but observe that everything vegetable or animal was put by Cornish people into a pie. He saw and heard of fishy pie, star-gazy pie, conger pie, and, indeed, pies of all the fishes of the sea; of parsley pie, and herby pie, of lamy pie, and pies without number. Therefore, fearing they might take a fancy to a devilly pie, he took himself back into Devonshire'.

ROBERT HUNT, *Popular Romances of the West of England*

[1] The annual value of the vicarage rentcharge—R.S.H.

16. How to Make a Witch

'LET him go to chancel,' said he, 'to sacrament, and let him hide and bring away the bread from the hands of the priest; then, next midnight let him take it and carry it round the church, widdershins —that is, from south to north, crossing by east three times: the third time there will meet him a big, ugly, venomous toad, gaping and gasping with his mouth opened wide, let him put the bread between the lips of the ghastly creature, and as soon as ever it is swallowed down his throat he will breathe three times upon the man, and he will be made a strong witch for evermore.'

R. S. HAWKER, *Footprints of Former Men in Far Cornwall*

17. In St. Ewe Churchyard

Here lies the body of Joan Carthew,
Born at St Mewan, died at St Ewe;
Children had she five,
Three is dead and two's alive;
They that are dead choosin rather
To die with mother than to live with father.

18. The Levan Stone

When, with panniers astride
A pack-horse can ride
Through the Levan Stone,
The world will be done.

19. Charm to Extract a Thorn

Happy man that Christ was born!
He was crownèd with a thorn:
He was piercèd through the skin,
For to let the poison in;
But His five wounds, so they say,
Closed before He passed away.
In with healing, out with thorn:
Happy man that Christ was born!

R. S. HAWKER, *Footprints of Former Men in Far Cornwall*

20. Charm for Adder-bite

DID you ever hear, sir, how I heal an adder's bite? You cut a piece of hazelwood, sir, and you fasten a long bit and a short one together into the form of a cross; then you lay it softly upon the wound, and you say, thrice, blowing out the words aloud like one of the commandments—

Underneath this hazelin mote
There's a Braggoty worm with a speckled throat,
    Nine double is he:
Now from nine double to eight double,
And from eight double to seven double,
And from seven double to six double,
And from six double to five double,
And from five double to four double,
And from four double to three double,
And from three double to two double,
And from two double to one double,
And from one double to no double,
    No double hath he!

R. S. HAWKER, *Footprints of Former Men in Far Cornwall*

21. A Cornish Folk Song

Now, of all the birds that keep the tree,
  Which is the wittiest fowl?
Oh, the Cuckoo—the Cuckoo's the one!—for he
  Is wiser than the owl!

He dresses his wife in her Sunday best,
  And they never have rent to pay;
For she folds her feathers in a neighbour's nest,
  And thither she goes to lay!

He winked with his eye, and he buttoned his purse,
  When the breeding time began;
For he'd put his children out to nurse
  In the house of another man!

Then his child, though born in a stranger's bed,
  Is his own true father's son;
For he gobbles the lawful children's bread,
  And he starves them one by one!

So, of all the birds that keep the tree,
  This is the wittiest fowl!
Oh, the Cuckoo—the Cuckoo's the one!—for he
  Is wiser than the owl!

R. S. HAWKER, *Cornish Ballads*

22. Weather Rhyme

Mist from the sea
Brings fine weather to thee;
Mist from the hills
Brings water to the mills.

———

On Sea-Mist: 'All for 'eat an' pilchards.'

229

23. *In St. Buryan Churchyard*

Sleep Here A While
Thou Dearest part of Me;
   In Little Time
I'll Come and Sleep With Thee.

Our life is but a Winter's day;
Some only Breakfast and away;
Others to Dinner stay and are Full fed;
The oldest only Sups and goes to Bed.
Large is his Depth, who lingers out the Day:
Who goes the soonest has the least to pay.

24. *The Price of Empire*

OVER the chancel door:

'In loving memory of James Olivey, R.N. master's assistant of H.M.S. "Spy", fifth son of Hugh Oliver Olivey and Peggy his wife, who died at sea May 25th, 1855, aged 16.

'And of Richard Olivey, R.N. Paymaster of H.M.S. "Kestrel", sixth son of the above, who died at Hankow, North China, Sept. 9th, 1876, aged 36.

'Also of Walter Rice Olivey, Lieut. 66th Regt. son of Lieut.-Col. W. R. Olivey, Army Pay department, who was killed whilst carrying the Queen's colour of his Regiment at the battle of Maiwand, Afghanistan, on the 27th July, 1886, aged 20. "Until the day dawn".

'Also of his youngest brother, Herbert Edward Olivey, Capt. Suffolk Regt. who was killed in action in Somaliland while serving with the 2nd Battalion King's African Rifles on 17th April, 1903, aged 32.'

In Mylor Church

25. *Going to Bed*

From ghoulies and ghosties,
And long-leggèd beasties,
And things that go bump in the night—
    Good Lord deliver us.

VIII. Birds, Beasts, Flowers, Gardens

1. The Cornish Chough

THE Chough's existing stronghold to-day lies within a coastline stretch of about thirty miles on our Northern sea-board. Outside this, the birds are to be found nowhere in Cornwall unless very occasionally as casual wanderers. On this stretch, there are six known nesting sites but two of them are only exceptionally tenanted, the remaining four being occupied more or less regularly. I believe that no other nesting site remains undiscovered. Never, to my knowledge, have all been occupied in any one year. If broods from as many as three of them are safely reared, there is good cause for satisfaction.

This elegant and charming bird is a member of the Corvidae family. If one did not know that it has been scientifically classified as such, one might well find it difficult to believe that it is, in fact, one of the seven species of Crows which are regular residents in the British Isles. Except that it is black like some others of its cousins, I can find little in it that resembles any Crow. Its graceful form, its delightful manners, and its whole way of life stamp it as well nigh unique among British Birds.

Its long curved red bill and red legs, its comely figure, its lively gait, its glossy blue-black plumage, tinged with green which glitters as it flashes through the sunlight, all these pronounce it a thorough-bred. Its clear ringing call, once its characteristic timbre is imprinted on the mind, can be mistaken for that of no other bird. In company with others of its kind, it is at once playful and talkative but never aggressive. It seeks no quarrel with any other bird, yet it is no coward and knows how to look after itself. It desires acquaintance of none but those of its own breed. Gentle of manner, it displays no resentment towards birds which intrude themselves upon it but it makes no advances to them. Unperturbed, and heedless of their presence, it completes the job in hand.

B. H. RYVES, *Bird Life in Cornwall*

2. *Dr. Borlase's Tame Chough*

OUR chough is now I think in its fourteenth year. It has some-times been sick, Mrs. Borlase is the doctor, and when its appetite appeared to be disordered she has grated rubarb made up with a little meal into a paste with success; if his spirits are low we infuse saffron into his water; and as he has free egress and ingress, he appears generally at dinner, knocking at the door if it be shut with his bill till 'tis opened; his place is to perch behind my chair, his favourite dish is the yolk of a boiled egg, which he will take off my plate without leave; if there is any white meat, particularly chicken or veal, he expects his share minced for him, and he flies upon the table and back to his perch without ceremony and manners. It is a bird that loves such familiarity and I apprehend cannot live in solitude where he has not liberties of ranging and varying the scene.

DR. BORLASE, in P. A. S. Pool, 'William Borlase', in *Journal of the Royal Institution of Cornwall* (1966)

3. The Eagles

The mighty birds still upward rose,
In slow but constant and most steady flight,
The young ones following; and they would pause,
As if to teach them how to bear the light,
And keep the solar glory full in sight.
So went they on till, from excess of pain,
I could no longer bear the scorching rays;
And when I looked again they were not seen,
Lost in the brightness of the solar blaze.
Their memory left a type, and a desire;
So should I wish towards the light to rise,
Instructing younger spirits to aspire
Where I could never reach amidst the skies;
And joy below to see them lifted higher,
Seeking the light of purest glory's prize.
So would I look on splendour's brightest day
With an undazzled eye, and steadily
Soar upwards full in the immortal ray,
Through the blue depths of the unbounded sky,
Portraying wisdom's boundless purity.
Before me still a lingering ray appears,
But broken and prismatic, seen thro' tears,
The light of joy and immortality.

SIR HUMPHRY DAVY

4. Birds of Pelynt

PELYNT, between valley and valley, has every kind of likely habitat
for birds. It has little marshes fed by a spring bubbling up from
the clay, it has thick scrubby woods and clear oak woods and

furze brakes, saltings and mud flats in the West Looe River, the dells of rock hung with ivy, the streams for dipper and kingfisher and all the miles of thorn-capped hedge and bank. Scene after scene is framed for me in different portions of this medley. Typical of the parish, an elm stands by itself under a wet sky, along one of the hedges. While I am fifty yards away, a carrion crow slides furtively out. Climb and I shall discover the eggs lying in the cup, which is cosy with sheep's wool and binder twine and perhaps even a piece of the *Cornish Times* a month or two old. Or an old blackthorn hunched between luxuriant hollies, a goldcrest flicking through the blossoms, too light to shake one of them to the ground, creeping this way and that, hanging in all manner of attitudes from the lichen-covered twigs, uttering a *sip, sip* to another goldcrest a few yards up the hedgerow. Every year in the vicarage garden these birds hung a cradle from the lower branches of a Californian Redwood; and I have a slightly incongruous note of a goldcrest feeding among the sharp prickles of a monkey-puzzle near-by. Much else comes back. The scolding of sedgewarblers in the Looe valley, or in the winter the melancholy flocks of lapwing, alternately like black and white snowflakes, and the winnards (the redwings, that is) flipping on those upland pastures above the village, and the occasional curlews down from the moorland, which looked black, heavy and outlandish as they disappeared between field and low evening sky. The tale of the year's expeditions included one by the green roads out to Lizzen (once, after all, a part of the manor of Pelynt), to peer into a raven's nest over the sea, in a sharp easterly wind, and observe the young birds in their coarse cradle of furze branches, cow hair, horse hair, sacking and old rope. Yet the two eminent species of the parish are, so I have always felt, the grey wagtails and the buzzards. They speak for the coombes; the wagtails for that intimacy I have pictured, of rock and moss and ivy and spring water, the buzzards for the wide roll of the coombe-divided landscape and the clean oak woods.

GEOFFREY GRIGSON, *Freedom of the Parish*

5. Birds in Cold Weather

No sooner had I gone away than the bitterly cold weather with snow and sleet, which prevailed over a great part of the country at Christmas, swept over the southern and western counties and drove the birds before it. The first news I had of it was in a letter, dated December 30, from a naturalist friend, Mr. G. A. B. Dewar, who was staying on the towans, overlooking St. Ives Bay, close to Hayle.

I wonder [he wrote] did you see much of the marvellous migration scene which took place here on Friday morning? For hours— till about midday—redwings, thrushes, larks and fieldfares streamed across St. Ives Bay, coming from the east. There was a great highway of birds, which must have been miles broad. We saw them first from the window as we dressed. ... Most of the birds crossed the Bay, going towards Land's End, but thousands and tens of thousands dropped exhausted among the sand dunes, or towans, here, and among these I found golden plover, ring plover, sanderlings, lapwings, etc.—altogether an extraordinary assemblage. On Saturday morning, lasting till one o'clock P.M., the birds returned in a great highway east again. Mingled among them were many small birds, linnets, etc. A most wonderful pathetic scene, I assure you. I wondered if any of the travellers crossed the Channel, or whether they all stopped in this extreme westerly bit of land. I did not think England had so many fieldfares and redwings.

On my return a few days later, I found on inquiring along the coast that large numbers of the birds had appeared at the Land's End towards evening and settled down to roost in the furze and heath and among the stones. At one house, I was told, numbers of thrushes and starlings crowded on the window-sills, and some of them that were stiff with cold were taken in, but were found dead in the morning. From all I could hear the migration appears to have spent itself at this spot.

To me the 'pathetic' part of it was the reception the starved fugitives met with from the good people along the coast, especially at St. Ives with its horn or 'island' beyond the town thrust out into the sea, a convenient resting-place for the birds after flying across the bay. My information on the subject, which would fill some twenty pages of a Blue Book, was gathered from men and lads, mostly fishermen, who had taken part in the massacre. Each person buys a handful of small fish-hooks, manufactured for the purpose and sold, a dozen for a penny, by a tradesman in the town. Ten to twenty baited hooks are fastened with short threads to a string, two or three feet long, called a 'teagle', and placed on a strip of ground from which the snow has been cleared. To these strips of mould or turf the birds fly and seize the hooks, and so blind to danger are they made by hunger that they are not deterred by the frantic struggles of those already hooked. Many birds succeed in freeing themselves by breaking the thread in their struggles, but always with that bit of barbed or bent wire in their mouths or stomachs, which must eventually cause their death. In one garden where food was placed for the birds and their hunters kept out, eleven dead and dying birds were picked up in one day among the shrubs, all with hooks in their gullets.

One young fisherman told me with great glee that he had found two hooks besides his own in the mouth of a blackbird he had taken with his teagle.

W. H. HUDSON, *The Land's End*

6. Chough

Desolate that cry as though world were unworthy.
See now, rounding the headland, a forlorn hopeless bird,
trembling black wings fingering the blowy air,
dainty and ghostly, careless of the scattering salt.

This is the cave-dweller that flies like a butterfly,
buffeted by daws, almost extinct, who has chosen,
so gentle a bird, to live on furious coasts.

Here where sea whistles in funnels, and slaps the back
of burly granite slabs, and hisses over holes,
in bellowing hollows that shelter the female seal
the Cornish chough wavers over the waves.

By lion rocks, rocks like the heads of queens,
sailing with ragged plumes upturned, into the wind
goes delicate indifferent the doomed bird.

REX WARNER

7. *A Young Seal*

THE north side of the walled garden was sheltered from the wind
by a large shrubbery of laurels and a grove of these elms; these
sheltered the west side of the house, against which grew right up to
the gutter round the roof two large trees of *Magnolia grandiflora*.
When they were in full August bloom the air of the lawn was
scented by their great flowers. The lawn itself sloped down into the
elms through the laurels, under which a path led to the road along
the estuary, ending by the Lelant ferry a mile or so along. The
ferryman was a captivating figure who stood in the bows and
ferried his passengers across the hundred yards of river with the
power and grace of a gondolier. I see now his slanting eyebrows as
he told me that autumn of a tragedy. Throughout the summer a
baby seal which had lost its mother had made a habit of following
his boat backward and forward each time he crossed.

'It was like a child,' he told me, 'and belonged to cuddle up
against me when I would stroke his head. Then one day in August
month when I was ferrying over some of these furrin visitors I
asked them what they thought of my baby seal and one of they
bloody visitors up and shot my baby seal. Man, I don't know how I
didn't throw him into the river; I suppose the Lord stopped me

241

because if I had thrown him in he'd have drowned dead sure because the tide would have swept the bugger out to sea. I believe I'll give up the ferry come October month because I'm for ever looking behind for my baby seal and you never know what I might do to the boat one day.'

SIR COMPTON MACKENZIE, My Life and Times

8. Seagull and Adder

IT is very lovely here. I am sitting with my back against a boulder, a few yards above the houses. Below, the gorse is yellow, and the sea is blue. It is very still, no sound but the birds and the wind among the stones. A very big seagull just flew up from the east, white like lime-stone, and hovered just in front of me, then turned back in the sky. It seemed like a messenger.

The sun is very hot, it is like summer. Yesterday I saw an adder sleeping on the grass. She was very slim and elegant with her black markings. At last she was disturbed, she lifted her slender head and listened with great delicacy. Then, very fine and undulating, she moved away. I admired her intensely, and liked her very much. If she were a familiar spirit, she was a dainty and superb princess.

D. H. LAWRENCE, Letters

9. A Merry Gentleman's Mishap

THIS mention of snakes called to my remembrance how not long since a merry Cornish gentleman tried that old fable to be no fable which sheweth the dangerous entertaining of such a guest: for he

having gotten one of that kind, and broken out his teeth (wherein
consisteth his venom), used to carry him about in his bosom, to set
him to his mouth, to make him lick his spittle, and when he came
among gentlewomen, would cast him out suddenly, to put them in
fear: but in the end, their vain dread proved safer than his fool-
hardiness; for as he once walked alone, and was kissing this gentle
playfellow, the snake in good earnest, with a stump, either newly
grown up, or not fully pulled out, bit him fast by the tongue, which
therewith began so to rankle and swell, that by the time he had
knocked this foul player on the head, and was come to his place of
abode, his mouth was scarce able to contain it. Fain was he therefore
to shew his mishap, and by gestures to crave aid in earnest of the
gentlewomen whom he had aforetime often scared in sport.

RICHARD CAREW, *Survey of Cornwall*

10. *Owl and the Owl-Woman*

HER password was 'Tu-whit-too-whoo', emitted from the throat
with head thrown back and chin drawn in. It was a vibrant note
that did not die away like any human speaking voice in the sunshine all about us; it was projected to hill and valley far beyond our
garden boundary. She gave the first call in the pleasure grounds and
in a few seconds there came an answering 'Tu-whit-too-whoo.' The
password was repeated and that answer came again, this time it was
not so far away. Now from every thicket there came a panic
chittering, about us the blackbirds and finches were a-twitter in the
bushes, it was like the beginning of an eclipse.

Then, like a spirit summoned from the unseen world, a brown
owl came, in swift and silent flight, looked down round-eyed and
questioning upon us from a branch, gave hooting answer to hooting
call and after a while withdrew to his secret haunt, silently as he
had come.

That evening we walked across the field above Relowas Bottom. We stood looking down into the wooded valley where tangled undergrowth had made a sanctuary for birds and animals. She threw back her head and gave the call. From the depth of the valley came reply: 'Tu-whit-too-whoo-oo-oo'. She varied her note a little as she answered. We were seated just within the wood, our backs against a hedge, and I clutched a trail of ivy in each hand and all my consciousness was centred in the power of listening; it seemed as if every muscle listened. Something strange was about us, revelation might be lurking in yonder trees. Far down the valley there sounded another 'Tu-whit-too-whoo-oo-oo', long-drawn, pitched a little higher than the first reply. In another moment it seemed as if the wood were but a vault for the echoing of those owl cries. Nearer and nearer they came.

Always before, when owls had hooted in the daylight, there had been a crooning, half-awakened sound in the calls; their greetings had been low-toned, slow and comfortable, but now in these owl-cries about us there was a note of urgency and flutter. The cries began to close in on us and then, noiseless and swift, two brown owls came and perched on low branches ten yards from where we sat. They perched there looking solemnly into our faces and I could not gaze ardently enough into those blinking eyes.

There was something occult, almost sinister, about this inter-course between a woman and a bird. From what hiding-place had these unfamiliar creatures been cozened? What was the nature of a summons that could lure the bird of night from his habitual world of shadows while the sun was high in heaven?

C. C. Vyvyan, *The Old Place*

11. *A Little Cat at Polruan*

No account of our life there would be complete without the history of the cat to whom we gave the name 'Little Soul'. This cat of whom I am writing wandered down as a kitten from the farm-place where her mother lived in a half-wild state, and attended my Mass at the church on the hill for three mornings in succession. As no one claimed her I picked her up and took her home. After a time she took to accompanying me each morning, with those short runs and stops which a cat adopts in going for a walk, to the church where I first discovered her. Sitting on the step, she would gravely me-ow when I turned to say 'Dominus tecum' and go before me to the vestry when Mass was ended. Later she took to coming to the Sunday evening service, walking sedately before me to the pulpit where, from the bookrest, she looked down on the people.

One Sunday evening a Miss Mahon, an old lady of Polruan, was sitting in the front pew. The glistening sequins that decorated her mantle proved an irresistible attraction to Little Soul that evening, for, springing from her place in the pulpit, she landed in the lap of the old lady. The following day I received a letter from the Vicar enumerating my many extravagances, concluding with the monstrous behaviour of my cat on the previous night. One phrase remains in my memory—'Your performing cat has made religion stink in the nostrils of the best people in Polruan'. In answering, I advanced the example of St. Philip Neri, whose cat always attended him at his devotions; but our little cat was forbidden ever to enter the church again. Later, Little Soul came with us to St. Hilary, where her religious observance was limited to producing kittens by some means or other on the great Feasts of the Church.

BERNARD WALKE, *Twenty Years at St. Hilary*

12. *Gallop Galliards in the Roof*

OF all manner of vermin, Cornish houses are most pestered with rats, a brood very hurtful for devouring of meat, clothes, and writings by day; and alike cumbersome through their crying and rattling, while they dance their gallop gallyards in the roof at night.

RICHARD CAREW, *Survey of Cornwall*

13. *Lanes and Hedges*

THE great thing about a Cornish lane is that it simulates the condition of a wood. The hedges on either side are damp, they do not get the full sun, they may even be thickly wooded along their crests. So they have a woodland flora, and something of a woodland fauna as well, even to the sprawling mound-like nests of the red and black wood ant, *Formica rufa*. The hedges are rinsed with bluebells (which Pelynt people called Guckoos), white with ramsons or anemonies, yellow in a few stretches with Lent-lilies (daffodils, that is to say), purple with foxgloves. Wood-sorrel (Rabbit's Meat—the white flowers attractively sharp in taste when you bite into them), primroses, dog's mercury, to say nothing of ferns—all these belong to the hedges; which also nourish some of the select plants of the West of England.

A Northerner walking through these green chasms would be unfamiliar with tutsan (its yellow flowers changing to black devil's berries), or wild columbine, or alkanet, or that foetid but lovely Cornish Balm. Irritating or no, because of the way they cut off the views, the hedges are indispensable to the Cornish scene. Without them each parish would be wind-scythed and less coloured, less floral above the shelter of the valleys. So here the human past conditions the present once more. All this valley-cleft plateau, ranging in elevation between 350 and 500 feet, was thrust up from under the sea, which had moulded and modified its surface. Before the early Celt or Cornishman went to work, one must imagine it, I suppose, as a plateau mainly of scrub—gorse, blackthorn, bramble, figwort and honeysuckle, over which the south-western gales sliced from the

Atlantic. The habitat of so many of the more excellent plants would have been a dell or a shaded corner here and there; from which, when the enclosure came, they spread to the endless miles of earthen bank. I reckon that within the 4,683 acres of Pelynt the criss-crossing hedges add up to about 120 miles. Making allowance for that amount of hedge fully open to the sun, the hedges, therefore, must represent about 96 acres of extra woodland or semi-woodland flora.

Man interfered in another way, because though the road and lane hedges are pared every so often, it is the flora precisely of these hedges which is fullest and most varied. The flowers of the field hedges, away from the roads, are disappointingly monotonous, the plants, I think, having found it easier to spread up and down the roadways. Their seeds—if they depend on seeds—have been carried by the road-long currents of air, or on the muddy boots, and hooves, and iron-bound wheels of cart and waggon. On the whole, too, the flowering and other plants of the real wood and coppice, of which there are more than four hundred acres in the parish, are meagre by contrast, and that in spite of anemonies, bluebells, primroses, the small delicate cow wheat, *Melampyrum pratense*, and the male ferns, which in some places are as immense, almost, as tree ferns from New Zealand in a sub-tropical garden; in spite, too, of the dry, brown and green woodrush, *Luzula sylvatica*, which is exquisite on woodland floors and banks. It is an odd thing that the Lent-lily sticks only to the road hedges or lane hedges, and extends nowhere—in Pelynt—into the woods. Perhaps, in its few habitats, it has really gone wild from cultivation. Woods, all told, if they are less rich, are less frequented; and they are also more of a stable and closed habitat than the earthen hedges.

GEOFFREY GRIGSON, *Freedom of the Parish*

14. *Herbs on the Cliffs*

OF herbs and roots for the pot and medicine, Cornishmen enjoy a like portion in proportion with other shires, which somewhere also receiveth an increase by the sowing and planting of such as are brought thither from beyond the seas. The like may be said of roots and salads for the table, save that (I suppose) Cornwall naturally bringeth forth greater store of seaholme and samphire, than is found in any other county of this realm. The seaholme root preserved either in sirup, or by candying, is accepted for a great restorative. Some of the gally grounds do also yield plenty of rosa solis. More-over nature's liberal hand decketh many of the sea cliffs with wild hyssop, sage, pelamountain, marjorum, rosemary, and such like well-savouring herbs.

RICHARD CAREW, *Survey of Cornwall*

15. *A Garden after the War*

WE are not an old garden, as gardens go in this part of the country. In 1918 there were only trees, laurels and aucubas in the shrubbery. The layout of the pleasure grounds is an almost flat and a comparatively narrow strip a quarter of a mile long and about a hundred and forty yards in width from the terrace to the green walk where a fuchsia hedge and a grass path face south, catching all the sunshine. Between these two a couple of narrow paths, with one or two connecting branches, run parallel along the whole length of the shrubbery; they run from Farm Corner in the west, within sight of the Home Farm, to the beech grove that looks across deep valleys and quiet fields to the far side of the hidden Helford river. Thus there is more than a mile of pathways to be kept up. The trusty and careful agent had allowed these paths to be overgrown so as to keep out the Americans who were nervous about dripping foliage on account of their smart 'pink' trousers. Even the broad terrace was overgrown, great bays of laurel and rhododendron had straggled across it in many places and were now like blots on the cleanness of its beautiful straight line.

I tried not to think about these paths and the work that would be entailed in clearing them and I set out, bill-hook in hand, on a tour of inspection round the shrubs. Some were hidden, all were straggling away from the undergrowth or sidegrowth of laurel and weeds, several were dead.

A lonicera hedge, always a greedy feeder, had surrounded on three sides our best rhododendron Griersonianum; rose-bay willow-herb in the sunniest glade was threatening all our treasures there, the little *Corylopsis pauciflora* and the big andromeda, a young dendromecon and a middle-aged group of azaleas. In another glade a happy family of forsythias, choice rhododendrons, a lorelia, two bamboos and a *Prunus autumnalis* still survived among nettles five feet high, but nowhere could I see our precious Moyesii rose. I slashed the nettles to right and left, cutting my way in to the spot where I remembered her standing ten feet high. There she lay, pushed over by an intrusive ash sapling, a mere skeleton of dead roots and dry branches. Opposite the glade that is known as the Nine Ashes I perceived, like a signal of distress, one flash of scarlet in a tangle of rhododendron and fallen cryptomeria. I chopped my way towards it and there was a young *Rhododendron eriogynum* which I had forgotten, struggling for light and air. One prisoner at any rate was now free.

Then I went on to the sycamore glade and found that the Major had not failed me. In every open space of the shrubbery there were disfiguring circular trenches, reminder of army tents, but this glade was inviolate. In old days we could glance from one clean sycamore stem after another over a carpet of daffodils and later over groups of Solomon's seal and monkshood and the little foreign treasures, but now each sycamore was feathered with low leafage sprouting from the base. Half an hour with the bill-hook, a beautifully balanced little tool, did wonders here, and then I cut the ivy on each tree, pulling it back from the trunks, leaving exposed a circle of leaf-mouldy earth. Hope revived again. Surely any sturdy and rabbit-proof plants that had survived in the herbaceous border could be transplanted to the glade? I thought of a little woodland that I knew well in that loveliest of Devon gardens, Chevithorne Barton, and my mind went hastening on into the future of my garden and thought how fortunate it is that in the matter of planting there is no copyright and that among true gardeners every one is generous. I knew where I could get plants for my glade.

The worst tragedy was that our Greek temple, the beech grove, had lost its purity of outline; no longer could one see the sky behind each base and crest of those Doric pillars. Standing beside the house in the hollow and looking up the long grass slope towards the beeches, one saw scrubby undergrowth in front and scrubby undergrowth behind the trees. From that distance it seemed to be very small stuff, but when I came close I found such a tangle of escallonia, of ilex shooting from an old stump, of sycamore saplings and fuchsia as would afford many hours' work for the chopper. Well, this tangle was cleared, and cleared quickly, in the first few days and laid aside until such time as I could collect a few visitors for a bonfire party.

On the third day, when I stood on the lawn beside the house and could look once again at the sky between straight stems, I drew a long breath of satisfaction. How quickly trees respond to freedom and how beautiful are their lines when they rise clear of undergrowth. How quickly the ivy that one has cut begins to wither. The trees seemed to soar above anxiety, regret, despair. Gone were the days of pottering with slow and careful toil about one's midget alpines and one's little herbs; gone were the days when every shrub was given appointed space, congenial soil and due top-dressing and pruning in its season. Each one must struggle for existence nowadays.

But the trees stood there unchanged, offering their ancient beauty and shelter and companionship. There was no cause for sadness now. Dirt, decay, jungle growth, weeds, all these were trifles. I was at home again, ready to devote myself to the trees.

C. C. Vyvyan, *The Old Place*

16. Ludgvan Rectory Garden

I was exceptionally fortunate in having within reach so many of the great Cornish gardeners, all of whom were always willing to give their advice, and what was more, some of their rarities, to a young enthusiast. Every visit to the Rev. A. T. Boscawen's garden on top of that hill at Ludgvan was a fresh inspiration. I remember his telling me that he was thinking of giving up everything except New Zealand plants, but as in a corner of his garden he had hundreds of seedlings from one of Forrest's or Kingdon-Ward's Chinese expeditions I doubt if the resolution was kept. Celmisias were his particular passion at the moment, a passion with which he fired me; he grew them wonderfully at Ludgvan Rectory; I never succeeded, with all his advice, in making much of any celmisias except *coriacea*. On the other hand I was able to grow that other New Zealand daisy *Olearia insignis* to perfection; I even dreamed of crossing it with one of the shrubby Olearias in order to produce an eight-feet bush covered with those fat *insignis* daisies which remain as fresh as a daisy for nearly two months. I grew it at the foot of a wall where it could keep as dry as it liked.

In a field near Ludgvan Rectory I saw what I believe I can call the most perfect combination of land- and sea-scape I ever saw. It was a ten-acre field of that vivid green Cornish grass, surrounded on three sides by a belt of dark pines—*insignis* probably—underneath which was growing a line of that black-stemmed hydrangea with panicles of intensely blue flowers. Southward the view was open to Mount's Bay; between the dark pines and blue hydrangeas St Michael's Mount seemed to float on an azure sea beneath an azure sky. The sky, the sea, the narrow bosket of blue hydrangeas, the emerald grass, and the dark green of the pines created an unforgettable vision of severe yet immensely rich colour to which was added the supreme simplicity of design one finds in a Chinese picture. I wished that one of the St Ives painters would preserve the picture of that field but nobody who is not a painter ever succeeds in recommending a landscape or seascape to a painter; Julius Ohlsen, Arnesby Brown, Lamorna Birch and others less renowned listened patiently to my plea for that field, but none of them was inspired to take a look for himself and preserve on canvas those pines and hydrangeas and grass with the sea and the sky and that castellated islet beyond.

SIR COMPTON MACKENZIE, *My Life and Times*

17. *Acclimatising Plants*

Is it not astonishing that plants from such diverse countries, soils, climates and altitudes should settle down as neighbours here? Nowhere can one see the miracle of acclimatisation more strikingly displayed. Within the space of a few feet plants from Switzerland, Ecuador, South Africa, the Chinese Alps, Chile, Corsica and Siberia are all thriving in the writer's garden on a Cornish moor; and such a triumph of adjustment by plants is so common that we take it too much for granted. A century ago Sir Joseph Hooker brought to Kew seeds of rhododendrons from Sikkim; seedlings of these were tried in various woodland gardens, and experience showed that under cultivation here the visitors grew quite as well—even better, it is claimed—as their parents do in the fiercely competitive conditions of the Indian forest. A similar claim has been made for some New Zealand shrubs. Canon Boscawen, of Ludgvan Rectory in Cornwall, after forty years of growing New Zealand shrubs sent to him by his brother in that country, compared notes with that brother on his return to England; and the Canon concluded that some of the plants under his care here made a braver show than ever they did in the New Zealand bush. But one need not go to the mild counties to find such examples of acclimatisation. Fifty years ago our gardens had no purple buddleias; today these Chinese plants are not only at home in our gardens everywhere, but have become wildlings, self-sown on ruins and railway embankments. Certainly we have much cause to be thankful for the singular fortune that plants from such different homes can flourish together in this alien land.

W. Arnold-Forster, *Shrubs for the Milder Counties*

18. *Garden-stealing*

The soil and climate of Cornwall are very propitious to shrub propagation from seeds or cuttings. This encouraged stealing, which everyone did. The more unscrupulous employed agents, but this was considered not quite the thing. You were expected to do your own dirty work. Because of this the owners of the great houses could not very well go round at dead of night slipping into their neighbours' plantations. The danger of ridicule was too great. We had to wait for invitations or for the public fêtes which occurred once a year in all the gardens. It was more difficult to achieve a coup during a private invitation because your host knew exactly what you would be doing and seldom took his eyes off you. General routine was: chatting in the drawing-room or salon, tea, and then the great test and trial of ingenuity, the stroll through the grounds. This fulfilled a twofold purpose; it gave the host an opportunity to show off, and the guest, fingers twitching and eyes skinned, an opportunity to pluck a seed or break a slip. Every conversational gambit was employed to one end, either to lull into security or distract. Sometimes the host fell a victim to his own pride. Intoxicated by victory and a little deft flattery, he would allow his attention to relax. Then like lightning—snip. Conversation would suddenly lapse, there being no more pretences to keep up. Host would come abruptly to his senses and start eyeing guest, particularly pocket, from which hand is withdrawn carelessly. Host has a panicky inclination to demand that guest empties pockets there and then. This with difficulty he resists. Nevertheless something in guest's manner implies satisfaction—which it certainly ought not to—particularly after viewing the first-to-flower-in-England of one of Kingdon-Ward's Sikkim tree-rhododendrons. Unless—! They stroll back to the car. Guest drives away to his own mansion glowing with fulfilled ambition. He will shortly pop the cutting into the damp manure and leaf-mould already prepared for it.

Everyone in Cornwall gave a fête. It was a sort of public showing-off. Of course, the dangers of such an enterprise were tremendous, but they had to be faced if one was ever to bask in the jealousy of one's neighbours or make any impression on the populace. All the local gentlemen flocked to each other's fêtes, accompanied by a mob of hangers-on. They compared notes, criticised their arrangements and snaffled a few seeds or cuttings which they had their eyes on. The supporters of the home team were mobilised and all the rare plants heavily guarded. The visitors used to send out their chauffeurs, bailiffs and head gardeners as scouts and spies, while they themselves lounged around the stalls or the tea tent. Action was generally deferred until evening, by which time they had got the lie of the land and the defenders were tired. Sometimes the visitors would send off their cars to lull suspicion and pretend they had left. Then there would be swift descent along previously reconnoitred paths to the centre of action. The guards should already have left, drawn away by promises, invitations to a quick beer, or false alarms for reinforcements from other points. The visitor stands alone in the twilight, confronting his treasure. His men have done their work well. He stretches out his hand. 'Excuse me, sir,' says a voice, 'but Mr. Bolitho (or Sir Courtenay, or Mrs. Clowance, or His Lordship) is very particular about not plucking the flowers. I'm very sorry, sir, but I'm sure you understand.'

'Oh, quite. Perfectly. Very reasonable. Silly of me.' Half a crown passes hands and the unlucky party marches off, concealing his chagrin as best he can.

FRANK BAINES, *Look Towards the Sea*

19. Planning and Planting

In very many places, especially near the sea, more planting would be desirable. But in recognising this we should also recognise that there are some places, treeless now, whose 'amenity value' would not be enhanced but injured by planting, however well done. In our small, much-domesticated islands some of the treeless wild places have a special value for at least a part of the community—a value largely dependent on their remaining treeless and wild. If you have visited those Cornish headlands where you can look westwards 'from the shore that hath no shore beyond it set in all the sea,' you will have done so, probably, in cheerful expectation that the winds you will face will be fresh off the Atlantic, winds untempered as yet by trees or hills; and when there you will not regret but enjoy the characteristic absence of growths taller than thrift and wind-nibbled gorse. The austere quality that makes these exceptional places precious should not lightly be destroyed or changed by planting. If their afforestation were proposed, it should not be permitted unless an impartial weighing of economic needs against the other values involved had shown compelling reasons why such sacrifice must be tolerated.

So much for the exceptional places where planting would be definitely *injurious* to amenities. Now, are there many places along our seaboard where more planting would be definitely *advantageous*? Surely the number of such places is great. In particular, many of our seaside towns and villages would be enormously improved in appearance, in comfort, and in economic value, if they were more amply furnished with trees and shrubs. I think, for example, of a Cornish seaside village. The old part of that village, huddled down by the cove, is pleasant and full of character; but the new part consists of white boxes spattered all over the place without coherent plan; and the whole place is far less attractive than it might be if it were better planned and better planted. Not a tree or shrub to give the white boxes screen or shelter. Good planting is specially called for in such a place; for this village, with its brilliant sands and almost frost-free climate, is likely to attract more visitors and more permanent residents in future.

That is but one example out of very many that might be given. A headland may have a beauty that is close-cropped; but few towns can afford to look positively bald, and little of our seaside architecture can well afford to dispense altogether with the softening shape and colour of trees or shrubs. Towns which live largely by attracting visitors should be at special pains, for economic reasons if for no others, to ensure that their seaward side does not become an unrelieved grey mass of cement and stone.

W. Arnold-Forster, *Shrubs for the Milder Counties*

IX. Customs and Beliefs

1. The Miracle Plays

THE guary miracle, in English, a miracle-play, is a kind of interlude, compiled in Cornish out of some scripture history, with that
grossness, which accompanied the Romans 'vetus comedia.' For
representing it, they raise an earthen amphitheatre in some open
field, having the diameter of his inclosed plain some forty or fifty
foot. The country people flock from all sides, many miles off, to
hear and see it; for they have therein devils and devices to delight as
well the eye as the ear: the players con not their parts without book,
but are prompted by one called the ordinary, who followeth at their
back with the book in his hand, and telleth them softly what they
must pronounce aloud. Which manner once gave occasion to a
pleasant conceited gentleman of practising a merry prank; for he
undertaking (perhaps of set purpose) an actor's room, was accordingly lessoned (before-hand) by the ordinary, that he must say after
him. His turn came: quoth the ordinary, 'Go forth, man, and shew
thyself.' The gentleman steps out upon the stage, and like a bad
clerk in scripture matters, cleaving more to the letter than the sense,
pronounced those words aloud. 'Oh (says the fellow softly in his
ear) you mar all the play.' And with this his passion, the actor
makes the audience in like sort acquainted. Hereon the prompter
falls to flat railing and cursing in the bitterest terms he could
devise; which the gentleman with a set gesture and countenance
still soberly related, until the ordinary, driven at last into mad rage,
was fain to give over all: which trousse, though it break off the

interlude, yet defrauded not the beholders, but dismissed them with a great deal more sport and laughter, than twenty such guaries could have afforded.

RICHARD CAREW, *Survey of Cornwall*

2. *A Conjurer Reproved*

I hope the rumours of your pretending to conjuration are not true, and I have so much charity as to believe that you have not been medling in the dangerous mysteries of a lower world, but rather, like a good Christian, defy and refuse all intercourse with the devil. Yet since there are such rumours, and you are said to take upon you to discover lost and stolen goods, I hope you will think that to retrieve and vindicate your character it will be necessary for you to use abundant caution that you give no encouragement to silly women to come to you on such foolish and wicked errants; and particularly I am obliged to desire that no such encouragements may be given to those persons who are the flock, and must be the care, of your most humble servant, William Borlase.

DR. BORLASE, in P. A. S. Pool, 'William Borlase', in
Journal of the Royal Institution of Cornwall (1966)

3. *The Piskies*

AFTER some discourse Betty Martin began to talk about the pisgies (*sic*). She said that at St. Ive there was a house in the hollow of a hill, and that near it was a large hollow tree and that the pisgies were in the habit of dancing round it. That one night the women

260

of the house, getting out of bed and looking out of the window, heard the pisgies dancing violently with much laughter, and that the next morning there was a circle of a peculiar colour on the grass around the tree. That the pisgies were very fond of riding the cattle at night, and that frequently they were heard 'coursing' them violently round the fields, and the next morning the horses would be found all in a sweat, their mane here and there twisted into stirrups for the pisgies to mount by.—I gave the child sixpence and went away.

January 31. Looe Down.—I asked Mr. Henry Borrow if he believed in Pisgies. Mr. Taylor interposed by saying that he himself did not believe in them. Mr. Henry confessed that he scarcely knew what to say about the pisgies; he had never seen them, but he supposed there might be such things, as he had himself heard the 'durdy dogs'. When a boy he was sent to Liskeard one evening for salt and other articles; as he was riding back to Tredinnock at night, passing by Treworgy he heard over his head in the air the most beautiful cry of hounds that he had ever heard in his life. It was the cry of the 'durdy dogs'.

W. I. KNAPP, *George Borrow*

4. By Talland Church as I Did Go

By Talland Church as I did go,
I passed my kindred all in a row;

Straight and silent there by the spade
Each in his narrow chamber laid.

While I passed, each kinsman's clay
Stole some virtue of mine away:

Till my shoes on the muddy road
Left not a print, so light they trod.

Back I went to the Bearers' Lane,
Begged the dead for my own again.

Answered the eldest one of my line—
'Thy heart was no one's heart but mine'.

The second claimed my working skill,
The third my wit, the fourth my will:

The fifth one said, 'Thy feet I gave;
But want no fleetness here in the grave'.

'For feet a man need have no care,
If they no weight of his own may bear.

'If I own naught by separate birth,
What binds my heel e'en now to the earth?'

The dead together answered back—
'Naught but the wealth in thy knapsack'.

'Nay, then,' said I, 'that's quick to unload':
And strewed my few pence out on the road.

'O kinsmen, now be quick, resume
Each rag of me to its rightful tomb!'

The dead were silent then for a space.
Still I stood upright in my place.

Said one, 'Some strength he will yet conceal.
Belike 'tis pride of a planted heel?

'Man has but one perduring pride:
Of knowledge alone he is justified.

'Lie down, lie down by us in the sod:
Thou shalt be wise in the ways of God'.

'Nay, so I stand upright in the dust,
I'll take God's purposes all on trust.

'An inch of heel for a yard of spine,—
So give me again the goods that are mine!'

I planted my heel by their headstones,
And wrestled an hour with my kinsmen's bones.

I shook their dust thrice into a sieve,
And gathered all that they had to give.

I winnowed knowledge out of the heap:
'Take it,' I said, 'to warm your sleep'.

I cast their knowledge back on the sod,
And went on my journey, praising God.

Of all their knowledge I thought me rid:
But one little grain in my pack had hid.—

Now, as I go, myself I tell,
'On a planted heel man wrestles well'.

But that little grain keeps whispering me—
'Better, perhaps, on a planted knee'.

Q, *Poems*

5. The Mayor of Halgaver

THE youthlier sort of Bodmin townsmen use sometimes to sport themselves, by playing the box with strangers, whom they summon to Halgaver. The name signifieth the Goat's Moor, and such a place it is, lying a little without the town, and very full of quagmires. When these mates meet with any raw servingman, or other young master, who may serve and deserve to make pastime, they cause him to be solemnly arrested, for his appearance before the mayor of Halgaver, where he is charged with wearing one spur, or going untrussed, or wanting a girdle, or some such like felony: and after he hath been arraigned and tried, with all requisite circumstances, judgment is given in formal terms, and executed in some ungracious prank or other, more to the scorn than hurt of the party condemned.

Hence is sprung the proverb, when we see one slovenly apparelled, to say, 'He shall be presented in Halgaver court.'

But now and then they extend this merriment with the largest, to the prejudice of over-credulous people, persuading them to fight with a dragon lurking in Halgaver, or to see some strange matter there; which concludeth at least with a training them into the mire.

RICHARD CAREW, *Survey of Cornwall*

6. Hurling and Wrestling

THE game called the Hurlers is a thing the Cornish men value themselves much upon. I confess I see nothing in it, but that it is a rude violent play among the boors or country people; brutish and furious, and a sort of an evidence that they were once a kind of barbarians. It seems to me something to resemble the old way of play, as it was then called, with Whirle-Bats, with which Hercules slew the giant, when he undertook to clean the Augean stable.

The wrestling in Cornwall is, indeed, a much more manly and generous exercise, and that closure, which they call the Cornish hug has made them eminent in the wrestling rings all over England, as the Norfolk and Suffolk men are for their dexterity at the hand and foot, and throwing up the heels of their adversary without taking hold of him.

DANIEL DEFOE, *A Tour Through Great Britain*

7. *Padstow Hobby-Horse*

ST. PETROC may be neglected in Padstow today. But the Hobby-horse is not. Whether it came in with the Danes who sacked the town in 981 and drove St. Petroc's monks to Bodmin or whether it was a pagan rite which St. Petroc himself may have witnessed with displeasure, I leave to antiquarians to dispute. The Padstow Hobby-horse is a folk revival which is almost certainly of pagan origin. Moreover, it is as genuine and unselfconscious as the Morris Dancing at Bampton-in-the-Bush, Oxfordshire, and not even broadcasting it or an influx of tourists will take the strange and secret character from the ceremonies connected with it. For this is what happens. On the day before May Day, green boughs are put up against the houses. And that night every man and woman in Padstow is awake with excitement. I knew someone who was next to a Padstow man in the trenches in the 1914 war. On the night before May Day, the Padstow man became so excited he couldn't keep still. The old 'obby 'oss was mounting in his blood and his mates had to hold him back from jumping over the top and dancing about in No-man's-land.

Now imagine a still night, the last of April, the first of May. Starlight above the chimney pots. Moon on the harbour. Moonlight shadows of houses on opposite slate walls. At about two in the morning the song begins. Here are the words.

> *With a merry ring and with the joyful spring,*
>> *For summer is a-come unto day*
> *How happy are those little birds which so merrily do sing*
>> *In the merry morning of May.*

Then the men go round to the big houses of the town singing below the windows a variety of verses—

> *'Arise up Mr. Brabyn I know you well afine*
> *You have a shilling in your purse and I wish it were in mine.'*

And then on to a house where a young girl lives—

> *'Arise up Miss Lobb all in your smock of silk*
> *And all your body under as white as any milk.'*

Morning light shines on the water and the green-grey houses. Out on the quay comes the Hobby-horse—it used to be taken for a drink to a pool a mile away from the town. It is a man in a weird mask, painted red and black and white, and he wears a huge hooped skirt made of black tarpaulin which he is meant to lift up, rushing at the ladies to put it over one of their heads. The skirt used to have soot in it. A man dances with the Hobby-horse carrying a club. Suddenly, at about 11.30 in the morning, there is a pause. The Hobby-horse bows down to the ground. The attendant lays his club on its head and the day song begins, a dirge-like strain.

> *'Oh where is St. George? Oh, where is he, O?*
> *He's down in his long boat. All on the salt sea, O.'*

Then up jumps the Hobby-horse, loud shriek the girls, louder sings the crowd and wilder grows the dance—

> *With a merry ring and with the joyful spring*
>> *For summer is a-come unto day*
> *How happy are those little birds which so merrily do sing*
>> *In the merry morning of May.*

JOHN BETJEMAN, *First and Last Loves*

8. St. Nunn's Well

IN our forefathers' day, when devotion as much exceeded knowledge, as knowledge now cometh short of devotion, there were many bowsening places for curing mad men, and amongst the rest, one at Alternunne, in this hundred, called S. Nunn's Pool, which saint's altar (it may be) by 'pars pro toto', gave name to the church. And because the manor of this bowsening is not so unpleasing to hear, as it is uneasy to feel, I will (if you please) deliver you the practice, as I received it from the beholders.

The water running from S. Nunn's well fell into a square and close walled plot, which might be filled at what depth they listed. Upon this wall was the frantic person set to stand, his back toward the pool, and from thence, with a sudden blow in the breast, tumbled headlong into the pond; where a strong fellow, provided for the nonce, took him, and tossed him up and down, alongst and athwart the water, until the patient, by foregoing his strength, had somewhat forgot his fury. Then was he conveyed to the church, and certain masses sung over him; upon which handling, if his right wits returned, S. Nunn had the thanks; but if there appeared small amendment, he was bowsened again and again, while there remained in him any hope of life, for recovery.

It may be, this device took original from that master of Bedlam, who (the fable saith) used to cure his patients of that patience, by keeping them bound in pools, up to the middle, and so more or less, after the fit of their fury.

RICHARD CAREW, *Survey of Cornwall*

9. An Image at Launceston

THERE is a fine image, or figure of Mary Magdalen, upon the tower of the church, which the Catholics fail not to pay their reverence to, as they pass by.

DANIEL DEFOE, *A Tour Through England*

10. *The Red Lion at Truro*

To Hon. C. B. Agar—20th April 1805

The Red Lyon Inn in Truro is undoubtedly the best Inn there—but as the Innkeeper (whose name is Blight) behaved extremely improper towards my Mistress's interest respecting the late law-suit betwixt her and Lord de Dunstanville I have never been at his house since. The King's Head Inn is a tolerable good house and is patronised by Sir William Lemon and many other respectable characters.

WILLIAM JENKIN, in A. K. H. JENKIN, *News From Cornwall*

11. *The Bodmin Riding*

THE festival called Bodmin Riding, of which the remembrance lingers only among people past middle age, and which is never likely to be revived, was kept on Sunday and Monday after S. Thomas Becket's day, July 7. A puncheon of beer having been brewed in the previous October, and duly bottled in anticipation of the time, two or more young men who were entrusted with the chief management of the affair, and who represented the 'wardens', went round the town attended by a band of drums and fifes or other instruments. The Crier saluted each house with: 'To the people of this house a prosperous morning, long life, health, and a merry riding!' The musicians then struck up the Riding tune, a quick and inspiriting measure, said by some to be old as the Feast itself. The householder was solicited to taste the Riding ale, which was carried round in baskets. A bottle was usually taken in, and it was acknowledged by such a sum as the means or humour of the towns-man permitted, to be spent on the public festivities of the season. Next morning a procession was formed, all who could afford to ride mounted on horse or ass, which proceeded first to the Priory, to

268

receive two large garlands of flowers fixed on staves, and then in due order through the principal streets to the Town-end, where the games were formally opened. The sports, which lasted two days, were of the ordinary sort; wrestling, foot-racing, jumping in sacks, etc. It should be remarked that a second or inferior brewing, from the same wort, was drunk at a minor merry-making at Whitsuntide.

J. POLSUE, *Parochial History of Cornwall*

12. The Diversions of Mount's Bay

I have had the pleasure of seeing some of the most considerable places in England, and I think there is hardly any place where I could so willingly wish that my lot had fallen as where it has. There is no part of England that abounds so much in the necessaries and at the same time has so many of the elegancies of life as that of Mount's Bay. The gentry, most of whom are our near relations, are of a free frolicking disposition. In the Summer time we meet (some ten or a dozen) at a Bowling Green, there we have built a little pleasure house and there we dine, after dinner at bowls, and by so frequently meeting together we are as it were like so many brothers of one family, so united, and so glad to see one the other.[1] For my particular part since I have had the good fortune of a settlement it has required all my care and attention to gett my habitation, which was a most ruinous one when I came to it, in some tolerable order. I have now I thank God made it somewhat comfortable and easy and to my great satisfaction not only made the house tenantable, but from a wilderness or rather brake of briars and thorns have shap't out a little garden, where I may have plenty one time or other, and where I have at present some pretty airy walks, thriving

[1] This was the famous Marazion Bowling Club for which William Gwavas composed a Cornish rhyme. Borlase remained a member until 1750, when he resigned on health grounds.

plantations, and clear running water; neither is my water barren cold or uninhabited, but there are little fish in store which leap and play together in a little pond I have, and supply me with a little dish of excellent shots upon any emergent occasion. In my garden I spend most of my time without doors, having not the good fortune to delight much in hunting or in shooting, diversions which I am however far from finding fault with in others and for which our country is abundantly well provided.

DR. BORLASE, in P. A. S. Pool, 'William Borlase', in
Journal of the Royal Institution of Cornwall (1966)

13. *A Duel*

MAY 10, 1811.—Lane of Cornwall called. He told me the duel which was fought last summer between Lord de Dunstanville and Sir Christopher Hawkins arose as follows,—Lord de Dunstanville was the principal interest in two boroughs, viz. Bodmin and Penryn; near the latter place he has large estates. At the last election for members of Parliament Sir Christopher Hawkins obtained a return of one member for Penryn, but it was afterwards proved to have been effected by bribery. One of the bribed voters swore that 24 guineas was paid to each of many voters. This caused the election of Sir Christopher's Member to be set aside, and Lord de Dunstanville obtained the return of a member in his room. Sir Christopher had long acted towards His Lordship in a manner the contrary of friendly behaviour.

At a public meeting on some occasion an assertion which had been made by Sir Christopher was directly contradicted by His Lordship. This was told to Sir Christopher. On coming home from the Opera one evening His Lordship found a letter from Sir Christopher requiring him to explain his conduct in having contradicted what Sir Christopher had asserted. Lord de Dunstanville wrote an answer declaring he would give no explanation, and added that Sir Christopher might do whatever his mind dictated. A few days afterwards Lord D. received a challenge from Sir Christopher. Lord D. got Admiral Sir Edwd. Buller to be his second, and Mr. Davies Giddy also knew his situation. Sir Christopher had a military officer for his second.

On the morning appointed for the meeting Lord D. rose at six o'clock, which surprised Lady D. who said to him that there must be something very particular to cause his rising so early.—Lord D. went to a place appointed and found Sir Edward Buller, and with him, in a chaise, proceed[ed] to meet Sir Christopher. Two shots were fired by each. The first ball fired by Sir Christopher touched the hair of Lord de Dunstanville. After the two shots had been fired the seconds interfered, and would not allow the matter to go any farther.—The morning before that on which the duel was fought, Lane called upon Lord D., but did not see him. His Lordship afterwards told him that he was then employed in adding codicils to his will and in settling his affairs.

JOSEPH FARINGTON, *The Farington Diary*

Belief

Cross a stile and a gate hard by,
And you'll be a widow before you die.

14. *Culver-houses*

IN many old Cornish farm-yards holes were made for pigeons in the thickness of walls. There was a fine array of such pigeon-holes to be seen at Mewdon, near Mawnan, until the recent alterations there. At Penwarne, in the same parish, the ghosts were so numerous and troublesome in the eighteenth century that Parson Jago, of

Wendron, and those of the neighbouring clergy noted as ghost-layers were called in to exorcise them. They hit upon the happy expedient of driving them with whips into pigeon-holes and sealing them up there under a spell. Whether the ghosts were released when the old houses were pulled down many years ago has not been recorded.

In many places, where all traces of the pigeon-house have gone, the field-name of 'Culver-House Park' recalls them. At St. Cadix (or St. Carroc's), the site of a small priory, in St. Veep, is a field so called. Close by at Cliff in Manelly was a 'Columbarium' which William FitzWalter granted to Henry Score in 1373, as appears from a deed in my possession. In the vicinity, at Dorset in Lanteglos, is another 'Culver-House Park', and at Fowey across the river was yet another, in 1602 belonging to the Treffry family. The Canons of St. Germans Priory had their 'Culver-House' at St. Winnols or Eglaroose on the high lands two miles away from their house. There was a 'Columbarium' at Kernick in St. Stephens-in-Branel in 1342, and a map of 1696 shows a 'Culver-House' at Treloggas in Kea, in the orchard at the creek-head.

Fields called 'Culver-House Meadow' are named at Portlooe in Talland, Kestle in Egloshayle, Roscarrock in Endellion, Trenance in St. Columb Minor, and Tregrylls in Lesnewth. More common still are such field-names as 'Culver Park', 'Culver Hay', 'Culver Well', and 'Culver Hill'. In some instances (though not all) these are shortened forms of 'Culver-House'. 'Columbaria' are frequently mentioned as appendages of Cornish manors in conveyances and other documents. From this fact and from the field-names already mentioned it is clear that pigeon-houses were once as common in Cornwall as in other parts of England.

Those few that remain, in whole or in part, are nearly all the same type and of about the same dimensions. The best preserved are those at Bussow, Crafthole, Halwyn, Nanswhyden, Trevannion, and Tintagel.

CHARLES HENDERSON, *Essays in Cornish History*

Cradles

Rock the cradle empty,
You'll rock the babies plenty.

15. Bells

MR. DUNKIN in 1872 found about fifty pre-Reformation bells in Cornwall. Most of our church towers were built or rebuilt in the fifteenth century, to hold three bells only, and in a very few cases the original trio of fifteenth-century bells remains. This is the case at St. Michael Carhays, Landewednack, and Gunwalloe, remote little sanctuaries on the southern coast. Gunwalloe has a detached 'campanile' on the edge of the cliff. When the Commissioners visited it in 1551 they noted the 'iij Bellys', which are there to-day, all bearing medieval symbols and jingling inscriptions, dear to the bell-founders of all ages, such as:

> Voce mea viva, Depello cuncta nociva
> With my living voice, I ward off what annoys

and
> Eternis Annis, resonet campana Johannis
> Let the Bell of (St.) John, for ever ring on

and
> Plebs omnis plaudit ut me tam sepius audit
> All people cheer, when they me hear.

Not far off, the venerable tower of Landewednack, near the Lizard, houses its original trio of fifteenth-century bells called after St. Anne, St. Mary Magdalene, and St. Nicholas. The Gothic lettering of the inscriptions is well executed, each word on a separate block in relief. The founders' emblems appear on shields. These emblems and verses are, of course, common all over southern England. At St. Anthony-in-Meneage, also in the Lizard district, one medieval bell with an invocation to Our Lady lay shattered on the tower floor for many years. It has recently been recast and now sings with its two old brethren (recast in 1674 by John Lakes) and some younger companions. At St. Just-in-Penwith two medieval bells survive, one with an invocation to St. Michael, the patron of Cornwall, the other with an inscription to the Virgin Mary.

Protege Virgo Pia; Quos Convoco Sancta Maria
St. Mary Holy Virgin! guard them all, whom I to church do call.

An alleged translation of this couplet, 'Pray for the Virgin Mary', appears from the pen of a clergyman in the reports of a learned society of the middle of the last century. Such a translation reveals a surprising ignorance of the popular estimation of the Blessed Virgin's status in medieval England.

At Lanhydrock is a very curious bell with a reversed inscription difficult to decipher, but apparently a prayer for the soul of Athelstan. This has evidently been reproduced from a much older bell. King Athelstan was (in the Middle Ages) regarded as the founder of Bodmin Priory, to which Lanhydrock then belonged. The King's effigy still appears on the seal of the borough. At Kilkhampton the sixteenth-century font of granite has inverted initials in relief round the rim which look as if they were reproduced from the marks on a bell, by way of record. On the whole, however, when bells were recast in the seventeenth and eighteenth centuries no care was taken to reproduce older inscriptions. A great deal of ringing was done by our Stuart and Georgian ancestors for whose benefit quaint 'Ringers' Rules' in rhyming verse painted on boards were set up in many towers. A good many of these remain, but in most cases the verses are the same.

The accounts of churchwardens in the seventeenth and eighteenth centuries show that a great deal of public money was expended annually on the bells. The ringers were given money, beer, and candlelight by the parish on November 5th, Christmas Eve, and other festivals. Occasions of public rejoicing, battles won, and royal birthdays were also celebrated by ringing. It is to be feared that the old bells received much rough treatment on these occasions. In one parish the blacksmith and his friends are reputed to have cracked all the bells by pounding them with sledge-hammers at weddings when the decayed state of the cages made it impossible to ring them properly.

In the eighteenth century the two great families of bell-founders who had the recasting of more than half the bells of Cornwall between them were the Rudhalls, of Gloucester, and the Penningtons, of Bodmin and Lezant. Their marks and inscriptions do not equal those of the medieval founders in beauty or interest. One of the Rudhalls was appropriately christened 'Abell', and used the symbol of 'a bell' for his 'rebus'. Their couplets and rhyming tags generally bless the King or wish prosperity to the Church of England. The initials of the churchwardens appear in addition to those of the founder. A bell at St. Just which was cast in 1741 bears the name of Admiral Vernon, 'Old Grog', who happened to be the hero of the hour and was therefore made an honorary churchwarden of a parish in which he had never set foot!

CHARLES HENDERSON, Essays in Cornish History

16. The Ringers of Lancells' Tower

THESE ancient men rang at the accession of George the Third and all again at his jubilee. Three of them lived on to ring in George the Fourth; and two survived to celebrate, in their native tower, the coronation of King William the Fourth.

> They meet once more! that ancient band,
> With furrow'd cheek and failing hand;
> One peal today they fain would ring,
> The jubilee of England's king!
>
> They meet once more! but where are now
> The sinewy arm, the laughing brow,
> The strength that hailed, in happier times,
> King George the Third with lusty chimes?

Yet proudly gaze on that lone tower,
No goodlier sight hath hall or bower;
Meekly they strive—and closing day
Gilds with soft light their locks of grey.

Hark! proudly hark! with that true tone
They welcomed him to land and throne;
So ere they die they fain would ring
The jubilee of England's king.

Hearts of old Cornwall, fare ye well!
Fast fade such scenes from field and dell;
How wilt thou lack, my own dear land,
Those trusty arms, that faithful band!

R. S. HAWKER, *Cornish Ballads*

17. *'Shoring'*

ONE can hardly mention the Bishop and his Clerks, as they are call'd, or the rocks of Scilly, without letting fall a tear to the memory of Sir Cloudesly Shovel, and all the gallant spirits that were with him at one blow, and without a moments warning dash'd into a state of immortality; the admiral with three men of war, and all their men (running upon these rocks, right afore the wind, and in a dark night) being lost there, and not a man sav'd. But all our annals and histories are full of this, so I need say no more. . . .

This may be the reason why, as we observed during our short stay here, several mornings after, it had blown something hard in the night, the sands were cover'd with country people running to and fro' to see if the sea had cast up anything of value. This the seamen call 'going a shoring'; and it seems they do often find good purchase: Sometimes also dead bodies are cast up here, the consequence of shipwrecks among those fatal rocks and islands; as also broken pieces of ships, casks, chests, and almost everything that will float, or roll on shore by the surges of the sea.

DANIEL DEFOE, *A Tour Through England*

18. *Fare*

THE squab pye, the herb pye, the leek and pork pye, on which clouted cream was poured profusely, the goose and parsnip and the fish and apple pye were frequent in Meneague. And pilchards, herrings and potatoes, and barley bread baked under the kettle, were the chief sustenance of the poor.

RICHARD POLWHELE, *Traditions and Recollections*

19. *Parish Feasts*

On the Sunday after the last Thursday in April
　　　　　Lanivet men fare well;
On the Sunday after the first Tuesday in May
　　　　　Lanlivery men fare as well as they.

20. *Lord, When the Wise Men Came from Far*

Lord, when the wise men came from far
Led to thy cradle by a star,
Then did the shepherds too rejoice,
Instructed by thy angel's voice,
Blest were the wise men in their skill,
And shepherds in their harmless will.

Wise men in tracing Nature's laws
Ascend unto the highest cause,
Shepherds with humble fearfulness
Walk safely, though their light be less,
Though wise men better know the way
It seems no honest heart can stray:

There is no merit in the wise
But love, the shepherds' sacrifice,
Wise men all ways of knowledge past,
To the shepherds' wonder come at last,
To know, can only wonder breed,
And not to know, is wonder's seed.

A wise man at the altar bows
And offers up his studied vows
And is received, may not the tears,
Which spring too from a shepherd's fears,
And sighs upon his frailty spent,
Though not distinct, be eloquent.

'Tis true, the object sanctifies
All passions which within us rise,
But since no creature comprehends
The cause of causes, end of ends,
He who himself vouchsafes to know
Best pleases his creator so.

When then our sorrows we apply
To our own wants and poverty,
When we look up in all distress
And our own misery confess,
Sending both thanks and prayers above,
Then though we do not know, we love.

SIDNEY GODOLPHIN

21. Christ at the Cheesewring

As I walked on the wicked moor
Where seven smashed stones lie
I met a man with a skin of tan
And an emerald in his eye.

All naked was his burning back
And naked was his thigh,
His only cloak it was the smoke
Out of the failing sky.

O loudly did he nail my name
Upon the mine-stacks three
And louder rose the ragged crows
That sail above the sea.

> *O will you drink my body deep*
> *And wash my five wounds dry*
> *That shot with snow now gravely grow*
> *As scarlet as the sky?*

> *All down, he said, the drowning day*
> *And down the damaged sky*
> *God's naked son his fingers won*
> *About my thieving eye,*

> *And like a bough about my brow*
> *Planted a hand of horn*
> *That men may see mirrored in me*
> *The image of the thorn.*

I see no badge upon your brow
I drink no five wounds dry
I see no thief wrecked on the reef
Where seven smashed stones lie.

Above the stone, above the sun,
Above the swinging sky
The King of Heaven the days seven
Is hanging out to die!

Softly he touched my turning head
And softly touched my side
And blessed with bread the waters red
That on the sea-bay slide.

I saw him climb the canvas sun
The strapped world to untie,
On its sharp strand with splintered hand
The flags of heaven fly.

I scattered in a sand of stars
His hand, his lip, his thigh,
I plucked the thorn that he had worn
Above his beating eye.

And on the land where seven stones stand
He stretched his hand to me
And on my brow of staring snow
Printed a gallows-tree.

CHARLES CAUSLEY, *Johnny Alleluia*

X. Victoriana

1. *Thackeray Enjoys Himself at Looe*

THURSDAY June 21, 1832. When we crossed the water to Tor point & set off to Liskeard by the mail here our first act was a blunder we went to the wrong inn—this however was soon remedied, our trunks were withdrawn & ourselves breakfasted at Mr. Lynes the Atty's—a shrewd sensible snob of a fellow with whom we afterwards dined —but the journey had so knocked me up that I had but a weary day of it—my face burning with the sun & the wind. Most of the day was occupied in composing an address for Charles Buller, the one he sent down being considered very unsatisfactory—Arthur's was fixed upon it was good but too wordy. Then we went to see two more attornies to con over the address & to drink tea. The address was finally delivered into the hands of the Printer; & at about half past 10 we set off in a pouring rain for Polvellan where we arrived at 12 & went gladly to bed—

Friday, June 22. Woke & forgot all my travelling troubles after a long sweet sleep. & found myself in a very charming house, in a pretty room & with a pleasant family—the servants all mistook me for Charles Buller this created a sentiment in my favour & I was very kindly received by Mr. & Mrs. Buller. The day was passed pleasantly enough with a walk & a lunch & a ride & a dinner & a long talk afterwards about subjects of wh. none of the talkers knew anything—I find here Sir John Lewis & two Miss Bullers, at dinner was a gentleman remarkable for nothing but his name—Capt. Toop Nicholas. The house is very pleasant, the master of it most kind hearted & honest & the mistress a very charming woman, an ancient flame of my fathers—We rode to Morval, Mr. Bullers,[1] & saw a nice plain Elizabethan house, & some noble woods the country in the immediate neighbourhood is very bold & fertile— & Polvellan itself as sweet a little snuggery as ever I saw.

Thursday 28. A pleasant week passed in idleness—dined on Tuesday at Morval, a fine house & an excellent Master. on Wednesday rode with A. Buller for 12 hours canvassing & found much more intelligence and good feeling among the farmers than I had expected. There seems a class of farmers here unknown to our part of Devonshire—men with a tolerable education though not of a large property, like the Scotch farmers—

Mr. Buller's house & park at Morval are very gentlemanly & English, & he himself as he sits at his table surrounded by his family portraits a fine specimen of a breed almost gone out now— The country about here is very charming—well wooded & hilly— The house where I am staying very pretty & all the present inmates very agreeable—in fact I have spent a most pleasant week with little reason to regret having left the Temple so suddenly.

Letters of Thackeray, ed. Gordon R. Ray

2. John Sterling at Falmouth

At Falmouth, as usual, he was soon at home in his new environment; resumed his labours; had his new small circle of acquaintance, the ready and constant centre of which was the Fox family, with whom he lived on an altogether intimate, honoured and beloved footing; realising his best anticipations in that respect, which doubt-

[1] John Buller (1771–1849) of Morval, the uncle of Thackeray's friends, a wealthy country gentleman who owned the Cornish seat of West Looe for which Charles Buller had been sitting since 1830. The Miss Bullers were no doubt his daughters.

less were among his first inducements to settle in this new place. Open cheery heights, rather bare of wood; fresh south-western breezes; a brisk laughing sea, swept by industrious sails, and the nets of a most stalwart, wholesome, frank and interesting population: the clean little fishing, trading and packet Town; hanging on its slope towards the Eastern sun, close on the waters of its basin and intricate bay,—with the miniature Pendennis Castle seaward on the right, the miniature St. Mawes landward to left, and the mining world and the farming world open boundlessly to the rear:—all this made a pleasant outlook and environment. And in all this, as in the other new elements of his position, Sterling, open beyond most men to the worth of things about him, took his frank share. From the first, he had liked the general aspect of the population, and their healthy, lively ways; not to speak of the special friendships he had formed there, which shed a charm over them all. 'Men of strong character, clear heads and genuine goodness,' writes he, 'are by no means wanting.' And long after: 'The common people here dress better than in most parts of England; and on Sundays, if the weather be at all fine, their appearance is very pleasant. One sees them all round the Town, especially towards Pendennis Castle, streaming in a succession of little groups, and seeming for the most part really and quietly happy.' On the whole he reckoned himself lucky; and, so far as locality went, found this a handsome shelter for the next two years of his life.

THOMAS CARLYLE, *John Sterling*

3. *Godrevy*

THURSDAY, 21 July, 1870.

Breakfast 6.45. Mrs. Hockin drove us in the pony carriage to Perranwell Station in time for the 7.35 train to Hayle. The journey lay through a great mining district chiefly tin. 'Thou art Lord of the world-bright tin' (Miners' Song). The bowels of the earth ripped open, turned inside out in the search for metal ore, the land defiled and cumbered with heaps and wastes of slag and rubbish, and the waters poisoned with tin and copper washings. The Cornish villages bare bleak barren and ugly, whitewashed and often unsheltered by a single tree, grouped or scattered about mountainous wastes.

About Godrevy and all along the North coast there are a great many seals. Once at Godrevy the Hockins saw a fearful battle between a seal and a large conger eel. The seal had got his teeth into the conger and the conger had coiled his folds round the seal's neck and was trying to choke him. The seal kept on throwing up his head and trying to toss the conger up out of the water that he might have more power than the eel. It was a fierce and dreadful fight, but at last the seal killed the conger.

The Vicar of St. Ives says the smell of fish there is sometimes so terrific as to stop the church clock.

We did not know it at the time but while we were enjoying ourselves on the beach a poor miner who had gone out to bathe in his dinner hour was drowning in the bay very near us.

The sea fog came rolling up from the Atlantic in a dense purple bank, and the sea changed colour to a deep dark green.

FRANCIS KILVERT, *Diary*

4. *Shopping in Truro*

(WEDNESDAY, 20 July, 1870)

At ten we went to Truro in the pony carriage, Mrs. Hockin driving. A pretty road with long hills and fine views back over the country and mining districts from the crests of the hills. Market day at Truro, and the road lively with market folk. The Cornish people seem fine tall folk, especially the women, much taller, larger people than the Welsh, and most of them appear to be dark-haired.

The hedges along these fine broad roads are brilliant with purple heather growing in bushes, taller and finer than ours in Wales. It seems to be very early here. We shall not have heather in bloom in Wales for another month. Descending the hill into Truro, a glimpse of the white tall monument of Lander, the African traveller, a column surmounted by an erect statue. Entering the town the road passed close beneath the monument, past the ugly cupola Church with round-headed windows, and we drove to the Royal Hotel. I went with Mrs. Hockin into the market where she bought some fish, red mullet and whiting, poultry &c. There was a good supply of fish, a number of conger eels, turbot, John Dory, ray &c.

It is a nice market house and all sorts of things are sold there besides eatable provisions, e.g. boots, clothes, earthenware &c.

Then we went to a pastry cook's and bought some Cornish 'pasties' for lunch, a sort of turnover with meat and potatoes inside instead of fruit or preserve. As we waited on the quay for our boat to come round an old invalid man, who had been in the Infirmary for some time and had only just been sent out, was being tenderly helped into a boat off the quay steps and covered up with cloaks in the stern by two or three men. Mrs. Hockin says the Cornish are very kind and neighbourly to each other, especially when they are in trouble. Certainly these boatmen were very kind to this old infirm man.

We waited some time for our boat. It was boiling hot on the blazing quay, and Mrs. Hockin sat down on the steps. The tide was ebbing low before we embarked and dropped down the river with oars and mizzen sail between the steaming mud banks and sand flats, leaving Truro town in a dim haze of heat. Danish and Norwegian ships, three-masted vessels, from 200 to 400 tons, were lying anchored lower down the river above, below Malpas. They had brought timber and were waiting to take back miscellaneous cargoes, among other things tin and copper. Hockin and I landed at Malpas leaving Mrs. Hockin sitting in the boat. We went up a flight of wooden steps and by a winding garden path to a little inn standing by the side of the high road which here runs parallel with the river. We brought down a basket full of ginger beer and pushed off again immediately as the boatman was a temperance man, had not touched beer &c for years, and would not have anything to drink. This boatman was a shrewd fellow, very original, with a quaint caustic turn of humour, but very independent and not always over complimentary in his replies. Mrs. Hockin said to him that she supposed he had put by some money since he had taken the pledge. How was he to put by money, he said. Oh yes, it was likely that he could put by a lot of money with the children and sometimes not a penny to be earned for five weeks together.

He also remarked quaintly that he had a good many teeth yet to 'let out' for beef when he came across it. He was very wrath with Lord Falmouth for his tyranny and meanness in shutting up his park and not allowing any picnics in his woods. However the boatman said he would land parties of pleasure on the estate whenever he chose in defiance of his Lordship.

We passed the mouth of the gorge and creek of Restronget above which stands Tullimaar. The wind was dead against us from the South all the way down and at last the boatman took down the mizzen sail. Oyster dredgers were at work, the men rowing their boats out into midstream, pushing their oars with their faces to the bow Venetian gondola fashion. The boat rope was fixed to an anchor at one end and a windlass on board at the other and as the man rowed away from the anchor the wheel flew round whirling and plied out as much rope as was wanted. Then the man worked the boat back to the anchor by the windlass and rope, scraping the oyster bank at the bottom meanwhile with his dredge. There used to be a great many oysters in the Fal.

FRANCIS KILVERT, *Diary*

5. *Garibaldi and Colonel Peard*

APRIL 17, 1864.—Garibaldi came to Par to see his Englishman, and we, armed with a friendly introduction from the Colonel and

Mrs. Peard, went to meet him. Amongst the flags erecting to welcome him was a grim Austrian banner, which was soon lugged down. It was moonlight before he arrived; there was a pause as the train drew up at the platform, and then the General was almost lifted out of the carriage, and stood with the lamps lighting up his face. It was full of deep lines of pain and care and weariness, but over and through it all such a spiritual beauty and moral dignity. His dress was picturesque in form and colour—the red shirt, the grey cloak lined with red, the corner flung gracefully over one shoulder. Colonel Peard was there, his duty being to protect his chief from the enthusiasm of the crowd. The next morning he gave us a cordial reception; a good night had done wonders for him, and had taken off twenty years from his apparent age. We talked of his last night's reception, and I asked if he had ever been at Falmouth as was reported. 'Never', he said: 'but I was at Portsmouth in '55': he hopes to come and visit us some day.

CAROLINE FOX, *Journals and Letters*

6. *Morning Service at St. Michael Penkivel*

(SUNDAY, 27 August, 1871).

At dinner to-night I told Roland Venables the story that Hockin told me about poor Lanyon who used to live at Tullimaar. He had money and other troubles and went out of his mind. Unfortunately the outbreak happened in church. He was living in Falmouth and one Sunday morning he went to Tregothnan Church.[1] During the celebration of the Communion Lanyon went to the desk and began reading the Litany aloud. The curate came down the Chancel and asked him to desist. Lanyon turned on the curate. 'Get thee behind me, Satan,' he said severely, and went on reading the Litany aloud. The curate went behind him and returned to the Altar. The

[1] St. Michael Penkivel is the parish church of Tregothnan.

Rector now came down and remonstrated with Lanyon. Lanyon
made no answer but took up the great Prayer Book and knocked
the Rector on the head.

FRANCIS KILVERT, *Diary*

7. *Tennyson on Holiday*

THE next day we were all down on the white shore admiring the
purple marble rock polished and made lustrous by the sea washing
it in calm and storm. Each of us found his own particular object of
interest apart from those which appealed equally to all. Perhaps it
was the peaceful noise made by the laughing waters, or the bellowing of the cave-entrapped wave, that made Palgrave less mindful
than his wont, and again he was heard calling out the Laureate's
name whenever for a moment he had escaped observation.

Prinsep and I each began a drawing of Asparagus Island, and as
we settled to work, Tennyson proved how, despite his short-
sightedness, he had acquired the knowledge of details found in his
poems.

THE EAGLE

He clasps the crag with hooked hands;
Close to the sun in lonely lands,
Ring'd with the azure world, he stands.

The wrinkled sea beneath him crawls;
He watches from his mountain walls,
And like a thunderbolt he falls.

He was not satisfied with the first casual impression made by a
new experience; he went about from point to point of his first
observations, and conferred over each impression with his companions. We painters had placed ourselves upon a tongue of cliff
which divided a large bight into two smaller bays; thence we could,

290

to right and left, see down to the emerald waves breaking with foam white as snow on to the porphyry rocks. Our seats were approached by a shelving saddle of a kind that required keen sight and firm feet to tread. The poet had made up his mind to look down into the gulf, and we had to find an abutting crag over which he could lean and survey the scene. In the original sense of the word, he was truly nervous, but looked steadily and scrutinisingly. The gulls and choughs were whirling about to the tune of their music, with the pulsing sea acting as bass, and it was difficult for eye or ear to decide whether the sound or the sight were most delightful. Tennyson, when led away to a broader and safer standpoint, said, 'I could have stayed there all day'. He sat and talked for a time, then strolled away with Palgrave out of our sight and hearing. That night after dinner the conversation began again about the English classics, and while it lasted there was little said that was not of inexhaustible interest, for Palgrave, as his books show, was an ardent appreciator of high thought and polished scholarship; but in time the divergent note was struck. 'You're always losing your temper,' said Palgrave.

'I should be sorry to do that, unless the reason were a very weighty one,' said Tennyson.

'Surely,' said Palgrave, 'you must see that you've been offended with the most inadequate cause ever since our start. I appeal to the others', and after referring to the objection of the poet to the use of his name and the alternative epithets, he made it his text that Tennyson had complained to me about the revelation of his name to the Misses Stirling.

I at once said that Tennyson was quite right on this point, that I had been foolish in making the blunder, and that the alertness of the ladies had proved how well founded was his dread of being lionised.

The poet, taking up his candlestick, said, 'Each must do as he thinks best, but I have no doubt what to do. There is no pleasure for any of us in this wrangling, and I shall to-morrow go on to Falmouth and take the train home.'

'There now,' said Palgrave as Tennyson was at the door, 'you're always most unreasonable; if things that you have a whim for are not absolutely yielded, no one else is to have a voice in the matter.' When the poet had gone, Palgrave said to us, 'You've no idea of the perpetual worry he causes me.'

Val ejaculated, 'Did you say that he caused *you*?'

'Yes', he returned. 'The last words that Mrs. Tennyson said to me on leaving were that I must promise her faithfully that I would never on any account let Tennyson out of my sight for a minute, because with his short-sight, in the neighbourhood of the cliffs or on the beach of the sea, he might be in the greatest danger if left alone. I'm ever thinking of my promise, and he continually trying to elude me; if I turn my head one minute, on looking back I find him gone, and when I call out for him he studiously avoids answering.'

'But you call him by his name?' we pleaded for the poet.

'Of course I do, for I find that his fear of being discovered gives me the best chance of making him avow himself.'

Gradually Palgrave gathered that our sympathy for him was limited, and then he took his candle and went off to bed. Val and I, when quietly talking together afterwards after the dispute, had our attention arrested by creaking steps on the stairs, the door was quietly opened and Tennyson appeared in his slippers. Putting his candle down and taking a chair, he spread both his hands out afar on the table and said, 'I've come down to say to you young fellows that I'm very sorry if I seem to be the cause of all the bickerings that go on between Palgrave and myself. It is I know calculated to spoil your holiday, and that would be a great shame. I don't mean to quarrel with any one, but all day long I am trying to get a quiet moment for reflection about things. Sometimes I want to compose a stanza or two, and find a quiet nook where I may wind off my words, but ere I have completed a couplet I hear Palgrave's voice like a bee in a bottle making the neighbourhood resound with my name, and I have to give myself up to escape the consequences.' We explained that all this arose from Palgrave's desire to keep him from danger, for he felt responsible. 'Oh, I know he means very well,' said Tennyson, 'but it worries me, and I am going away to-morrow morning, but I hope you all will stay and enjoy yourselves.'

The next morning before we had finished breakfast a dog-cart stood before the window, and the landlord came in to say that the trap was ready for the luggage. Palgrave cut short the speaker, deciding that it was not for our party, but the Laureate interposed with the explanation that he had ordered it, and he held to his determination to go to Falmouth at once.

When he had already got up into the dog-cart, and Palgrave found that further remonstrance would be in vain, he darted back into the inn, entreating his friend to wait a minute. It was fully ten minutes ere he reappeared, preceded by his luggage, and then jumped up beside Tennyson, greatly to the poet's surprise. He protested, but the remonstrance was met by Palgrave appealing to us to come too, and declaring that he was under promise to Mrs. Tennyson never to leave him on the journey, and as the pair were driven away we heard the two arguing as to whether such watchfulness were necessary.

HOLMAN HUNT, *Pre-Raphaelitism and the Pre-Raphaelite Brotherhood*

8. Birth and Dedication of 'The Golden Treasury'

Francis Turner Palgrave to Tennyson, 30 October 1860: Since I have returned I have worked steadily for two or three hours a day at making the collection of English Lyrical Poems which we discussed in Cornwall; and I have spoken about it to Macmillan, who gives a conditional consent to act publisher.

G. F. PALGRAVE, *Francis Turner Palgrave*

Dedication of *The Golden Treasury*

To Alfred Tennyson, Poet Laureate:

'Your encouragement, given while traversing the wild scenery of Treryn Dinas, led me to begin the work.' . . .

F. T. P.

XI. Epilogue

Our Time

In memory of six children of William Grigson, priest, sometime vicar of Pelynt, and Mary Beatrice his wife.

John Grigson, D.S.O., D.F.C., Air Commodore R.A.F., killed on active service at Bulawayo, Rhodesia, 3 July 1943.

Kenneth Grigson, M.C., Captain West Yorkshire Regt., killed in action in France, 20 July 1918.

Sir Wilfrid Grigson, C.S.I., Indian Civil Service, killed in an air accident in the Punjab, 26 November 1948.

Lionel Grigson, 2nd Lieutenant Devonshire Regt., killed in action in France, 9 May 1917.

Claude Grigson, Cadet R.A.F., died at Shorncliffe, 15 October 1918.

Aubrey Grigson, Captain, Army of Burma Reserve of Officers, killed on active service Shivebo, Burma, 27 April 1942. They were christened in this church and were lovers of this parish.

In Pelynt Church

Index of Contributors